First World War
and Army of Occupation
War Diary
France, Belgium and Germany

46 DIVISION
Divisional Troops
Royal Army Medical Corps
1/3 North Midland Field Ambulance
19 February 1915 - 31 January 1917

WO95/2681/1

The Naval & Military Press Ltd
www.nmarchive.com
Published in association with The National Archives

Published by

The Naval & Military Press Ltd

Unit 10 Ridgewood Industrial Park,

Uckfield, East Sussex,

TN22 5QE England

Tel: +44 (0) 1825 749494

www.naval-military-press.com

www.nmarchive.com

This diary has been reprinted in facsimile from the original. Any imperfections are inevitably reproduced and the quality may fall short of modern type and cartographic standards.

Contents

Document type	Place/Title	Date From	Date To
Heading	46th Division Medical 1/3rd Nth Midland Fd Amb. Mar 1915-1919 May		
War Diary	Labourse	23/10/1915	27/10/1915
War Diary	Cooker Quarry	27/10/1915	27/10/1915
War Diary	Vendelles	30/09/1915	30/09/1915
War Diary	Labourse	18/09/1917	28/10/1917
War Diary	Bruay	20/04/1918	21/04/1918
War Diary	Labourse	22/09/1917	30/09/1917
War Diary	He Sdigneul	09/06/1918	12/06/1918
War Diary	Bailleul	18/05/1915	19/05/1915
War Diary	Fouquieres	19/11/1917	28/11/1917
War Diary	Labourse	26/08/1917	17/09/1917
War Diary	Labourse	20/04/1915	20/04/1915
War Diary	Labourse	11/09/1917	16/09/1917
War Diary	Bailleul	01/05/1915	05/05/1915
War Diary	Fresnoy Le Grand	01/03/1919	04/03/1919
War Diary	Troisvilles	05/03/1919	28/04/1919
War Diary	Labourse	11/10/1917	15/10/1917
War Diary	Labourse	07/07/1917	13/07/1917
War Diary	Labourse	11/05/1915	11/05/1915
War Diary	Labourse	05/10/1917	06/10/1917
War Diary	Bailleul	21/06/1915	23/06/1915
War Diary	Labourse	05/08/1917	07/08/1917
War Diary	Hesdigneul	06/07/1918	09/07/1918
War Diary	Bailleul	20/05/1915	20/06/1915
War Diary	Labourse	20/08/1917	06/09/1917
War Diary	Laherliere	31/08/1916	31/08/1916
War Diary	Labourse	28/08/1917	10/09/1917
War Diary	Labourse	11/08/1917	13/08/1917
War Diary	Hesdigneul	29/04/1918	30/04/1918
War Diary	Labourse	18/10/1917	20/10/1917
War Diary	Labourse	14/07/1915	15/07/1915
War Diary	Gaudiempre	23/03/1916	31/03/1916
War Diary	Labeuvriere	01/07/1917	06/07/1917
War Diary	Labeuvriere	23/07/1915	31/07/1915
War Diary	Labourse	21/10/1917	23/10/1917
War Diary	Isbergues	09/01/1916	09/01/1916
War Diary	Marseille	11/01/1916	16/01/1916
War Diary	Baillevl	07/05/1915	17/05/1915
War Diary	Hesdigneul	27/07/1918	31/07/1918
War Diary	Bailleul	08/05/1915	10/05/1915
War Diary	Labourse	14/08/1917	16/08/1917
War Diary	Hesdigneul	14/05/1918	15/05/1918
War Diary	Labourse	23/08/1917	26/08/1917
War Diary	Labourse	19/08/1917	19/08/1917
War Diary	Labourse	04/05/1915	30/06/1915
War Diary	Fresnoy-Le-Grand	23/10/1918	25/10/1918
War Diary		20/04/1915	22/04/1915
War Diary	Hesdigneul	31/03/1918	31/03/1918
War Diary	Labourse	02/08/1917	05/08/1917

War Diary	Labourse	27/07/1917	29/07/1917
War Diary	Labourse	05/11/1917	10/11/1917
War Diary	Troisvilles	16/03/1919	30/03/1919
War Diary	Near Poperinghe	09/07/1915	14/07/1915
War Diary	Labourse	18/08/1917	19/08/1917
War Diary	No Poperinghe	17/07/1915	07/08/1915
War Diary	Labourse	07/08/1917	11/08/1917
War Diary	Bruay	24/04/1918	24/04/1918
War Diary		07/09/1915	20/09/1915
War Diary	Gaudiempre	18/06/1916	29/06/1916
War Diary	Bailleul	05/05/1915	07/05/1915
War Diary	La Herliere	01/08/1916	06/08/1916
War Diary	Maison Rolland	01/02/1916	10/02/1916
War Diary	Labourse	16/08/1917	17/08/1917
War Diary	Fouquires	29/10/1915	31/10/1915
War Diary	Labourse	01/09/1917	05/09/1917
War Diary	Fouquieres	10/12/1917	14/12/1917
War Diary	La Herliere	30/08/1916	30/08/1916
War Diary	Fresnoy-Le Grand	13/10/1918	18/10/1918
War Diary	Gaudiempre	30/06/1916	30/06/1916
War Diary		02/07/1916	04/07/1916
Heading	War Diary of 1/3rd Midland Field Ambulance. From 1/8/18 to 31/8/18 Vol 42		
War Diary	Bailleul	27/05/1915	31/05/1915
War Diary	Bruay	18/04/1918	20/04/1918
War Diary	Labourse	01/10/1917	04/10/1917
War Diary	Predefin (Pdec)	14/02/1918	16/02/1918
War Diary	Bailleul	24/06/1915	24/06/1915
War Diary	Near Poperinghe	24/06/1915	25/06/1915
War Diary	Labeuvriere	03/04/1918	05/04/1918
War Diary		26/04/1915	28/04/1915
War Diary	Labeuvriere	08/04/1918	10/04/1918
War Diary	Fouquieres	22/12/1917	24/12/1917
War Diary	Hesdigneul	17/05/1918	19/05/1918
War Diary	Bailleul	31/05/1915	09/08/1915
War Diary	Vendelles	21/09/1918	22/09/1918
War Diary	Bonnay	14/09/1918	18/09/1918
War Diary	Tertry	19/09/1918	20/09/1918
War Diary	Fouquieres	09/10/1915	17/10/1915
War Diary	Hayettes	07/11/1918	08/11/1918
War Diary	Boulogne Sur Helpe	09/11/1918	12/11/1918
War Diary	Avesnes	13/11/1918	13/11/1918
War Diary	Preux	14/11/1918	14/11/1918
War Diary	Preux	12/08/1915	20/08/1915
War Diary		21/03/1915	26/03/1915
War Diary	Ecoivres	14/03/1916	31/03/1916
War Diary	Bailleul Aux Cornailles U 19b. ? 36 B.	01/05/1916	05/05/1916
War Diary	Hesdigneul	12/05/1918	13/05/1918
War Diary	Labourse	31/08/1917	31/08/1917
War Diary	Fouquieres Les Bethune	06/12/1917	08/12/1917
War Diary	Hesdigneul	04/06/1918	05/06/1918
War Diary	Hesdigneul	04/05/1918	05/05/1918
War Diary	Fouquieres	02/11/1915	02/11/1915
War Diary	Zelobes	07/11/1915	07/11/1915
War Diary	Labourse	16/10/1917	17/10/1917
War Diary		25/06/1915	25/06/1915

War Diary	Farm 1 1/2 Miles South Of Poperinghe	26/06/1915	27/06/1915
War Diary	La Herliere	22/08/1916	30/08/1916
War Diary	Bailleul	07/06/1915	11/06/1915
War Diary		25/08/1915	25/08/1915
War Diary	Bailleul	01/06/1915	06/06/1915
War Diary	Labeuvriere	16/06/1915	20/06/1915
War Diary	Hesdigneul	20/05/1918	22/05/1918
War Diary	Bailleul	12/05/1915	14/05/1915
War Diary	Near Poperinghe	02/07/1915	08/07/1915
War Diary	Busnes St Venant Rd	26/12/1915	31/12/1915
War Diary	La Herliere	02/09/1916	05/09/1916
War Diary	Cooker Quarry	29/09/1918	29/09/1918
War Diary	Cooker Quarry	04/10/1918	05/10/1918
War Diary	Hesdigneul	03/05/1918	03/05/1918
War Diary	Labourse	01/11/1917	04/11/1917
War Diary	La Herliere	22/08/1916	22/08/1916
War Diary	Aix Noulette	05/05/1917	08/05/1917
War Diary	Fouquieres	29/11/1917	30/11/1917
War Diary	Hiesdigneul	27/04/1918	28/04/1918
War Diary	Preux	15/11/1918	26/11/1918
War Diary	Fouquieres Les Bethune	12/01/1918	14/01/1918
War Diary	Cooker Quarry	05/10/1918	08/10/1918
War Diary	Magny La Fosse	09/10/1918	09/10/1918
War Diary	Bethune	14/03/1918	18/03/1918
War Diary	Hesdigneul	09/05/1918	10/05/1918
War Diary	Bailleul	12/06/1915	15/06/1915
War Diary	Hesdigneul	07/06/1918	09/06/1918
War Diary	Isbergue	01/01/1916	07/01/1916
War Diary	Bethune	05/03/1918	05/03/1918
War Diary	Gaudiempre	12/05/1916	12/05/1916
War Diary	Hesdigneul	05/05/1918	07/05/1918
War Diary	Gaudiempre	10/05/1916	11/05/1916
War Diary	Hesdigneul	01/08/1918	05/08/1918
War Diary	Bruay	24/04/1918	24/04/1918
War Diary	Hesdigneul	25/04/1918	04/07/1918
War Diary	Hesdigneul	05/06/1918	06/06/1918
War Diary	Monplaisir Near Hem Ref Lens 11	02/03/1916	06/03/1916
War Diary	Canettemont (Lens II)	09/03/1916	09/03/1916
War Diary	Magnicourt	10/03/1916	11/03/1916
War Diary	Hesdigneul	15/05/1918	17/05/1918
War Diary	La Herliere	14/08/1916	14/08/1916
War Diary	La Bourse	07/10/1917	10/10/1917
War Diary	Troisvilles	04/05/1919	30/05/1919
War Diary	Hesdigneul	22/05/1918	30/05/1918
War Diary	Cooker Quarry R.11. A. 9.7 Sheet 62C	01/10/1918	03/10/1918
War Diary	Predefin	11/02/1918	13/02/1918
War Diary		09/03/1915	13/03/1915
War Diary		14/07/1917	20/07/1917
War Diary	La Beuvriere	01/04/1918	03/04/1918
War Diary	Hesdigneul	21/07/1918	26/07/1918
War Diary	Vendelles	27/09/1918	27/09/1918
War Diary	Cooker Quarry	28/09/1918	28/09/1918
War Diary	La Herliere	10/09/1916	16/09/1916
War Diary	La Beuvriere	06/04/1918	07/04/1918
War Diary	Bailleul	25/05/1915	27/05/1915
War Diary	Gaudiempre	14/05/1916	22/05/1916

War Diary	La Beuvriere	24/03/1918	24/03/1918
War Diary	Marseille	18/01/1916	25/01/1916
War Diary	Hesdigneul	06/08/1918	10/08/1918
War Diary	Aix Noulette	21/05/1917	23/05/1917
War Diary	Annezin	25/01/1918	28/01/1918
War Diary	ACQ	12/03/1916	13/03/1916
War Diary	Hesdigneul	01/05/1918	01/05/1918
War Diary	Gaudiempre	01/06/1916	04/06/1916
War Diary	Busigny	01/11/1918	04/11/1918
War Diary	Cartillon	05/11/1918	05/11/1918
War Diary	Burbure	06/09/1918	11/09/1918
War Diary	In The Train	12/09/1918	12/09/1918
War Diary	Bonnay	13/09/1918	13/09/1918
War Diary	St Amand	06/12/1916	07/12/1916
War Diary	Gaudiempre	01/07/1916	01/07/1916
War Diary	Hesdigneul	01/06/1918	03/06/1918
War Diary	La Herliere	06/08/1916	11/08/1916
War Diary	Gapennes	08/11/1916	08/11/1916
War Diary	Froyelles	11/11/1916	13/11/1916
War Diary	Fouquieres	25/12/1917	31/12/1917
War Diary	Gaodiempre	30/06/1916	30/06/1916
War Diary	Near Poperinghe	02/10/1915	06/10/1915
War Diary	Fresnoy	29/10/1918	29/10/1918
War Diary	Busigny	31/10/1918	31/10/1918
War Diary	Hesdigneul	10/07/1918	20/07/1918
War Diary	Hesdigneul	30/04/1918	03/05/1918
War Diary	Fouquieres	17/10/1915	20/10/1915
War Diary	Allouagne	21/10/1915	28/10/1915
War Diary	Neuve Eglise		
Miscellaneous	Appendix I War Diary. Medical Arrangements For Evacuations From Front For Which this Field Ambulance is responsible.	30/09/1917	30/09/1917
Miscellaneous	Evacuation Of Casualties. Appendix II	17/07/1915	17/07/1915
War Diary	Maison Rolland	15/02/1916	23/02/1916
War Diary	Aix-Noulette	08/05/1917	09/05/1917
War Diary	La Herliere	29/10/1916	30/10/1916
War Diary	La Beuvriere	21/07/1917	24/07/1917
War Diary	Hesdigneul	12/06/1918	17/06/1918
War Diary	Maison Rolland	10/02/1916	15/02/1916
War Diary	Bruay	23/08/1918	30/08/1918
War Diary	Labeuvriere	29/03/1918	29/03/1918
War Diary	Fresnoy Le Grand	03/01/1919	27/01/1919
Heading	War Diary Of Major T.A. Barron O.C. 1/3 N.M.F. AMB 1st June To 30th June 1917		
War Diary		14/03/1915	20/03/1915
War Diary	Hesdigneul	07/05/1918	27/05/1918
War Diary	La Beuvriere	27/03/1918	28/03/1918
War Diary	La Beuvriere	25/03/1918	27/03/1918
War Diary	Vendelles	23/09/1918	26/09/1918
War Diary		04/03/1915	09/03/1915
War Diary	Fresnoy	22/12/1918	30/12/1918
War Diary	St Amand	17/12/1916	21/12/1916
War Diary	Gaudiempre	11/06/1916	16/06/1916
War Diary		19/02/1915	03/03/1915
War Diary		26/11/1915	29/11/1915
War Diary	Fouquteres	20/01/1918	24/01/1918

War Diary	Gaudiempre	20/03/1917	22/03/1917
War Diary	Bus Les Artois	23/03/1917	24/03/1917
War Diary	Contay	25/03/1917	25/03/1917
War Diary	Villers Bocage	26/03/1917	26/03/1917
War Diary	Predefin	20/02/1918	20/02/1918
War Diary	Predefin	17/02/1918	19/02/1918
War Diary	Mericourt	10/10/1918	12/10/1918
Heading	War Diary Of 1/3. North Midland. Field Ambulance. From 1/7/18. To 31/7/18. Vol 41		
Heading	Labeuvriere	25/03/1918	27/03/1918
War Diary	Bailleul Aux Cornailles	22/04/1916	22/04/1916
War Diary	Map Sheet 36B. V 19 B	24/04/1916	30/04/1916
War Diary	La Beuvriere	13/06/1916	15/06/1916
War Diary		22/04/1915	25/04/1915
War Diary	Bruay	21/04/1918	05/09/1918
War Diary	Predefin	20/02/1918	23/02/1918
War Diary	Ecoivres	12/04/1916	21/04/1916
War Diary	Fresnoy Le Grand	19/10/1918	22/10/1918
War Diary	La Herliere	17/10/1916	27/10/1916
War Diary	Line Of March	01/11/1916	07/11/1916
War Diary	La Herliere	13/07/1916	09/09/1916
War Diary		03/04/1915	30/04/1915
War Diary	Maison Rolland	24/02/1916	25/02/1916
War Diary	Mesnil Domqueur	26/02/1916	29/02/1916
War Diary	Hesdigneul	18/06/1918	23/06/1918
War Diary	La Herliere	25/07/1916	14/08/1916
War Diary	La Bourse	25/07/1917	25/07/1917
War Diary	Bruay	31/08/1918	31/08/1918
Miscellaneous	I Corps Main Dressing Station. Appendix I		
War Diary	Hesdigneul	10/05/1918	11/05/1918
War Diary	Aix-Noulette	19/04/1917	23/04/1917
War Diary	Fresnoy Le Grand	03/02/1919	28/02/1919
War Diary	Brevillers	01/12/1916	05/12/1916
War Diary	Annezin (P de C)	07/02/1918	09/02/1918
War Diary	Nedon (P de C)	10/02/1918	10/02/1918
War Diary	Predefin (P de C)	11/02/1918	11/02/1918
War Diary		12/12/1915	19/12/1915
War Diary	Busnes St Venant Road	20/12/1915	20/12/1915
Heading	War Diary Of 1/3rd N.M. Field Ambulance. 1st December 1918 to 31st December 1918. Vol 46		
War Diary	Ivergny	06/05/1916	08/05/1916
War Diary	Predefin	24/02/1918	27/02/1918
War Diary	Annezin	29/01/1918	06/02/1918
War Diary	Fouquieres	15/12/1917	19/12/1917
War Diary	Hesdigneul	11/08/1918	14/08/1918
War Diary	Bruay	15/08/1918	15/08/1918
War Diary	Labeuvriere	06/06/1917	09/06/1917
War Diary	Maison Rolland	30/01/1916	30/01/1916
War Diary	Aix-Noulette	09/05/1917	11/05/1917
War Diary	La Bourse	25/07/1917	27/07/1917
War Diary	La Beuvriere	10/04/1918	12/04/1918
War Diary	Divion	13/04/1918	13/04/1918
Heading	Medical From November 1st. 1918 to November 31st. 1918. O.C. 1/3rd. N.M. Field Ambulance. Vol 45-		
War Diary	St Amand	04/01/1917	08/01/1917
Diagram etc	Appendix III		

War Diary	St Amand	30/12/1916	31/12/1916
War Diary	Ecquedecques	05/04/1917	09/04/1917
War Diary	Aix-Noulette	28/04/1917	28/04/1917
War Diary	Bethune	06/03/1918	08/03/1918
War Diary	Gaudiempre	24/02/1917	28/02/1917
War Diary	Gaudiempre	05/06/1916	09/06/1916
War Diary	St Amand	01/01/1917	03/01/1917
War Diary	Predefin	27/02/1918	28/02/1918
War Diary	Brevillers	26/11/1916	29/11/1916
War Diary		18/09/1916	28/09/1916
War Diary	Fouquieres	15/01/1918	19/01/1918
War Diary	Cux Noulette	25/05/1917	26/05/1917
War Diary	Gaudiempre	20/02/1917	23/02/1917
War Diary	La Herliere	02/10/1916	11/10/1916
War Diary	Aix-Noulette	01/05/1917	05/05/1917
War Diary	Hesdigneul	30/06/1918	30/06/1918
War Diary	Gaudiempre	17/02/1917	18/02/1917
War Diary	Neuve Eglise	16/06/1915	16/06/1915
War Diary	Bailleul	16/06/1915	16/06/1915
War Diary	Fouquieres Lez Bethune	01/01/1918	11/01/1918
War Diary	Fouquieres Lez Bethune	01/12/1917	05/12/1917
War Diary		15/11/1915	20/11/1915
War Diary	Preux	01/12/1918	09/12/1918
War Diary	Busigny	11/12/1918	11/12/1918
War Diary	Fresnoy Le Grand	12/12/1918	20/12/1918
War Diary	Cux Naulette	18/05/1917	21/05/1917
War Diary	La Herliere	01/09/1916	01/09/1916
War Diary	Gaudiempre	30/06/1916	30/06/1916
Miscellaneous	106 Men Of 1/5th. Leicestershire Regt. Under Observation In 1/3rd. N.M. Field Ambulance. App I		
War Diary	Aix Noulette	29/04/1917	30/04/1917
War Diary	Marseille	26/01/1916	27/01/1916
War Diary	Pont Remy Maison Rolland	29/01/1916	29/01/1916
War Diary	Cux Naulette	15/05/1917	17/05/1917
War Diary	Aix Noulette	23/04/1917	28/04/1917
War Diary	St Amand	08/12/1916	17/12/1916
Heading	Medical War Diary Of The 1/3 North Midland. Field Ambulance. For June. 1918. Vol 40		
Miscellaneous	Subject:- Improvement to Billets. see D.R.O. 130 of 8/2/16. App I	18/05/1916	18/05/1916
War Diary	La Bourse	30/09/1917	10/11/1917
War Diary	Fouquieres	12/11/1917	19/12/1917
War Diary	La Beuvriere	03/06/1917	05/06/1917
War Diary	La Beuvriere	01/06/1917	02/06/1917
War Diary	La Bourse	30/07/1917	31/07/1917
War Diary	St Amand	02/02/1917	03/02/1917
War Diary	Gaudiempre	04/02/1917	10/02/1917
War Diary	Ecquedecques	10/04/1917	13/04/1917
War Diary	Bethune	16/04/1917	18/04/1917
War Diary	La Bourse	31/07/1917	31/07/1917
War Diary	Gaudiempre	23/02/1917	23/02/1917
War Diary	La Beuvriere	09/06/1917	12/06/1917
War Diary	La Beuvriere	29/03/1918	30/03/1918
War Diary	St Amand	19/01/1917	26/01/1917
War Diary	Westrehem	01/03/1918	04/03/1918

Miscellaneous	1/3rd N. Mid. F.A. 46th Divn. 2nd Corps. Western Front. O.C. Lt. Col. A.E. Hodder D.S.O. April. 17. 1st Army.	19/04/1917	19/04/1917
War Diary	Gaudiempre	06/03/1917	11/03/1917
War Diary	La Herliere	10/07/1916	12/07/1916
War Diary	Bethune	22/03/1918	23/03/1918
War Diary	Labeuvriere	23/03/1918	23/03/1918
War Diary	Hesdigneul	24/06/1918	29/06/1918
War Diary	Saveuse	27/03/1917	30/03/1917
War Diary	Ecquedecques	31/03/1917	31/03/1917
War Diary	St Amand	12/01/1917	17/01/1917
War Diary	La Bourse	31/08/1917	31/08/1917
War Diary	Gaudiempre	01/03/1917	06/03/1917
War Diary	St Amand	24/12/1916	29/12/1916
War Diary	La Herliere	14/08/1916	22/08/1916
War Diary	Zelobes	01/12/1915	09/12/1915
War Diary	Bethune	09/03/1918	13/03/1918
War Diary	Ecquedecques	01/04/1917	04/04/1917
War Diary	Bethune	15/03/1918	21/03/1918
War Diary	Near Poperinghe	01/07/1915	02/07/1915
War Diary	Gaudiempre	11/02/1917	16/02/1917
War Diary		25/04/1915	25/04/1915
Miscellaneous	1/3rd N. Mid F.A. 46th Divn. 1st Corps. Western Front. O.C. Major T.A. Barron From 15/4/17. May. 17. 1st Army.		
War Diary	St Amand	22/12/1916	23/12/1916
War Diary	Anwezin	31/01/1918	31/01/1918
War Diary	Cux Naulette	23/05/1917	24/05/1917
War Diary	Labeuvriere	31/03/1918	31/03/1918
Miscellaneous	To Officer Commanding 1/3 N. Midland Field Ambulance		
War Diary	Labeuvriere	23/00/1918	24/00/1918
Miscellaneous	1/3rd N. Mid. F.A. 46th Divn. 1st Corps. Western Front. O.C. Lt. Col. A.E. Hodder D.S.O. O.C. Maj. T.A. Barron From 15/4/17. 1st Army.	15/04/1917	15/04/1917
War Diary		30/04/1915	30/04/1915
War Diary	Labeuvriere	31/05/1917	31/05/1917
War Diary	Appendix I		
War Diary	Gaudiempre	12/03/1917	19/03/1917
Miscellaneous	1/3rd N. Mid. F.A. 46th Divn. 1st Corps. Western Front. O.C. Lt. Col. A.E. Hodder D.S.O. April. 17. 1st Army.		
War Diary	Bruay	16/08/1918	22/08/1918
War Diary	La Bourse	31/10/1918	31/10/1918
Miscellaneous	Appendix VI		
War Diary	Cux Naulette	12/05/1917	14/05/1917
Miscellaneous	War Diary.	06/09/1915	06/09/1915
Miscellaneous	April 1915 Appendix IV		
War Diary	La Herliere	04/07/1916	08/07/1916
War Diary	La Beuvriere	27/07/1916	30/07/1916
Miscellaneous	1/3rd N. Mid. F.A. 46th Divn. 1st Corps Western Front. O.C. Lt. Col. A.E. Hodder D.S.O. May. 17. O.E. Maj. T.A. Barron From 15/4/17. 1st Army.	15/04/1917	15/04/1917
Diagram etc	Appendix II		
Miscellaneous	War Diary.	14/03/1915	14/03/1915
War Diary	St Amand	09/01/1917	11/01/1917

War Diary	Ecoivres	22/03/1916	27/04/1916
Miscellaneous		16/06/1915	16/06/1915
War Diary	Gaudiempre		
War Diary	Divion	14/04/1918	16/04/1918
War Diary	Bruay	17/04/1918	17/04/1918
Miscellaneous	Fire Orders & Appendix No. 1	05/03/1916	05/03/1916
War Diary	Froyelles	14/11/1916	22/11/1916
War Diary	Yvrench	23/11/1916	23/11/1916
War Diary	Bachimont	24/11/1916	25/11/1916
Heading	War Diary Of 1/3rd North Midland Field Ambulance. Jan 1st To Jan 31st 1919. Vol 47		
Miscellaneous	Summary Of Medical War Diaries For 1/3rd N. Mid. F.A. 46th Divn. 2nd Corps. 1st Corps From 19/4/17. 1st Army.		
Miscellaneous	War Diary		
Heading	War Diary Of 1/3 North Midland Field Ambulance For Month Ending 30/9/18. Vol 43		
Miscellaneous		27/08/1917	27/08/1917
Miscellaneous	War Diary.	31/07/1915	31/07/1915
Miscellaneous	Appendix II June 1915		
War Diary	1/3 North Midland F.A. Mar 1918		
War Diary	Labeuvriere	27/05/1917	31/05/1917
War Diary	St Amand	28/01/1917	31/01/1917
Diagram etc	Garden		
Miscellaneous	3rd: Field. Ambulance. 46th: Division. Advanced Dressing Stn: No: 1. Appendix I		
Miscellaneous	Detail Of Duties.		
Miscellaneous	War Diary.	30/04/1915	30/04/1915
Miscellaneous			
Miscellaneous	1/3rd N. Mid F.A. 46th Divn. 1st Corps. Western Front. O.C. Major T.A. Barron From 15/4/17. May. 17. 1st Army.	15/04/1917	15/04/1917
Miscellaneous	Colonel W. Beevor, A.D.M.S. 46th: Division. Appendix I	16/07/1915	16/07/1915
Miscellaneous	1/3rd N. Mid F.A. 46th Divn. 1st Corps. Western Front. O.C. Lt. Col. A.E. Hodder D.S.O. April. 17. 1st Army.		
Heading	War Diary Of 1/3 North Midland Field Ambulance For The Month of October. 1918. Vol 44		
Miscellaneous	3rd: Field. Ambulance. 46th: Division. Advanced Dressing Station. No: 2 Appendix II		
Miscellaneous	46th Div 3rd N.M. Field Ambulance Jan 1917		
Heading	WO95/2681/1		
Heading	46th Division 1/3rd NM F. Amb Jan Vol XI Jan 1916		
Miscellaneous	R.A.M.C.T.	27/02/1916	27/02/1916
Heading	46th Division 3rd N.M. Field Ambulance Vol VII Sept 15		
Heading	46th Division No 3 N.M. Field Ambulance Vol IV June 1915		
Heading	46th Division 1/3rd N.M. Field Ambulance Vol VI August 15		
Miscellaneous	Summary Of Medical War Diaries For 1/3rd N. Mid. F.A 46th Divn. 2nd Corps. 1st Corps From 19/4/17. 1st Army.	19/04/1917	19/04/1917
Heading	46th Division 1/3 N. Midland Field Ambulance Vol I Feb 19th To March 26th 1915		
Heading	1/3rd North Midland F.A. Jan 1918		

Heading	War Diary Of 1/3rd N.M. Field Ambulance. 1/2/19. To 28/2/19 Vol 48 Feb 1919		
Heading	1/3rd North Midland F.A. July 1917		
Heading	1/3rd N.M.F.A. May 1917		
Heading	46th Div 1/3rd N.M. Field Amb Oct 1916		
Heading	46th Div 1/3rd N. Midland Field Ambulance June 1916		
Heading	46th Div 1/3rd N.M. F Amb Dec 1916 Vol X		
Heading	46th Div 3rd North Mid. Fld Amb Vol VIII Oct 15		
Heading	46th Division 1/3 N. Midland Field Amb Feb Mar 1916		
Heading	46th Division 1/3rd N.M.F. Amb Nov 1915 Vol IX		
Miscellaneous	1/3rd N. Mid. F.A. 46th Divn. 2nd Corps. Western Front. O.C. Lt. Col. A.E. Hodder D.S.O. April 17. 1st Army.	19/04/1917	19/04/1917
Heading	1/3rd North Midland F.A. Oct. 1917		
Heading	46th Division 1/3rd N.M. Field Ambulance Vol V July 1915		
Heading	1/3rd North Midland F A June 1917		
Miscellaneous	46th Div 1/3rd N.M. Field Ambulance Sept 1916		
Heading	1/3rd North Midland F.A. Nov 1917		
Heading	46th Div 1/3rd N.M. Field Ambulance Dec 1916		
Heading	46th Div. 1/3rd N.M. Field Ambulance Mar 1917		
Heading	46th Div 1/3rd North Midland F.A. April 19		
Heading	1/3rd North Midland F.A. Dec 1917		
Miscellaneous	46th Div 1/3rd N.M. Field Ambulance Sept 1916		
Heading	46th Div 1/3rd N.M. Field Ambulance Nov 1916		
Heading	46th Div 1/3rd N.M. Field Ambulance Feb 1917		
Heading	1/3 Nth. Mid. Field Ambulance March 1918		
Heading	1/3 N.M.F.A. August 1916		
Heading	1/3rd North Midland F.A. Feb 1918		
Heading	1/3rd North Midland F.A. Sept 1917		
Heading	1/3 N. Midland F A. May 1915		
Heading	1/3 N.M.F.A. Apr 1918-		
Heading	46th Division 1/3rd North Midland Field Ambulance Vol II April 1915		
Heading	46th Div 1/3rd N Midland F Amb April 1916		
Miscellaneous	46 Div 1/3rd N Mid Field Amb May 1919		
Heading	46th Div 3rd N.M. F. Amb May 1916		
Heading	1/3rd North Midland F.A. Aug 1917		
Heading	1/3rd Nor. Mid F.A. May 1918		
Heading	1/3 N. Mid F.A. April 1919		
Heading	46th Division No 3 N.M. Field Ambulance July 1916		
Miscellaneous	List Of Appendices Of War Diary Of O.C. 1/3 N. Mid F.A. May 1915.		
Miscellaneous	O.C. 3rd N.M. Fd Amb A.D.M.S. Office	28/02/1917	28/02/1917
Heading	O.C. 3rd N.M. Fd Amb		
Heading	1/3 N M Fd Amb Vol XIV		
Heading	3 N M F A Amb Feb Vol XII		
Heading	1/3 N M Fd Amb Vol XIII		

46TH DIVISION

MEDICAL

1/3RD NTH MIDLAND FD AMB.

MAR 1915-~~DEC 1918~~ 1919 MAY

Instructions regarding War Diaries and Intelligence Summaries are contained in F. S. Regs., Part II. and the Staff Manual respectively. Title pages will be prepared in manuscript.

WAR DIARY
or
INTELLIGENCE SUMMARY.
(Erase heading not required.)

Army Form C. 2118.

Place	Date	Hour	Summary of Events and Information	Remarks and references to Appendices
LABOURSE	23/10		Foden Thresh is not in good order but one chamber is doing quite well so have continued to work one only. Some experiments with hens eggs showed that the time of exposure in the chamber could safely be reduced to 30 minutes: improved methods of handling enabled the changing to be effected in 5 minutes. ie 50 blankets or their equivalent of clothing can be dealt with every 35 minutes: so that even with one chamber only working 1000 blankets per day can be put through. With both working, the theoretical maximum will be about 2400 but the actual will not exceed 2000. Have instituted a "running" book & will report each Saturday to ADMS on the weeks work.	
	24/10		Attended ADMS conference 10 am.	
	26/10		Lieut W B Jack to 1/5 Leicester Regt. for duty. In order to have 2 medical officers at ADS: RMO for [illegible]TOSH KEEP will live at FORT GLATZ.	
	27/10		Inspected draft of 1/5 South Staffs. Reported on weeks working of Foden Thresh to ADMS: this has improved greatly & I am now satisfied that it will deal with at least 1500 blankets per day efficiently. In afternoon inspected hay racks & wire hay nets at La FONTANELLE FARM.	

A7092. Wt. W12859/M1293. [illegible] Forms/C2118/[illegible]

Army Form C. 2118.

Instructions regarding War Diaries and Intelligence Summaries are contained in F. S. Regs., Part II. and the Staff Manual respectively. Title pages will be prepared in manuscript.

WAR DIARY
or
INTELLIGENCE SUMMARY.
(Erase heading not required.)

Place	Date	Hour	Summary of Events and Information	Remarks and references to Appendices
COOKER QUARRY			CHOPPER RAVINE with a relay post at G.33.a.7.2. Walking wounded were directed to the collecting post at VADENCOURT which was staffed by 1/2nd. N.M.F. Amb. About 3 P.M. the 32nd. Division went through the 46th Div & made a further advance DDMS IXth Corps. called at COOKER QUARRY	ACY
VENDELLES	30/9/18		Few casualties dealt with during night. At 6 AM Major Lane MC opened an ADS in cellar in BELLENGLISE at G.34.d.75.80. At the same time Major Graham's ADS at M.2.d.8.6 was closed. At 11 AM visited BELLENGLISE & found numerous casualties of 32nd. Division coming in & apparently no arrangements for clearing them. Sent two motor lorries & every available motor ambulance up to BELLENGLISE & got all wounded away soon after NOON. In afternoon visited BELLENGLISE together with ADMS, to look for better accomodation for ADS. GOC 46th Div called at COOKER QUARRY. In evening bearers of 1/1st & 1/2nd N.M.F. Ambs. & divisional bearers returned to their units. Capt. Reid proceeded to BELLENGLISE	

D. D. & L., London, E.C. (A8o94) Wt W1771/M2031 750,000 5/17 Sch. 52 Forms/C2118/14

Instructions regarding War Diaries and Intelligence Summaries are contained in F. S. Regs., Part II. and the Staff Manual respectively. Title pages will be prepared in manuscript.

WAR DIARY
or
INTELLIGENCE SUMMARY.
(Erase heading not required.)

Army Form C. 2118.

Place	Date	Hour	Summary of Events and Information	Remarks and references to Appendices
LABOURSE	18/9/17		Visited ADS CAMBRIN in afternoon.	
	19/9/17		All men lent to RE + ASC as working parties returned to Field ambulance.	
	20/9/17		A advanced party under Captain O. Steele MC left to take over ADS. PHILOSOPHE and an advanced party of 1 NCO + 5 OR. went to FORT GLATZ and posts in connection therewith. Captain Miller & part of "A" section reported at Hdqrs having handed over ADS CAMBRIN & posts to 6th Field Amb. Held court of enquiry into loss of kit of Gunner Gallagher 26/TMB. - and adjourned enquiry for further evidence.	
	21/9/17		Taking over of Advanced Dressing Stations PHILOSOPHE and FORT GLATZ with their forward posts completed. Distribution of personnel as follows.	
			ADS - PHILOSOPHE 2 officers + 26 O.R.: PONT ST POST - 4. OR.; St GEORGES " - 1 NCO + 4 OR.; ~~Halfway~~ " - 4. O.R.	
			ADS - FORT GLATZ 2 officers + 19 OR.: CHALK PIT - 4. OR.; TOSH KEEP - 4. OR; SOLENT POST - 4. OR; TUNNEL " - 4. OR.; NATAL " - 4. OR.	
			SOLENT POST shared with 6th Div. units: last 3 posts all in 6 Div Area.	

Army Form C. 2118.

Instructions regarding War Diaries and Intelligence Summaries are contained in F. S. Regs., Part II. and the Staff Manual respectively. Title pages will be prepared in manuscript.

WAR DIARY
or
INTELLIGENCE SUMMARY.
(Erase heading not required.)

Place	Date	Hour	Summary of Events and Information	Remarks and references to Appendices
LABOURSE	28/10		Inspected Baths NOYELLES & found the working much improved & now satisfactory, but the ironing facilities are unchanged. Visited A.D.S. PHILOSOPHE and gave Capt Steel the O/c detail of duties in connection with impending minor operation. Paid unit.	
	30/10		Visited advanced dressing stations in morning. Capt Ullman returned from duty with 67 H.A.G. Inspected all RAMC at Headquarters ~~ditto~~ for classification A and B.	
	31/10		Raid by 1/6 N. Staffs about 4.30 pm today. First casualties reached main dressing station 7.40 pm: the last at 11.40 and all had been transferred to C.C.S by midnight. Total 3 officers 8 O.R. with 12 wounded prisoners. Evacuation was via CHALK PIT ALLEY past to FORT GLATZ. There was evidently no hitch in the medical arrangements. Reported on number of Category A & B men with unit. 142 A: 40 B. all men wearing glasses being put into the latter provisionally.	

A7092. Wt. W12839/M1293. 750,000. 1/17. D. D & L., Ltd. Forms/C2118/14.

Army Form C. 2118.

WAR DIARY
or
INTELLIGENCE SUMMARY.
(Erase heading not required.)

Instructions regarding War Diaries and Intelligence Summaries are contained in F. S. Regs., Part II. and the Staff Manual respectively. Title pages will be prepared in manuscript.

Place	Date	Hour	Summary of Events and Information	Remarks and references to Appendices
BRUAY	20/4/18		Enemy put harassing fire from H.V. gun on town near Fosse 3. some casualties among civilians who were evacuated to St POL. Some civilians killed & buried under debris. Four accidentally wounded British [illegible] at 5.30 pm HAILLICOURT: machine gun mishap. The weather slightly warmer – last night E.A. rather active about midnight: some bombs dropped at a distance from here.	
	21/4/18		Further harassing fire from H.V. gun on BRUAY resulting in a number of casualties among troops and civilians. Extension of catarrhal epidemic fever among units of 138 Infantry Brigade. 1/5th Lincolns and 1/4th Leicesters being involved including some officers. Consulting physician I Army visited Field Amb. & expressed general satisfaction with the progress in controlling the epidemic. In all but a small amount of cases temperature & pulse rate become normal in 48 hours & remain down and convalescence is uninterrupted. It is expected that at least 80 will be able to go back to light duty on 22nd.	

Instructions regarding War Diaries and Intelligence Summaries are contained in F. S. Regs., Part II. and the Staff Manual respectively. Title pages will be prepared in manuscript.

WAR DIARY
or
INTELLIGENCE SUMMARY.
(Erase heading not required.)

Army Form C. 2118.

Place	Date	Hour	Summary of Events and Information	Remarks and references to Appendices
LABOURSE	22/9/17		New ADMS of 46 Division visited Main Dressing Station. Capt Cowell RAMC from 23 C.C.S. who is investigating "Shock" problems, to be quartered at FORT GLATZ. Capt J Miller leave from 22nd Sept to 2 Oct.	
	24/9/17		Attended weekly conference at ADMS office 10 am. Borrowed 1 Motor Ambulance from 1/2 N Mid. Fd. Amb. Conducted ADMS ~~to~~ round the area from which this unit is responsible for clearing. Posts in HULLUCH sector satisfactory but those in LOOS area overcrowded particularly TOSH KEEP where there are 8 regimental SB and 4 RAMC bearers besides 2 medical orderlies. Both ~~of~~ this and CHALK PIT RAP are I consider too far from the front line. Right Battn of 137 IB. has two RAPs, CHALK PIT and PONT St A good deal of shelling of ~~the~~ LOOS generally ~~and~~ during the morning and the TOSH ALLEY and ENGLISH ALLEY were blown in ~~in~~ several places shortly before we went along them. — An alternative method of evacuation from the Hill 70 area is greatly to be desired. At present everything has to go to FORT GLATZ at G35 b.3.8. thence by Motor Amb. along main LENS-BETHUNE ROAD.	

Instructions regarding War Diaries and Intelligence Summaries are contained in F. S. Regs., Part II. and the Staff Manual respectively. Title pages will be prepared in manuscript.

WAR DIARY
or
INTELLIGENCE SUMMARY.
(Erase heading not required.)

Army Form C. 2118.

Place	Date	Hour	Summary of Events and Information	Remarks and references to Appendices
LABOURSE	24/9/17		The only alternative seems to be by hand carriage from CHALK PIT post via CHALK PIT ALLEY to HALF WAY HOUSE G22b 2.2. This would be slow & would necessitate at least two relay posts en route: if this were adopted it would be possible to eliminate carriage through LOOS from Right Section and also ADS FORT GLATZ and TOSH KEEP POST. The present disposition of RAPs in this section is not satisfactory but the conditions are very difficult.	
	25/9/17		Inspected Baths at LABOURSE and VERQUIN with ADMS in morning. Sent 32 bearers up to attend cylinder carrying parties HULLUCH section.	
	26/9/17		Capt Herga came down from A.D.S. to report on his careful examination of evacuation routes from HILL 70. Bearers at SOLENT POST G36c.8.5 have been moved forward to NEW SOLENT POST at G36d.2.2. as the situation is better for all purposes. Evacuation from NATAL POST H31d.1.2. via OG1 or OB1 to CHALK PIT is not practicable and for the present it is essential to bring cases via TUNNEL POST H31c5.2., SOLENT POST and LOOS to FORT GLATZ G.35b.2.7. where there is the immense advantage of getting wounded in to a motor ambulance which ensures rapid and easy evacuation. Evacuation by hand carriage to Halfway House via CHALK PIT ALLEY should be reserved for occasions when the former route is rendered too unsafe.	

Army Form C. 2118.

WAR DIARY
or
INTELLIGENCE SUMMARY.
(Erase heading not required.)

Instructions regarding War Diaries and Intelligence Summaries are contained in F. S. Regs., Part II. and the Staff Manual respectively. Title pages will be prepared in manuscript.

Place	Date	Hour	Summary of Events and Information	Remarks and references to Appendices
LABOURSE	27/9/17		Visited A.D. Stations PHILOSOPHE & FORT GLATZ and the bearer posts from the latter to Hill 70. – all in good order and the day quiet. First relief of bearers from the posts effected in afternoon. 32 bearers detailed to accompany carrying parties up to HULLUCH section at night for 4 nights. New bearer post at G36d 2.2 – New Solent Post very good indeed: well secured in galleries under & connecting with small mine crater. Ample accommodation for bearers & fair for about a dozen stretchers & a large number of lightly wounded. G.O.C. 46 Division inspected horse lines & expressed unqualified approval of them.	
	30/9/17		Visited A.D.S. PHILOSOPHE in morning – DDMS 1 Corps visited main dressing station in my absence. – Sent two men as carpenter and tinsmith for temporary duty with No 8 Sanitary Section. Summary of changes in personnel for month of September 1917 10 Class A. batmen ASC sent to Base Depot 10 P.B. men received as batmen instead 2 officers off to other posting 2 " on from other posting 4 O.R. taken on strength 7 O.R. struck off strength. Net total reduction of strength 3 O.R.	

A7092. Wt. W12839/M1293. 750,000. 1/17. D. D. & L. Ltd. Forms/C2118/14.

Army Form C. 2118.

Instructions regarding War Diaries and Intelligence Summaries are contained in F. S. Regs., Part II. and the Staff Manual respectively. Title pages will be prepared in manuscript.

WAR DIARY
or
INTELLIGENCE SUMMARY.
(Erase heading not required.)

Place	Date	Hour	Summary of Events and Information	Remarks and references to Appendices
HESDIGNEUL	9/6/18		Normal relief of C section by A section at ADS GORRE effected by Tram service & completed 6 am. Capt Patlanski RAMC 1/2 NMFA attached to OC ADS for instruction for six days. A few enemy gas shells were put into BEUVRY and of LE QUESNOY about 10 pm – otherwise situation normal and quiet. AUH	
	10/6/18		1 NCO and 20 men from 1/2 NMFA arrived as reinforcement bearers for emergency and were attached to A sec. for administration & discipline. Pte SCHAEFFER RAMC left on 1 months probationary attachment to Intelligence Police I Army as interpreter. AUH	
	11/6/18		20 reinforcement bearers from 1/2 NMFA reported for duty.	
	12/6/18		ADMS conference 10 am: examined cellars at CHAMBORD Barracks and Civil & Military Hospital BETHUNE with a view to [illegible] the latter the most suitable & being best known, evacuation route direct to MDS and less work will be required to adapt them. There are large amounts of medical stores left in the building which I have applied to ADMS to be allowed to salvage. Visited ADS GORRE in afternoon. This is becoming quite palatial and strengthening proceeds steadily. [illegible] S. Staff Stys and arranged for instruction of a further batch of stretcher bearers. AUH	

D. D. & L., London, E.C. (A8604) Wt W1771/M2031 750,000 5/17 Sch. 52 Forms/C2118/14

10

Instructions regarding War Diaries and Intelligence Summaries are contained in F. S. Regs., Part II. and the Staff Manual respectively. Title pages will be prepared in manuscript.

WAR DIARY
or
~~INTELLIGENCE SUMMARY.~~
(Erase heading not required.)

Army Form C. 2118.

1/3 N M F Ambce

Hour, Date, Place	Summary of Events and Information	Remarks and references to Appendices
BAILLEUL 18-5-15	State :- Remained 3 Admissions 8 Evacuations 1 Remaining 10	
	Sgt Murray of the unit examined at the request of the D.D.M.S. a sample of artificial manure sent to a local resident through SWITZERLAND. This was found to be free from Arsenic & to be as far as could be found out what it was stated to be viz:- Calcium Cyanamide = a harmless artificial manure.	
	500 Respirators complete in waterproof bags + 500 bags issued to O C 7. Sherwood Foresters –	
19-5-15 BAILLEUL	Remained 10 – Admitted 4 – Evacuated nil Remaining 14.	
	Lt Boyd detailed to assist Lt McNee in investigating a supposed outbreak of Paratyphoid in the Division –	

Instructions regarding War Diaries and Intelligence Summaries are contained in F. S. Regs., Part II. and the Staff Manual respectively. Title pages will be prepared in manuscript.

WAR DIARY
or
INTELLIGENCE SUMMARY.
(Erase heading not required.)

Army Form C. 2118.

Place	Date	Hour	Summary of Events and Information	Remarks and references to Appendices
FOUQUIERES	19.11.17		Cases of Scabies bathed under the shower bath, instead of using tubs.	
			Concert given by No 1. CCS.	
	21.11.17.		Whist drive for Patients.	
	23.11.17.		Sink in Kitchen moved to side, new grease traps fixed. and drain to main drain down garden finished	
			Lieut Colonel Hodder returned from short leave.	
			Concert by Very lights.	
	24.11.17		Reported in person to ADMS.	
			C.R.S. inspected by G.O.C. 46 Div. & by DDMS 1 Corps.	
			Capt G.D. Fairley returned from temporary duty with 4 CCS.	
	25.11.17		ADMS visited C.R.S. and inspected improvements in progress.	
	27.11.17		Capt E.L. Henga M.C. reported in relief from temporary duty with 1/2 N.M.F.A.	
			New drainage from Kitchens laid & connected up to sink etc: New incinerator completed & working satisfactorily. Mixed whist drive for patients & RAMC personnel.	
	28.11.17		O.C. attended weekly conference at ADMS.	
			Capt Henga went to G.B. on 14 days leave.	
			Capt Doyle O.S. MORC. & 2 Sergeants went to course at 1 Army RAMC school.	

A5092. Wt. W12839/M1293. 750,000. 1/17. D. D. & L., Ltd. Forms/C2118/14.

Instructions regarding War Diaries and Intelligence Summaries are contained in F. S. Regs., Part II. and the Staff Manual respectively. Title pages will be prepared in manuscript.

WAR DIARY
or
INTELLIGENCE SUMMARY.
(Erase heading not required.)

Army Form C. 2118.

Place	Date	Hour	Summary of Events and Information	Remarks and references to Appendices
LABOURSE	26/8/17		Main dressing station LABOURSE now serving as CORPS-MDS and not merely divisional drawing cases from 46th and 6th divisions and attached corps details. All "gassed cases" diverted to No 16 Field Amb. at NOEUX les MINES. Drew up and promulgated measures to be taken at Main Dressing station in the event of ~~[struck through, illegible]~~ sustained heavy casualties being expected. - copy attached to W.D. -	App. I
	27/8/17		Attended conference at ADMS office 10 am. at which Field Ambulance commanders were instructed to furnish Regimental Aid Posts in their sections with alkaline solutions, Paraffin No 7 and pyjama suits so that complete treatment of yellow cross gassed cases may be initiated in R.A.Ps. I do not regard this as particularly feasible as the space is very limited and RMO is likely at such a time to have his hands very full and his quarters congested with patients. Facilities for this treatment are available at ADS once put into operation there eventually. ADMS instructions of course were carried out. Inspected ADS CAMBRIN in afternoon - a good deal of cleaning had been done but there is more to do as the place was very dirty and lime wash badly needed to improve the lighting. While there at 3.28pm a tremendous explosion was heard & felt + glass of windows broken. ? cause. The great concussion was also felt at LABOURSE and GOSNAY.	
	28/8/17		Sent party of 20 men to be administered by 465 Coy RE in ANNEQUIN and work under their orders on communication trenches	

A7092 Wt. W12839/M1293 750,000. 1/17. D. D & L., Ltd. Forms/C2118/14.

Instructions regarding War Diaries and Intelligence Summaries are contained in F. S. Regs., Part II. and the Staff Manual respectively. Title pages will be prepared in manuscript.

WAR DIARY
or
INTELLIGENCE SUMMARY.
(Erase heading not required.)

Army Form C. 2118.

Place	Date	Hour	Summary of Events and Information	Remarks and references to Appendices
LABOURSE	7/9/17		Attended ADMS conference 10 am. Principal subject under discussion impending alteration of divisional front & consequent Field Ambulance changes. Was informed that this unit would have responsibility for ~~collect~~ removal of casualties from whole of front south of HULLUCH TUNNEL and would resume charge of A.D.S. PHILOSOPHE and take over charge of A.D.S. Fort GLATZ & posts in connection therewith. In afternoon with Capt Herga, visited Fort GLATZ and posts TOSH KEEP; CHALK PIT ALLEY; SOLENT POST; TUNNEL POST and NATAL POST. Total personnel required 2 officers and 35 O.R. c̄ 2 drivers motor cyclist. Frequent reliefs necessary & will be made from Headquarters. ADS PHILOSOPHE will act as advanced base for supplies to LOOS posts. At Philosophe - 2 Motor Ambs will be stationed in addition to 1 from MAC and a water cart c̄ driver & 2 mules. Total Personnel at Philosophe - 2 officers 45 O.R.	

Army Form C. 2118.

Instructions regarding War Diaries and Intelligence Summaries are contained in F. S. Regs., Part II. and the Staff Manual respectively. Title pages will be prepared in manuscript.

WAR DIARY
or
INTELLIGENCE SUMMARY.
(Erase heading not required.)

Hour, Date, Place	Summary of Events and Information	Remarks and references to Appendices
20 - 4 - 15.	Patients in the Hospital as follows:- On 12th April 53 13th 70 - 14th 72 - 15th 86 - 16th 99 - 17th 84 - 18th 92. 19th 97 - 20th 100 = Three patients have been employed in cleaning the patients' rifles, bayonets + equipment in the Store - Dubbing has been indented for and each man able has been made to clean his boots - Baths have been established in the Hospital - Every man has a bath on admission, is served out with clean underclothing + his tunic + trousers are ironed to kill vermin - The dirty underclothing is washed, disinfected + dried + reissued = 100 sets of new underclothing have been obtained to carry this out - Extras in diet such as eggs, milk, porridge Cocoa + green vegetables have been procured in order to expedite the patients' recovery -	

(9 29 6) W4141—463 100,000 9/14 H W V Forms/C. 2118/10

Instructions regarding War Diaries and Intelligence Summaries are contained in F. S. Regs., Part II. and the Staff Manual respectively. Title pages will be prepared in manuscript.

WAR DIARY
or
INTELLIGENCE SUMMARY.
(Erase heading not required.)

Army Form C. 2118.

Place	Date	Hour	Summary of Events and Information	Remarks and references to Appendices
LABOURSE	11/9/17		Lieut W. B. Jack went on short leave to England.	
	12/9/17		Capt J. S. Ullman US. M.O.R.C. reported for duty - temporarily attached during absence of Capt Gavin with 1/5 Leic^r.	
	13/9/17		Drew Elephant for making emergency dressing room at Corps Main Dressing Station, and final instalment of RE. material for stable construction.	
			Visited A.D.S. CAMBRIN in afternoon.	
			All 20 men attached 466 Field Coy RE. returned to Field Ambulance for duty.	
	14/9/17		Started to rebuild farrier's shop & billet so as to provide better building and an overhang ~~roof~~ roof enabling horses to stand dry in wet weather while being shod.	
	15/9/17		Sent 40 Bearers to CAMBRIN section 6pm in connection with cylinder carrying parties.	
	16/9/17		Repeated bearers as for 15th all carrying completed ~~by~~ without incident.	

A.7092 Wt. W12839/M1293 750,000. 1/17. D. D & L., Ltd. Forms/C2118/14.

CONFIDENTIAL

Instructions regarding War Diaries and Intelligence Summaries are contained in F. S. Regs., Part II. and the Staff Manual respectively. Title pages will be prepared in manuscript.

1/3 North Midland Field Ambulance RAMC T.F

WAR DIARY
or
~~INTELLIGENCE~~ SUMMARY.
(*Erase heading not required.*)

Army Form C. 2118.

Hour, Date, Place	Summary of Events and Information	Remarks and references to Appendices
1st May 1915 BAILLEUL	Sgt James - ASC - Motor Driver attached to the unit - Sent to ENGLAND by orders of GHQ to have made the Collapsible wheeled Stretcher Carrier he had invented & to return with the finished article to GHQ = Attached are photographs of the "MILLER-JAMES" Carrier See Appendix I	Appendix I HHCD
2 = May = 1915	See Appendix II for the position of the 1/3 N M Field Ambulance + its Regimental Aid Posts. State 6 pm of the Section of the unit acting as a Casualty Clearing Hospital :- Remained 1. Admitted 49. Remaining 50	Appendix II HHCD
3 - May - 15	State :- Remained 50 Admitted 131 (60 gassed cases) Died 2 Transferred 12. Remaining 167.	
~~May 15~~	See Appendix III for the situation in BAILLEUL of the various medical departments that have been administered by the 1/3 N.M.F AMB. since April 5.15	Appendix III HHCD

(9 29 6) W 4141—463 100,000 9/14 H W V Forms/C. 2118/10

5

Army Form C. 2118.

Instructions regarding War Diaries and Intelligence Summaries are contained in F. S. Regs., Part II. and the Staff Manual respectively. Title pages will be prepared in manuscript.

WAR DIARY
or
~~INTELLIGENCE SUMMARY.~~
(Erase heading not required.)

1/3 N M F Amb
RAMC T

Hour, Date, Place	Summary of Events and Information	Remarks and references to Appendices
	divided - I suggested to the ADMS (Col Beevor) & to the DDMS (Col Geddes) that these sprays might be used in the Trenches for spraying the "Gasses" used by the Enemy - a solution of Sodium Carbonate or "Hypo" being used for this purpose - The spray is shown in Appendix V	Appendix V HAED
5 - 5 - 15 BAILLEUL	Experimented with Bromine vapour before the DDMS & the Commander of the II Corps = It was found that spraying the vapour with "Hypo" solution made a considerable impression the room filled with Bromine vapour being made clearer & possible to breath in - This experiment justified a trial of the sprays at the front & the Commander of the II Corps told me to purchase 40 - I purchased all in BAILLEUL - (18) & gave them to an Officer of the IIIrd DIVISION - supplying him with	

(9 29 6) W4141—463 100,000 9/14 H W V Forms/C. 2118/10

7

113 N Med F A

Army Form C. 2118.

WAR DIARY
or
INTELLIGENCE SUMMARY.
(Erase heading not required.)

Instructions regarding War Diaries and Intelligence Summaries are contained in F. S. Regs., Part II. and the Staff Manual respectively. Title pages will be prepared in manuscript.

Vol 49

Place	Date	Hour	Summary of Events and Information	Remarks and references to Appendices
FRESNOY LE GRAND	1/3/19		Capt. F. L. RICHARD RAMC reported for duty from 1/5th S. Staff. Inspected cookhouses, water-carts & latrines of 1/6th N. Staff. ACY	
	4/3/19		ADMS called. ACY	
TROISVILLES	5/3/19		Unit left FRESNOY at 9.30 AM & proceeded by route march to TROISVILLES arriving at 1.45 P.M. Billets fairly good. ACY	
"	6/3/19		Capt. G. R. SHARP RAMC reported for duty from 230 Bgde. RFA. ACY	
"	7/3/19		Major E. J. BRADLEY M.C. reported from leave. Capt. T. HARPER M.C., C.F. departed for duty with 58 CCS.	
"	9/3/19		Lt Col. A. C. Turner DSO left unit for demobilisation. MAJOR G.H.H. MANFIELD M.C. took over Command. 5 Other Ranks left for demobilisation. Capt. G R SHARP left unit for duty with AD.M.S. [initials]	
"	11.3.19		Capt G R SHARP returned to duty with the unit [initials]	
"	12.3.19		ADMS called [initials]	
"	14.3.19		MAJOR E.J. BRADLEY MC evacuated to C.C.S. 5 Other Ranks left for demobilisation [initials]	

D. D. & L., London, E.C.
(10560) Wt W5300/P713 750,000 3/18 E 2688 Forms C/2118/14.

Instructions regarding War Diaries and Intelligence Summaries are contained in F. S. Regs., Part II. and the Staff Manual respectively. Title pages will be prepared in manuscript.

WAR DIARY
or
INTELLIGENCE SUMMARY.
(Erase heading not required.)

Army Form C. 2118.

1/3 N M Fd Amb

Vol 50

Place	Date	Hour	Summary of Events and Information	Remarks and references to Appendices
TROISVILLES	5.4.19		CAPT J KING RAMC T.F returned from U.K short leave [initials]	
	8.4.19		CAPT E M MORRIS M.C. U.S.A. left unit for duty with 28th LABOUR GROUP. [initials]	
	9.4.19		CAPT F.L. RICHARD S.R. returned from U.K Special leave [initials]	
	14.4.19		CAPT F.L. RICHARD S.R. left unit for demobilisation [initials]	
	21.4.19		One O.R. left unit for demobilisation [initials]	
	28.4.19		Two O.R. RAMC left unit for demobilisation. RAMC now at CADRE Strength. [initials]	

[illegible signature]
Major RAMC

D. D. & L., London, E.C.
(10340) Wt.W2300/P713 750,000 2/18 E 2688 Forms/C2118/16.

Instructions regarding War Diaries and Intelligence Summaries are contained in F. S. Regs., Part II. and the Staff Manual respectively. Title pages will be prepared in manuscript.

Army Form C. 2118.

WAR DIARY
or
INTELLIGENCE SUMMARY.
(Erase heading not required.)

Place	Date	Hour	Summary of Events and Information	Remarks and references to Appendices
LABOURSE	11/10/17		Visited Advanced Dressing Station and the post & RAP on Hill 70 section: visited Hdqrs R^r Batt^n 139 Bde & discussed with C.O. measures relating to health of the men in trenches. Visited Battalion drying room & found a good place: if provision for washing feet could be added it should be of great value in the coming months.	
	12/10/17		Got out instructions for assistance of RMOs in combatting surgical shock in wounded.	
	13/10/17		Visited PHILOSOPHE in morning to investigate means of preventing rain water getting into the cellars. This a very difficult problem. R.E. officer inspected same ADS with a view to installation of steam heating.	
	15/10/17		Visited ADS. PHILOSOPHE & entertained at lunch there Capt CANNON. U.S. Army. the distinguished physiologist who is investigating phenomena of surgical shock (primary). Horse-master 1 Corps ~~[illegible]~~ inspected standings & animals & expressed approval.	

A7092. Wt. W12839/M1293 750,000. 1/17. D. D & L., Ltd. Forms/C2118/14.

Army Form C. 2118.

Instructions regarding War Diaries and Intelligence Summaries are contained in F. S. Regs., Part II. and the Staff Manual respectively. Title pages will be prepared in manuscript.

WAR DIARY
or
INTELLIGENCE SUMMARY.
(Erase heading not required.)

Place	Date	Hour	Summary of Events and Information	Remarks and references to Appendices
Labeuvrière	7/7/17		General routine. Paraded all available men in Full Marching Order this being the first opportunity after 11 weeks of work at advanced post. A.D.V.S. I Corps inspected the horses & mules & was extremely satisfied with their condition	
	8/7/17		Capt. E.E. Herga was decorated with the Military Cross by G.O.C. 46th Div. D.D.M.S. I Corps visited the Rest Station	
	9/7/17		Proceeded to conference A.D.M.S.'s office.	
	10/7/17		General routine	
	11/7/17		Sent all patients who were fit to walk & all available officers & men of the unit to line the route between Hesdigneul & Gosnay on the occasion of His Majesty the King	
	12/7/17			
	13/7/17		Major Baron left for duty with 1/1 North Midland Field Amb. Command taken over by Capt. J. Miller.	

(A7092). Wt. W12839/M1293. 750,000. 1/17. D. D. & L., Ltd. Forms/C.2118/14.

Instructions regarding War Diaries and Intelligence Summaries are contained in F. S. Regs., Part II. and the Staff Manual respectively. Title pages will be prepared in manuscript.

WAR DIARY

or

~~INTELLIGENCE SUMMARY.~~

(Erase heading not required.)

1/3 N.M. F. Ambce

Army Form C. 2118.

Hour, Date, Place	Summary of Events and Information	Remarks and references to Appendices
11 - 5 - 15	Number of wounded passed through the Field Ambulance acting as a detached Clearing Hospital during the last 14 days i.e. since the commencement of the F. Ambce so acting = 770 = The following Major Operations have been performed - Amputations 6 Decompressions :- 12 Abdominal Operations 1 =	
	The No of Deaths in the 14 days = 21 = (3 being from the Effects of Gas) - Gassed cases :- 122 -	
	State :- Remained 30 = Admissions 97 = Transferred 46 = Deaths 1 = Discharged to Duty 1 = Remaining 79 =	
	10 men of the unit still employed preparing cotton waste for Anti-gas Masks -	

(9 29 6) W 4141—463 100,000 9/14 H W V Forms/C. 2118/10

Instructions regarding War Diaries and Intelligence Summaries are contained in F. S. Regs., Part II. and the Staff Manual respectively. Title pages will be prepared in manuscript.

WAR DIARY
or
INTELLIGENCE SUMMARY.
(*Erase heading not required.*)

Army Form C. 2118.

Place	Date	Hour	Summary of Events and Information	Remarks and references to Appendices
LABOURSE	5/10/17		Projection of gas took place early this morning from HULLUCH section. Bearers sent up had no casualties above normal to bring in.	
			Bearer party from 1/2 NMFA. returned to their unit 10 am.	
			3 Officers and a number of OR of the Field Amb. attended lecture by Consulting Surgeon 1 Army in afternoon at YMCA hut NOEUX L/M.	
			Capt W.C. GAVIN RAMC deputed for duty as MO i/c 1 Corps Reinforcement Depot & is struck off strength of Field Ambulance.	
	6/10/17	2.30pm	Marching order inspection of all ranks at Headquarters.	
			Visited ADSs PHILOSOPHE and FORT GLATZ and inspected posts at TOSH KEEP, CHALK PIT and HALF WAY HOUSE.	
			Discussed with M.O. 8th NOTTS & DERBY Rgt means of improving conditions of his men as regards facilities for washing, feeding etc while in trenches.	
			All trenches traversed today were very wet and the going particularly bad between TOSH KEEP and FORT GLATZ.	

A7092 Wt. W12839/M1293 750,000. 1/17. D. D. & L., Ltd. Forms/C2118/14.

7

Instructions regarding War Diaries and Intelligence Summaries are contained in F. S. Regs., Part II. and the Staff Manual respectively. Title pages will be prepared in manuscript.

WAR DIARY
or
INTELLIGENCE SUMMARY.
(Erase heading not required.)

Army Form C. 2118.

Hour, Date, Place	Summary of Events and Information	Remarks and references to Appendices
21 - June 15 BAILLEUL	State of Rest Hospital BAILLEUL :- Remaining 41 Admitted 25 To Duty 1. Remaining 65 —	
22 6 15 BAILLEUL	Remained 65 Admitted 17. Duty 2 Transferred 3 Remaining 77	
	Received instructions that the unit is to move to STEENVOORDE + take over the Rest Hosp: there for the sick of the 46 DIVISION.	
	Motored there + inspected the Building with the ADMS.	
23 - 6 - 15 BAILLEUL	Remained 77 Admitted 10 Evacuated 5. Remaining 82	
	~~B section of the Field Ambulance marched at 9 p.m. to STEENVOORDE to take over the Divisional Rest Hospital there~~ —	

(9 29 6) W 4141—463 100,000 9/14 H W V Forms/C. 2118/10

Army Form C. 2118.

Instructions regarding War Diaries and Intelligence Summaries are contained in F. S. Regs., Part II. and the Staff Manual respectively. Title Pages will be prepared in manuscript.

WAR DIARY
or
INTELLIGENCE SUMMARY
(Erase heading not required.)

Place	Date	Hour	Summary of Events and Information	Remarks and references to Appendices
	5/8/17		and a number of casualties were incurred. Only 4 cases were brought down here and by midnight all was quiet and all cars back at H.qrs.	
	6/8/17		Attended at ADMS office usual weekly conference. 10 am. Nothing of special importance considered.	
LABOURSE	7/8/17		Visited Advanced Dressing Station and bearer posts in morning. Trenches a good deal improved in the past few days. Reported to ADMS the results of my inspection and the conclusions I came to in regard to evacuation of casualties from Right subsector, HULLUCH sector, in the event of certain operations. Shelters situated about the junction of VENDIN ALLEY and POSEN ALLEY with Reserve line would be untenable & probably blown in as these points are exactly registered and frequently strafed. VENDIN ALLEY forward of reserve trench is very wet and back from that point may easily be rendered impassible by shell fire. For small local operations it would probably be better to detain casualties in shelters in support line till dark and then evacuate across the top. This would expose them to less risk than attempting to carry them down POSEN or VENDIN ALLEYS during activity	

2449 Wt. W14957/M90 750,000 1/16 J.B.C. & A. Forms/C.2118/12.

Instructions regarding War Diaries and Intelligence Summaries are contained in F. S. Regs., Part II. and the Staff Manual respectively. Title pages will be prepared in manuscript.

Army Form C. 2118.

WAR DIARY
or
INTELLIGENCE SUMMARY.
(Erase heading not required.)

Place	Date	Hour	Summary of Events and Information	Remarks and references to Appendices
HESDIGNEUL	6/7/18		Harassing fire by enemy on HESDIGNEUL - GOSNAY area in afternoon. One shell dropped within 30 yards of Horsed transport billets. Routine inspection for scabies carried out. AAH	
	7/7/18		All hands employed in digging in. All huts sunk another foot. Officers mess hut protected by revetment and shelter trench in front of bivouacs deepened. Enemy aircraft over in evening from 11pm onwards but no bombs dropped near by. Lieut G.R. MORRIS MRC USA joined and was taken on strength: 1 Corporal transferred to 1/1 NM Fd Amb. AAH	
	8/7/18		Lt Morris sent to R'ADS for duty & instruction. 20 OR of NM Fd Amb reporting for duty & attached to B sec. for administration. Further progress with protection against bombing raids made but lack of material for revetting makes the work very slow. AAH.	
	9/7/18		Capt A. FLORIAN MRC USA left for C.O.D. SOS. AEF & was struck off strength of unit. 4 OR went on leave to PARIS.	

D. D. & L., London, E.C. (A8604) Wt W1771/M2031 750,000 5/17 Sch. 52 Forms/C2118/14

11

Army Form C. 2118.

Instructions regarding War Diaries and Intelligence Summaries are contained in F. S. Regs., Part II. and the Staff Manual respectively. Title pages will be prepared in manuscript.

WAR DIARY
or
INTELLIGENCE SUMMARY.
(Erase heading not required.)

1/3 N M F Ambce

Hour, Date, Place	Summary of Events and Information	Remarks and references to Appendices
May 20 1915 BAILLEUL	Remained 14 - Admissions 28 - Evacuated 4 Remaining 38.	
May 21 15 BAILLEUL	Remained 38 - Admitted 10 - Evacuated 13 Remaining 35.	
May 22 - 15 BAILLEUL.	Copy of circular letter from DMS II Army on "Precautionary Measures against the Introduction of Typhus Fever" received = Circulated to all M.O's in the 137th BRIGADE	
~~May 23 15~~	Remained 36 Admissions 16 Evacuated 10 Remaining 42	
May 23 - 15	Remained 44 admitted 7 Evacuated 5 Remaining 46 -	
May 24 - 15 BAILLEUL	Remained 46 admitted 9 Evacuated 0 Remaining 55 = At 6.45 pm 73 gassed cases were admitted to the Section acting as a Divisional Rest Station - Most of the cases had used respirators, some respirators however were poor & had not been properly damped.	

(9 29 6) W 4141—463 100,000 9/14 H W V Forms/C. 2118/10

6

Army Form C. 2118.

Instructions regarding War Diaries and Intelligence Summaries are contained in F. S. Regs., Part II. and the Staff Manual respectively. Title pages will be prepared in manuscript.

WAR DIARY
or
INTELLIGENCE SUMMARY.

(*Erase heading not required.*)

Hour, Date, Place	Summary of Events and Information	Remarks and references to Appendices
BAILLEUL June 17.15	State :- Remained 65 - Admitted 3. To Duty 8 Remaining 60 - Wire received from ADMS 4.30 pm to be prepared for a Move at short notice -	
BAILLEUL June 18.15	State of Rest Station :- Remained 60 Admitted 10 To Duty 29 Transferred 7. Remaining 34.	
BAILLEUL June 19.15.	Road Report on area near the Regimental Aid Post at NEUVE EGLISE attached as Appendix I Took the D.A.D.M.S 50 Division round the Rest Stn BAILLEUL and the A.D.S. NEUVE EGLISE in view of that Division replacing the 46th Division Remained 34 Admitted 3 ~~Discharged~~ To Duty 3 Remaining 34	Appendix I H.H.C.D.
June 20 = 15 BAILLEUL	Remained 34 Admitted 15 Duty 4 Transferred 4 Remaining 41.	

(9 29 6) W4141—463 100,000 9/14 H W V Forms/C. 2118/10

Instructions regarding War Diaries and Intelligence Summaries are contained in F. S. Regs., Part II. and the Staff Manual respectively. Title pages will be prepared in manuscript.

WAR DIARY
or
INTELLIGENCE SUMMARY.
(Erase heading not required.)

Army Form C. 2118.

Place	Date	Hour	Summary of Events and Information	Remarks and references to Appendices
LABOURSE	20/8/17		Attended conference at ADMS office 10 am.	
			Recommended that R.A.P. at present in DUMPDRIVE shaft should be moved nearer to outer end of HULLUCH TUNNEL either near Advanced Battalion H.Q. or further out still. ADMS approved & requested B.G. cdg 137 I.B. to allot a position.	
			Captain E.E. Herga M.C. ~~attended~~ commenced Anti-Gas course at Divisional School.	
			Canadian A.M.C. leave ADS PHILOSOPHE which is now run entirely by Imperial Field Amb.	
			In connection with reduction of establishment of riding horses 4 were today disposed of under orders of DADMS.	
	21/8/17		During last night ~~the~~ a party of RE & Lincolns in VERMELLES were caught by enemy shell and several casualties brought in to Field Ambulance. Later the enemy sent a number of Trench mortar gas bombs on to HULLUCH sector resulting in some slightly gassed cases being admitted here. The gas was not yellow cross but apparently of the phosgene type.	
	22/8/17		Visited ADS - CAMBRIN held by No 6 Field Ambulance and obtained information as to CAMBRIN sector and the medical arrangements thereon.	

A7092. Wt. W12839/M1293. 750,000. 1/17. D. D & L., Ltd. Forms/C2118/14.

Instructions regarding War Diaries and Intelligence Summaries are contained in F. S. Regs., Part II. and the Staff Manual respectively. Title pages will be prepared in manuscript.

WAR DIARY
or
INTELLIGENCE SUMMARY.
(Erase heading not required.)

Army Form C. 2118.

Place	Date	Hour	Summary of Events and Information	Remarks and references to Appendices
LABOURSE	5/9/17		In the early hours of the morning an alarm of gas was received and the necessary steps were taken. Apparently numerous gas shells were fired on MAZINGARBE neighbourhood and a small amount of the gas was wind borne here: it was inconsiderable in amount, but was sufficient to cause sneezing and irritation of conjunctivae to a small extent.	
	6/9/17		Represented to A/ADMS the need in connection with Corps Main Dressing Station here of some form of shelter from enemy shells for personnel essentially retained at M.D.S. during shelling and for any patients there may be in at the moment. This may take the form of a suitably placed deep trench or perhaps preferably elephant tube erected under cover of western end of church. All other personnel and animals may be removed to a flank during shelling, but the essential remainder should be able to work with the same feeling of security as obtains in the average Advanced Dressing Station.	
			Visited A.D.S. CAMBRIN in afternoon.	
			Received 10 men (? P.B) in replacement of 10 Bâtmen A.S.C. carried on Field Ambulance establishment.	

A7092 Wt. W12839/M1293 750,000. 1/17. D. D & L., Ltd. Forms/C2118/14.

Instructions regarding War Diaries and Intelligence Summaries are contained in F. S. Regs., Part II. and the Staff Manual respectively. Title pages will be prepared in manuscript.

WAR DIARY
or
INTELLIGENCE SUMMARY.
(Erase heading not required.)

Army Form C. 2118.

LA HERLIÈRE

Hour, Date, Place	Summary of Events and Information	Remarks and references to Appendices
31/8/16	Most of the cases of gassing occurred well after the gas was liberated – the enemy replied with a number of gas shells smelling strongly of phosphorus but beyond some irritation of throat no one was seriously affected. The long time taken to collect cases was due to difficulty in finding them the symptoms being somewhat delayed. – for this reason Capt Harrison kept the bearers in the trenches till 3.30 am by which time the line was fairly free from ~~gas~~ any gas smell. In the opinion of this officer the few cases that occurred were due to men removing respirators too early. Very few whiffs of the gas in slight concentration were enough to cause dizziness & vomiting after a variable period. Goggles were not necessary at any period.	
10 am	Capt Harrison reports a further 5 cases of slight gassing this morning among men who were working hard all the time the gas was in evidence.	

A E Hodds

LIEUT.-COLONEL
[...] 3rd N. MID FIELD AMB
R. A. M. CORPS.

Army Form C. 2118.

Instructions regarding War Diaries and Intelligence Summaries are contained in F. S. Regs., Part II. and the Staff Manual respectively. Title pages will be prepared in manuscript.

WAR DIARY
or
INTELLIGENCE SUMMARY.
(*Erase heading not required.*)

Place	Date	Hour	Summary of Events and Information	Remarks and references to Appendices
LABOURSE	28/8/17		At 10.30pm received orders to send 36 bearers in motor ambulances to PHILOSOPHE for collection & evacuation of gassed and other casualties consequent on raid in enemy lines. Requisite bearers dispatched promptly.	
	29/8/17		Casualties from the above passed through Field Amb. 2 officers 44 O.R. – about 25 gassed cases were sent through to Field Amb at NOEUX les MINES. Last bearers returned to Headquarters 7am. Ford Motor Ambulance sustained damage to an axle & remained all night at crossroads G 34 d. 65.70. and was recovered & towed home 10am. One large car had minor damage from shell fire while at ADS PHILOSOPHE including a cut petrol pipe. Both cars taken to D.S.C. workshop for repair. No casualties to RAMC personnel of this unit.	
	30/8/17		Enemy shelled LABOURSE with large (app 8") shell between 1.30 pm and 2.15 pm. One of these hit the billet at W. end of school killing one & wounding 4 RAMC personnel. Billet wrecked. Found other billets for personnel; cleared all patients & will continue to clear them as they arrive to CRS or CCS pending further orders. The objective of the shelling is apparently a Railway Construction Section just west of school and about 300 yards distant; if as seems probable the shelling becomes a habit LABOURSE will have to be given up as a Corps Main Dressing Station. Prospected VERQUIGNEUL and VERQUIN in afternoon but neither has any accommodation.	

A7092. Wt. W12839/M1293. 750,000. 1/17. D. D & L., Ltd. Forms/C2118/14.

Army Form C. 2118.

WAR DIARY
or
INTELLIGENCE SUMMARY.
(*Erase heading not required.*)

Instructions regarding War Diaries and Intelligence Summaries are contained in F. S. Regs., Part II, and the Staff Manual respectively. Title pages will be prepared in manuscript.

Place	Date	Hour	Summary of Events and Information	Remarks and references to Appendices
LABOURSE	7/9/17		Of the 10 P.B. men received 2 have V.D.H. and are fit for light duty only: only three of the ten have any knowledge of horses.	
			Four cases came through exhibiting skin lesions due to yellow cross gas poisoning.	
	8/9/17		8 Class A. A.S.C. batmen departed for H.T. & S. depot HAVRE two more to follow when available.	
			Capt. GAVIN returned from rendering temporary assistance to 16 Field Amb.	
			18 of the party of RAMC employed as working party under 468 Field Coy R.E. required to assist 1/1 N.M.F.A. at VERMELLES.	
	9/9/17		Inspected ADS, RAP CAMBRIN section and R.A.M.C. posts.	
	10/9/17		Attended ADMS weekly conference 10 am. The most important matter considered was the disposal of very slightly gassed cases who are under present orders evacuated but in the opinion of ADMS & Field Amb. Commanders will be fit for duty in about 48 hours: whole question referred to Corps.	
			Submitted name of 421301 Pte W.J. BURKITT of this unit for Military Medal on report of his conduct night of 8/9 Sept by Capt. J. Graham M.C. RAMC i/c stretcher bearers.	
			DDMS I Corps visited Corps Main Dressing Station.	

A7092 Wt. W1283/M1293. 750,000. 1/17. D. D. & L., Ltd. Forms/C2118/14.

Army Form C. 2118.

WAR DIARY
or
INTELLIGENCE SUMMARY
(Erase heading not required.)

Instructions regarding War Diaries and Intelligence Summaries are contained in F. S. Regs., Part II. and the Staff Manual respectively. Title Pages will be prepared in manuscript.

Place	Date	Hour	Summary of Events and Information	Remarks and references to Appendices
	11/8/17		Submitted for consideration of ADMS a War Establishment for a re-modelled Field Ambulance which should be capable of ~~the~~ carrying out the same duties as the present Field Ambulance with a considerable economy of personnel, material and animals.	
LABOURSE	12/8/17		Routine day – Church Service (voluntary) in YMCA hut 11.30 am. A batch of 19 shell gassed cases arrived from MAROC about 6 pm: submitted report on them to ADMS: this gas was distinctly perceptible at A.D.S. PHILOSOPHE 2500 yards down wind, rendering wearing of S.B.R. necessary for a short time. The lacrimatory effect was marked but at the A.D.S. no one suffered from any other symptoms. This did not present any of the features which have come to be associated with the "new gas" the enemy is using. O.C. ADS described the smell as rather pleasant not unlike oil of spearmint.	
	13/8/17		Attended conference at ADMS office 10 am: discussed operation orders in the event of active operations. Afterwards visited A.D.S. PHILOSOPHE – recommended to ADMS that 46 Div. assume all the work of ADS PHILOSOPHE thereby setting free the Canadian personnel at present there.	

2449 Wt. W14957/M90 750,000 1/16 J.B.C. & A. Forms/C.2118/12.

Instructions regarding War Diaries and Intelligence Summaries are contained in F. S. Regs., Part II. and the Staff Manual respectively. Title pages will be prepared in manuscript.

WAR DIARY
or
INTELLIGENCE SUMMARY.
(Erase heading not required.)

Army Form C. 2118.

Place	Date	Hour	Summary of Events and Information	Remarks and references to Appendices
HESDIGNEUL	29/4/18		Morning report from Major Bradley i/c GORRE A.D.S. gives evacuation during night 28/29 as 1 officer & 65 OR. He also gives very satisfactory account of the behaviour of the [illegible] RAMC bearer squad put at disposal of MO i/c 1/5 S. Staffs. Situation report from Major Haga i/c ESSARS A.D.S. records a fairly heavy drenching with Blue Cross & Phosgene gas shells last night. Most of the casualties in 138 Brigade units were due to this. Further that RAP of support Battalion 1/4th (ESSARS) subsection which was at ECLUSE d'ESSARS X 19 C. 5 8 has been moved to X 25 a. 95 80 (ESSARS) provisionally. The Field Amb. bearer post (4 OR) which was attached has been called in & returned to Hdqrs as no longer needed. Field Amb posts in ESSARS sector now only two, & staff 1 officer 17 O.R. 2 Motor Ambs & 1 Motor cycle. Seven men from staff at BRUAY sent down to Hdqrs today.	
	30/4/18		In company of ADMS visited ADS GORRE and posts & RAPs and ADS ESSARS: all in order. Staff at ESSARS ADS & post relieved by Lt Richard & 10 OR. Major Haga & 10 OR returning to Hdqrs. Steady shelling of ESSARS round church all morning. Prospected for sites for Walking wounded post & ADS (alternative) between VERQUIN and BETHUNE BEUVRY road but found all the most eligible positions already occupied by Artillery. Probably stations in an open field will be the best solution of the difficulty. Further 3 men from staff at BRUAY rejoined Hdqrs. Patients remaining at BRUAY tonight 50.	

D. D. & L., London, E.C.
(A8co4) Wt W1771/M2031 750,000 5/17 Sch. 52 Forms/C2118/14

Instructions regarding War Diaries and Intelligence Summaries are contained in F. S. Regs., Part II. and the Staff Manual respectively. Title pages will be prepared in manuscript.

WAR DIARY
or
INTELLIGENCE SUMMARY.
(Erase heading not required.)

Army Form C. 2118.

Place	Date	Hour	Summary of Events and Information	Remarks and references to Appendices
LABOURSE	18/10/17		Inspection of unit in marching order. Visited C.R.S. in afternoon to inspect recent improvements and perhaps get a few tips.	
	19/10/17		Inspected Baths at NOYELLES and PHILOSOPHE. Ironing arrangements faulty at latter as at former & for same reason. A disinfestation chamber for service dress is however being made which aspires to effect disinfestation in 5 minutes by exposing garments freely spread out to a temperature of 180° Fah. upwards. The temperature is apparently got by circulation of steam or hot air but the building is not yet sufficiently advanced to pass an opinion on.	
	20/10/17		Gas was projected successfully on night 19/20 from part of front covered by this Field Ambulance: three of our men were accidentally gassed owing to explosion of a T.M. bomb injuring a cylinder. Under verbal instructions from ADMS. sent 1 officer MAC car attached, to PHILOSOPHE for duty with instructions to officer i/c. that it is to be used for direct evacuation of wounded to C.C.S. in his discretion. Foden Thresh attached started work here but was sent into Supply Column Workshop in evening as only one chamber was working properly.	

Instructions regarding War Diaries and Intelligence Summaries are contained in F. S. Regs., Part II. and the Staff Manual respectively. Title pages will be prepared in manuscript.

WAR DIARY
or
INTELLIGENCE SUMMARY.
(Erase heading not required.)

Army Form C. 2118.

Hour, Date, Place	Summary of Events and Information	Remarks and references to Appendices
July 14 – 15.	L' Corpl Welch H. reported by Captn Miller as having done exceedingly good work. He has been in charge of Ambulance wagons going up to MAPLE COPSE at night – These wagons have been in difficulties from bad roads & shell holes when under shell fire – L. Corp Welch has shown coolness & courage & no wagon has been lost.	
July 15. 16.	Inspected Dug-outs at the Ry Embankment I 21 C 6.8 – Some want repairing – reported to A.D.M.S. – One horse killed & one wounded by Shrapnel in Transport field at KRUISSTAAT H.18 d 1.1 Transport moved back to H 23 (b) 4.8 Suggested Mobile Dentists surgeries be provided for each Division & attached to one of the 3 Field Ambulances.	Appendix I A.D.M.S.

Instructions regarding War Diaries and Intelligence Summaries are contained in F. S. Regs., Part II. and the Staff Manual respectively. Title Pages will be prepared in manuscript.

WAR DIARY
or
~~INTELLIGENCE SUMMARY~~
(Erase heading not required.)

Army Form C. 2118

Place	Date	Hour	Summary of Events and Information	Remarks and references to Appendices
GAUDIEMPRE	23/5/16		Took Capt Yates over line of trench & explained the work required. Made arrangements for transport etc of men & applied to R.E. for necessary tools.	
	25/5/16		Major C.A. Stedston went on temporary duty RMO 4th Lincolns in exchange for Capt PERRY temp. attd to F. Amb.	
	26/5/16		Accompanied ADMS to FONQUEVILLERS to inspect a set of dugouts about 600 yards N of present ADS with a view to converting them into a supplementary ADS.	
	27/5/16		Tools available for whole working party which starts digging tonight — New main dressing station site fixed & hut positions taped out.	
	31/5/16		In past 4 days work on trench has progressed well: also erection of huts of main dressing station making good progress: supplied 24 men to work at levelling ground under direction of R.E. for the erection of huts. A number of cases of diphtheria have passed	

14

Instructions regarding War Diaries and Intelligence Summaries are contained in F. S. Regs., Part II. and the Staff Manual respectively. Title pages will be prepared in manuscript.

WAR DIARY
or
INTELLIGENCE SUMMARY.
(Erase heading not required.)

1/3 N M Fd Amb

Army Form C. 2118.

Vol 29

MEDICAL

Place	Date	Hour	Summary of Events and Information	Remarks and references to Appendices
Labeuvrière	1/7/17		Proceeded to A D M S & was informed that it was improbable that this unit would move. Went to A D S Pont Grenay where Capt Miller was dealing with large numbers of wounded. Made arrangements with Capt Miller for his relief at Bully Grenay & Pont Grenay	
	2/7/17		Capt Hersa & all N.C.Os & Bearers from the Lievin sector returned.	
	3/7/17		Capt D.B. Sattie returned from Lievin & Capt J. Miller, Lieut Jack with A section & Transport complete returned to H.Qrs from Bully Grenay	
	4/7/17		Capt J. L. Chamberlain reported to duty from base. A D M S visited Hospital	
	5/7/17		Detailed 1 horse ambulance to report for duty to Capt D. C. Sattie at Medical Aid Station Allouagne	
	6/7/17		Lieut R. H. Oulton evacuated to Base 5/7/17 & struck off the strength of the unit	

(A7092). Wt. W12839/M1293. 750,000. 1/17. D. D. & L., Ltd. Forms/C.2118/14.

Army Form C. 2118.

WAR DIARY
or
INTELLIGENCE SUMMARY.
(Erase heading not required.)

Instructions regarding War Diaries and Intelligence Summaries are contained in F. S. Regs., Part II. and the Staff Manual respectively. Title pages will be prepared in manuscript.

Hour, Date, Place	Summary of Events and Information	Remarks and references to Appendices
JULY 23rd 15	Commenced taking in wounded at THE MILL VLAMERTINGHE 8. am.	
	My letter to the ADMS re Mobile Dental Clinics attached to one Field Ambulance sent on to G.O.C 46 Division. Returned by G.O.C with a memo that the subject has already been considered, and Dentists were already attached to some Corps + he did not consider it advisable to forward the correspondence.	See Appendix I. AHCD
July 25 15	Sent one Officer + one tent subdivision to take over a School at BRANDHOEK as a second ADVANCED DRESSING STATION.	
July 27 15.	Moved main camp to G 13 6 10.4	
July 30 15	Large number of Casualties through Advanced Dressing Stations	
July 31 15	Week ending 8 AM July 30.15 – 530 Cases through the ADS at VLAMERTINGHE.	AHCD Lt Col Comdg 1/3 N Mid Fd Amb 46 Div

(9 29 6) W4141—463 100,000 9/14 H W V Forms/C. 2118/10

Instructions regarding War Diaries and Intelligence Summaries are contained in F. S. Regs., Part II. and the Staff Manual respectively. Title pages will be prepared in manuscript.

WAR DIARY
or
INTELLIGENCE SUMMARY.
(Erase heading not required.)

Army Form C. 2118.

Place	Date	Hour	Summary of Events and Information	Remarks and references to Appendices
LABOURSE	21/10/17		Visited advanced dressing station Fort GLATZ and PHILOSOPHE & found all in order. At the latter place the constructional work towards diverting rainwater & keeping the cellars dry has been completed & is apparently satisfactory. Loose box for a sick horse or mule, completed at Transport lines and also necessary alterations to Latrine in these lines carried out. Drew up & issued necessary general orders relating to Gas alarm.	
	22/10/17		Capt Cowell RAMC who had been quartered with this unit for some weeks while investigating "primary shock" departed to take up other duties.	
	23/10/17		Revised syllabus of training of newly appointed officers. Visited hot air disinfecting & drying chamber at NOEUX. This appears to work satisfactorily - a temp of 160° Fahr. can easily be maintained, & it is economical of fuel. It can be made from routine R.E. materials & is inexpensive to erect. It is certainly the best thing I have seen out here in nearly three years. It is the idea of O.C. No 8 Sanitary Section.	

A7092. Wt. W12839. D. D. & L., Ltd. Forms/C2118/14.

WAR DIARY
or
INTELLIGENCE SUMMARY
(Erase heading not required.)

Army Form C. 2118

Place	Date	Hour	Summary of Events and Information	Remarks and references to Appendices
ISBERGUES	9/1/16		Entrainment of 4 officers RAMC + 157 O.R. + 2 patients effected without hitch – all wagons [illegible] accompanied but no horses. Train moved out 10.20 am.	
MARSEILLE	11/1/16		Arrived MARSEILLES 2:30 pm – detrained personnel & wagons and marched to Camp at PARC BORELY. – all accommodated under canvas.	
	12/1/16		Reported to ADMS base & received general instructions from him.	
	13/1/16		In consultation with Medical Officers of 46 Div units in camp devised measures for limiting incidence of Scabies & venereal disease in the troops.	
	15/1/16		Visited Lt Col Sir Hill Child Bt. cdg 2nd N.M. Bde RFA as senior officer i/c troops of 46 Div in Camp with a view to effecting improvements in certain sanitary matters about the lines.	
	16/1/16		Lieut C.H. ARMITAGE detached for duty as M.O. i/c troops travelling per S.S. CLAN MACCORQUODALE Lt H W GREIG reported on completion of duty with 4th N.M. (Howitzer) Bde R.F.A. Took over Camp Hospital PARC BORELY from 1/2nd N.M. F. Amb: Capt J. MILLER in charge.	

5

Instructions regarding War Diaries and Intelligence Summaries are contained in F. S. Regs., Part II. and the Staff Manual respectively. Title pages will be prepared in manuscript.

WAR DIARY
or
~~INTELLIGENCE~~ SUMMARY.
(*Erase heading not required.*) 1/3 N M F Amb.

Army Form C. 2118.

Hour, Date, Place	Summary of Events and Information	Remarks and references to Appendices
7-5-15 BAILLEUL	Lt Harrison of the Unit + 10 men detailed from the sections at NEUVE EGLISE to make up + soak in neutralizing solution cotton waste for sewing into the gauze Masks for the men in the Trenches to use against asphyxiating gasses – The sewing was carried out by a party of girls in a convent ~~[illegible]~~ in BAILLEUL – The construction of these Masks is as follows:– A large piece of cotton waste A (the size of a fist) is rolled up + soaked in a solution of Hypo, carbonate of soda, glycerine + water – This is loosely sewn into a double layer of gauze 1 metre long – The part B is for covering the eyes the ends C tie behind the head – The Pad A going over the mouth =	

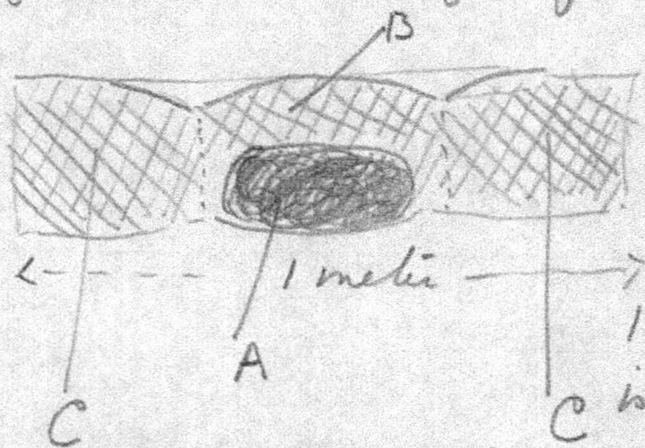

9

Instructions regarding War Diaries and Intelligence Summaries are contained in F. S. Regs., Part II. and the Staff Manual respectively. Title pages will be prepared in manuscript.

WAR DIARY
or
~~INTELLIGENCE~~ SUMMARY.
(Erase heading not required.)

1/3 N M 7 Ambce RAMCT. Army Form C. 2118.

Hour, Date, Place	Summary of Events and Information	Remarks and references to Appendices
15 - 5 - 15. BAILLEUL	Lt Harrison 1/3 N M 7 Ambce sent to HAZEBROUCK to purchase string for the tying up of waterproof bags - State - Remained 26 - Admissions 68. Evacuations 90 - Deaths 1. Remaining 3 =	
16 - 5 - 15 BAILLEUL	State :- Remained 3 Admissions 3 Evacuations 1 Deaths 1 Remaining 4	
17 - 5 - 15 BAILLEUL	The ADMS reports that Arsenic has been found in a stream coming from the GERMAN lines down to the section of trenches held by the 46th DIVISION - The amount found being 1 grain to the gallon - Col GEDDES DDMS II Corps came round the Hospital with Col Fleming RAMC. State :- Remained 4 - Admitted 11 Evacuations 12 Remaining 3 =	

(9 29 6) W 4141—463 100,000 9/14 H W V Forms/C. 2118/10

Army Form C. 2118.

Instructions regarding War Diaries and Intelligence Summaries are contained in F. S. Regs., Part II. and the Staff Manual respectively. Title pages will be prepared in manuscript.

WAR DIARY
or
INTELLIGENCE SUMMARY.
(Erase heading not required.)

Place	Date	Hour	Summary of Events and Information	Remarks and references to Appendices
HESDIGNEUL	27/7/18		Very wet most of day. Drew 500 francs in Imprest for payment of men. In afternoon visited A.D.S. GORRE: new exit being made on canal side of building and good progress with concreting first floor. Some trouble being caused in cellars by flood water coming down. A good deal of difficulty caused by flood water seeping in through the sunk sides of the orderly room tent. A.H.	
	29/7/18		Lt Col A.E. Hodder received verbal notice of appointment to No 57 C.C.S. in command. Closed Imprest a/c and transferred it to Major E.S. Herga M.C. Work started & progressing - drainage of camp site; incineration of horse manure; building of new orderly room of timber and corrugated iron. A.E.H.	
	30/7/18		Major E.S. Herga assumed command temporarily Col. A.E. Hodder having left to command 51 C.C.S. E.S.H.	
	31/7/18		O.C. visited A.D.S. Gorre - A.D.M.S. Conference attended	

E.S. Herga
1/10/18.
~~LIEUT.-COL~~ONEL
COMM'DG 3RD N. MID. FIELD AMB. R.A.M. CORPS

6

Instructions regarding War Diaries and Intelligence Summaries are contained in F. S. Regs., Part II. and the Staff Manual respectively. Title pages will be prepared in manuscript.

WAR DIARY
or
~~INTELLIGENCE~~ SUMMARY.
(Erase heading not required.)

1/3 N. M. F Amb.

Army Form C. 2118.

Hour, Date, Place	Summary of Events and Information	Remarks and references to Appendices
8 - MAY - 1915. BAILLEUL	State of Section of the Field Ambulance acting as a Casualty Clearing Hospital :- Remained 73 Transfers 68 Admissions 3 Remaining. 8.	
9 5 - 15	Sgt James returned from ENGLAND with his pattern Collapsible stretcher carrier - Sent with Captn J. Miller of the unit to GHQ	
	Lt S.S.B. Harrison sent to PARIS to buy waterproof material to ~~carry & keep in~~ make bags for carrying, in a moist condition, gauze Pads acting as respirators -	
	State :- Remained 8 Admitted 121 Transferred 111 Deaths 1. Remaining 17.	
	Miss Duncan transferred to Highland Casualty Clearing Hospital by orders of DMS II Army being sent to LILLERS by Motor Ambulance -	
10 - 5 - 15	State :- Remained 17 - Admitted 16 - Transferred Nil Deaths 3 Remaining 30 -	

Instructions regarding War Diaries and Intelligence Summaries are contained in F. S. Regs., Part II. and the Staff Manual respectively. Title Pages will be prepared in manuscript.

WAR DIARY
or
INTELLIGENCE SUMMARY
(Erase heading not required.)

Army Form C. 2118.

Place	Date	Hour	Summary of Events and Information	Remarks and references to Appendices
LABOURSE	14/8/17		At ADMS order despatched 10 O.R. to PHILOSOPHE to be attached to 3rd Australian Tunnelling Coy for work on DUMP DRIVE shaft of HULLUCH TUNNEL.	
			Reinforced A.D.S. with 1 officer and 21 O.R. for pending operations.	
			Staffs of RAMC posts on HULLUCH section doubled from 7pm.	
			Enemy aeroplane dropped 3 bombs (small) on this village about 11.45 pm. 1 man lightly wounded.	
	15/8/17		1 Officer and 60 O.R. wounded admitted between 6pm 14th and 3pm 15/8/17.	
			Visited A.D.S. PHILOSOPHE in afternoon: all in order there.	
			Successful operations carried out by Canadian Corps troops on our right resulting in an advance of their line about 1500 yards on section attacked.	
			Work on horse standings and other improvements suspended temporarily owing to scarcity of men at Headquarters.	
	16/8/17		C.S.M. (a/S.S.M) F.R. ROGERS i/c Horsed Transport of the Field Ambulance reduced to rank of Sergeant by Corps Commander under A.A. Sec 183(2) pm. 15/8/17 for inefficiency and neglect of duty.	

Instructions regarding War Diaries and Intelligence Summaries are contained in F. S. Regs., Part II. and the Staff Manual respectively. Title pages will be prepared in manuscript.

WAR DIARY
or
INTELLIGENCE SUMMARY.
(Erase heading not required.)

Army Form C. 2118.

Place	Date	Hour	Summary of Events and Information	Remarks and references to Appendices
HESDIGNEUL	14/5/18		Quiet night - no excursions or alarums. Attended with my officers at lecture by Consulting Physician I Army on Gas poisoning. A remarkably lucid lecture illustrated with coloured sketches & post mortem material. The lecturer differentiated clearly between the three types of Gas used: Blue cross - Diphenylchlorarsine; Green cross - Phosgene group; Yellow cross - Mustard Gas. The morbid effects produced as evidenced by the [post mortem material] pointing out that the Green cross group affect mainly the pulmonary alveoli after the initial irritation effect on the respiratory mucous membrane, the yellow cross gas the skin conjunctival mucous membrane and the lower respiratory effect, the action on the latter, trachea & larynx being remarkably delayed, and the blue cross as used by enemy at present mainly a stimulatory effect with perhaps some vomiting. From these facts indications for treatment were given.	
	15/5/18		G.S. Wagon and loading party collecting salvage in the BEUVRY - LE QUESNOY area in the morning came under shell fire - observation good & enemy balloons up.	

D. D. & L., London, E.C. (A8copy) Wt W1771/M2031 750,000 5/17 Sch. 52 Forms/C2118/14

Instructions regarding War Diaries and Intelligence Summaries are contained in F. S. Regs., Part II. and the Staff Manual respectively. Title pages will be prepared in manuscript.

WAR DIARY
or
INTELLIGENCE SUMMARY.
(Erase heading not required.)

Army Form C. 2118.

Place	Date	Hour	Summary of Events and Information	Remarks and references to Appendices
LABOURSE	23/8/17		Visited ADS and CAMBRIN sector with ADMS: inspected RAPs and Field Ambulance bearer posts and went on to A.D.S. VERMELLES. via trenches. Received RAMC. OO No 114 and 1 Corps Medical Instructions No 2. both dated 23/8/17 and issued the necessary orders to Section officers to comply. Captain Fairley started medical inspection of 46 D.S.C. personnel with object of re-classification of men for general service with infantry	
	24/8/17		Personnel and equipment of this unit at A.D.S. PHILOSOPHE withdrawn their place being taken by 1/2 N.M.F. Amb.	
	25/8/17		Lieut QMr King reported for duty from short leave. Capt J Miller returned from acting temporarily as DADMS. Lieuts Jack and Horman attended a lecture on Sanitation at 1 Corps central school.	
	26		DDMS I Corps visited Main Dressing Station and discussed the facilities for dealing with heavy casualties.	
	26/8/17		Captain Miller with Lieut Horman + 30 O.R. A section took over A.D.S. CAMBRIN [A26 a.0.7 BÉTHUNE Combined Sheet] with the dependent bearer posts at "BRAYS KEEP" A25 d 2.4 and "GUYS" G3 a 0.7. from No 6. Field Ambulance.	

A7092 Wt. W12839/M1293 750,000. 1/17. D. D & L., Ltd. Forms/C2118/14.

Instructions regarding War Diaries and Intelligence Summaries are contained in F. S. Regs., Part II. and the Staff Manual respectively. Title pages will be prepared in manuscript.

WAR DIARY
or
INTELLIGENCE SUMMARY.
(Erase heading not required.)

Army Form C. 2118.

Place	Date	Hour	Summary of Events and Information	Remarks and references to Appendices
LABOURSE	19/8/17		Repeated reinforcement of bearers for carrying party according to RAMC O.O. 113 of todays date.	
			Visited ADS - PHILOSOPHE and posts in right subsection and also Hdqrs 1/6 S. Staffs to discuss evacuation measures in connection with future operations.	
			In the 24 hours ending noon today over 100 Canadian gassed cases passed through A.D.S. All these were shell gassed and the gas used evidently "yellow cross", as many of the patients were suffering from "burns" of skin when seen at A.D.S. In all cases the conjunctival sacs were washed out with alkali; the men stripped + sponged with alkali before dressing the skin burns and clothed in pyjama suits before sending to Main Dressing Station. The clothing was exposed to the air before collection + return to Q.M's.	
			An interesting point in these cases was that the drink of tea given on arrival at A.D.S. made them vomit promptly - useful gastric lavage was thus effected.	
			Captain Fairley rejoined Hdqrs for duty and Lieut Homan went to duty at A.D.S.	

A7092. Wt. W12859/M1293. 750,000. 1/17. D. D & L., Ltd. Forms/C2118/14.

Instructions regarding War Diaries and Intelligence Summaries are contained in F. S. Regs., Part II. and the Staff Manual respectively. Title pages will be prepared in manuscript.

WAR DIARY
or
~~INTELLIGENCE SUMMARY.~~
(*Erase heading not required.*)

Army Form C. 2118.

1/3 N M 7 Amb
RAMC T

Hour, Date, Place	Summary of Events and Information	Remarks and references to Appendices
	at this date the Divisional Baths + the Infectious Hospital had been handed over to the III Corps	
4 – 5 – 15.	For Sick + wounded admitted to the unit through the Advanced Dressing Station at NEUVE EGLISE during the month of April see Appendix IV = This chart represents cases from the STAFFS INF. BRIGADE.	Appendix IV
	State :- Remained 167. Transferred 157 – Remaining 10	
	It was necessary to have some apparatus to spray walls & blankets in the Hospital = Locally I found one of these used for spraying hops, vines etc. It consists of a large copper container strapped on the back of the operator – The right hand works a pump handle, the pump being inside the container – The left hand holds a copper tube attached to the container by a rubber tube + the spray given is large + the fluid finely	

10

Instructions regarding War Diaries and Intelligence Summaries are contained in F. S. Regs., Part II. and the Staff Manual respectively. Title pages will be prepared in manuscript.

Army Form C. 2118.

WAR DIARY
or
INTELLIGENCE SUMMARY.
(Erase heading not required.)

Hour, Date, Place	Summary of Events and Information	Remarks and references to Appendices
27 - 6 - 15	The Officer of the Field Ambulance reaching the BRIGADE HEAD QUARTERS at the school on the MENIN ROAD ~~[illegible]~~ 3/4 mile outside YPRES he found this being heavily shelled & later set on fire necessitating its evacuation - The bearers were subjected to this fire on proceeding to the Regimental Aid posts - no casualties.	
28 - 6 - 15	Collection of wounded - The Ambulances & bearers were subjected to very severe shell fire & rifle fire - One officer & one driver on the front of the Car were slightly wounded.	
29 - 6 - 15	Collection of wounded -	
30 - 6 - 15	——— Ditto ———	
	Sick & wounded from the Staffs Brigade See Appendix II	Appendix II HHCD

HHCD Sml - Lt Col - O.C. 1/3 Field Ambce TF 46 Divn

(9 29 6) W 4141—463 100,000 9/14 H W V Forms/C. 2118/10

Instructions regarding War Diaries and Intelligence Summaries are contained in F. S. Regs., Part II. and the Staff Manual respectively. Title pages will be prepared in manuscript.

WAR DIARY
or
INTELLIGENCE SUMMARY.
(*Erase heading not required.*)

Army Form C. 2118.

Place	Date	Hour	Summary of Events and Information	Remarks and references to Appendices
FRESNOY-LE-GRAND	23.10.18		Lieut STEPHEN. J.W. reported from base for duty.	
			1/3 NMFA (-1 Section under Capt REID + Capt ELLENBOGEN) took over convent at FRESNOY from 1/1 NMFA in use as divisional dressing Stn. Main duty being clearing of sick + sick parades of many units around without MOs.	
			Capt GILLIES D. left for temporary duty at IX CMDS.	
	24.10.18		Cpl KENDERDINE + 11 men left for temporary duty at IX C.M.D.S.	
			Sgt THOMPSON. C, " WRIGHT. R.T. } RAMC reported from base for duty.	
			Lieut. Col. A.C. TURNER returned from leave. ACY	
	25.10.18		Visited ADMS. ACY	

D. D. & L., London, E.C. (A8C04) Wt W1771/M2031 750,000 5/17 Sch. 52 Forms/C2118/14

Instructions regarding War Diaries and Intelligence Summaries are contained in F. S. Regs., Part II. and the Staff Manual respectively. Title pages will be prepared in manuscript.

WAR DIARY
or
INTELLIGENCE SUMMARY.
(Erase heading not required.)

Army Form C. 2118.

Hour, Date, Place	Summary of Events and Information	Remarks and references to Appendices
20 – IV – 15	For disinfection of Blankets a Thresh's disinfector is urgently required but has not yet arrived altho' indented for. In the meantime the system adopted is to spray the blankets with Cresol solution & hang out in the open until dry.	
	A Nitrous Oxide gas apparatus has been obtained & extractions are painlessly carried out by one of the Officers of the Unit who is a Dentist.	
	For the MO's of Regiments Field Tourniquets have been issued. I have instructed them to give these to Officers in the Trenches & instruct the latter in their use.	
	100 patients in the Divisional Rest Hospital	
22 – IV – 15	Inspection of the Hospital by Col Geddes RAMC the D.D.M.S.	

(9 29 6) W 4141—463 100,000 9/14 H W V Forms/C. 2118/10

Instructions regarding War Diaries and Intelligence Summaries are contained in F. S. Regs., Part II. and the Staff Manual respectively. Title pages will be prepared in manuscript.

WAR DIARY
or
INTELLIGENCE SUMMARY.
(Erase heading not required.)

Army Form C. 2118.

Place	Date	Hour	Summary of Events and Information	Remarks and references to Appendices
HESDIGNEUL	31.5.18		Periodic shelling of HESDIGNEUL during day & last night with HV gun. Instruction of new personnel at Stage in various duties being carried out by section officers. Sent 4 addl. bearers to ADS GORRE as working party. Held inspection parade of Transport 3 pm. A pretty good turnout.	
			Personnel changes during month May.	

	on	off	net difference
Officers	3	2	+1
OR	44	49	−5

A. E. [illegible]
Lt Col cdg 1/3 W.R. F Amb.

D. D. & L., London, E.C. (A8004) Wt W1771/M2031 750,000 5/17 Sch. 52 Forms/C2118/14

Instructions regarding War Diaries and Intelligence Summaries are contained in F. S. Regs., Part II. and the Staff Manual respectively. Title Pages will be prepared in manuscript.

II

WAR DIARY
or
INTELLIGENCE SUMMARY
(Erase heading not required.)

Army Form C. 2118.

1/3 NM Fd Amb

Vol 30

MEDICAL

Place	Date	Hour	Summary of Events and Information	Remarks and references to Appendices
LABOURSE	2/8/17		Visited Advanced Dressing Station PHILOSOPHE in afternoon and made final arrangements for pending active operations. – Commenced extension of horsestandings but the work is much hindered by the wet weather.	
	3/8/17		Capt G. D. Fairlie and 17 O.R. went to reinforce ADS party. Lieut S. G. Stoman took over duties of M.O. attd 46 Div. Train which he will carry out from here till his period of one months attachment for instruction is completed.	
	4/8/17		Visited A.D.S. in afternoon: enemy shelling in close proximity. The smoke from the kitchen at A.D.S. is too conspicuous owing to the coal supplied being mostly "slack". Have applied for part issue of coke for this place to remedy the condition which is calculated to attract enemy fire. Received notice 7pm that pending operations were postponed indefinitely.	
	5/8/17		Reinforcements sent to A.D.S. for purpose of operations withdrawn to Hdqrs. 10.30 pm received wire from ADMS to send 1 M.O. and all available cars to PHILOSOPHE at once – complied – apparently a party of 22 Canadians was caught by enemy shell fire on the road in the village.	

2449 Wt. W14957/M90 750,000 1/16 J.B.C. & A. Forms/C.2118/12.

Instructions regarding War Diaries and Intelligence Summaries are contained in F. S. Regs., Part II. and the Staff Manual respectively. Title Pages will be prepared in manuscript.

WAR DIARY
or
INTELLIGENCE SUMMARY
(Erase heading not required.)

Army Form C. 2118.

Place	Date	Hour	Summary of Events and Information	Remarks and references to Appendices
LABOURSE	27/7/17		Attended meeting at ADMS office 2.30 relative to impending operations. Went on to A.D.S. Lieut Jack reported for duty in evening went to A.D.S to relieve Capt Herga due for leave. Continued instruction of L Homan & arranged for him to proceed to 1/5 N. Staffs to be attached to MO for practical instruction for three days.	
	28/7/17		All billets now settled and all personnel in billets & nearly all on wire beds.	
	29/7/17		Visited A.D.S. and all bearer posts in afternoon. Condition of trenches made a good deal worse by recent thunderstorms. R.A.P. left Battalion HULLOCH sector removed from WINGS WAY to DUMP DRIVE Tunnel G.18 a 1.5. Comfortable. Field Amb post at Wings way abolished and the men accommodated in sap adjoining R.A.P. — Capt G.D. Fairley RAMC (TC) reported from 230 Bde RFA for duty. Capt E.E. HERGA departed on leave	

Instructions regarding War Diaries and Intelligence Summaries are contained in F. S. Regs., Part II. and the Staff Manual respectively. Title pages will be prepared in manuscript.

WAR DIARY
or
INTELLIGENCE SUMMARY.
(Erase heading not required.)

Army Form C. 2118.

Place	Date	Hour	Summary of Events and Information	Remarks and references to Appendices
LABOURSE	5/11/17		Visited advanced dressing stations and all RAMC posts in HULLUCH & Hill 70 sections & found all in good order. Lower part of CHALK PIT alley very bad - about knee deep in tenacious mud & water. In Hill 70 section a track for stretcher bearers has been marked out over the tops & to a great extent avoiding the bad parts of the trenches. This is of great value as in the misty weather obtaining it can be used by day as well as by night.	
	7/11/17.		Lieut-Colonel Holder DSO. left on 14 days leave to England. Capt. J. MILLER. left in Charge of Field Ambulance.	
	8/11/17.		Conference at office of ADMS.. arranged. with OC 1/2. N. Mid Fd Amb. to take over B. Section 1st Corps Rest Station at FOUQUIERES. Relief to be completed by 6 pm. 12.11.17	
	9.11.17.		Tent ~~section~~ subdivision of C. Section relieved from ADSs at ~~Philosophe &~~ PHILOSOPHE & FORT. GLATZ.	
	10.11.17.		Tent subdivision of C. Section sent to No 18. CCS to relieve tent subdivision of 1/2. N. Mid Fd Amb. The ADSs. at PHILOSOPHE & FORT. GLATZ. handed over to 1/2. N. Mid Fd Amb.	

A7092. Wt. W12839/M1293. 750,000. 1/17. D. D & L., Ltd. Forms/C2118/14.

Instructions regarding War Diaries and Intelligence Summaries are contained in F. S. Regs., Part II. and the Staff Manual respectively. Title pages will be prepared in manuscript.

WAR DIARY
or
INTELLIGENCE SUMMARY.
(Erase heading not required.)

Army Form C. 2118.

Place	Date	Hour	Summary of Events and Information	Remarks and references to Appendices
TROISVILLES	16.3.19		Capt. J. KING proceeded on leave to U.K. [initials]	
"	19.3.19		2 other Ranks left unit for demobilisation 3 other Ranks RASC H.T. " " [initials] 5 other Ranks left unit for duty with 19 CCS [initials]	
"	23.3.19		Capt G.R. SHARP left for duty with Army of occupation Capt F.L. RICHARD proceeded on Special leave to U.K. [initials]	
"	24.3.19		4 other Ranks left unit for demobilisation [initials]	
"	25.3.19		8 other Ranks RAMC & 1 other Rank RASC HT left unit for demobilisation [initials]	
"	28.3.19		4 other Ranks left for duty with 49 C.C.S. 4 other Ranks left for duty with 58 CCS [initials]	
"	29.3.19		Capt E.M. MORRIS M.C. USA & Capt. F.L. RICHARD RAMC (SR) struck off strength of unit. [initials]	
"	30.3.19		12 other Ranks left unit for demobilisation [initials]	

[signature] Capt RAMC

D. D. & L., London, E.C.
(10540) Wt W3300/P713 750,000 3/18 E 2688 Forms C/2118/16.

Army Form C. 2118.

Instructions regarding War Diaries and Intelligence Summaries are contained in F. S. Regs., Part II. and the Staff Manual respectively. Title pages will be prepared in manuscript.

WAR DIARY
or
INTELLIGENCE SUMMARY.
(Erase heading not required.)

Hour, Date, Place	Summary of Events and Information	Remarks and references to Appendices
July 9. 15. Near POPERINGHE	Collection by day started - 1 NCO + 8 men sent to a dug-out at the N.E. Corner of MAPLE COPSE. The Dug-outs at H 24 a 4.8 KRUISSTAAT not yet completed but 2 Officers and 12 men stationed there.	
July 10 15.	Visited dug-outs KRUISSTAAT. Went to ZILLEBEKE LAKE - Sent extra personnel there. Now at Dug out in MAPLE COPSE 1 NCO 7 men. at KRUISSTAAT 20 NCO's + men + 2 Officers - One MOTOR Ambulance to be on permanent duty at KRUISSTAAT.	
July 12 15.	Sent one Officer + 20 men to Dug-outs I 21 C 6.8 1/40.000. These to learn the way to R.A.P. at I 27 b 5.3 + I 29 C 3.5 with a view of relieving the 100 Bearers of the 15th Brigade situated here -	
July 14 15.	Sent 56 extra men to dug outs I 21. c 6.8 + took over from 15th F Ambce - Cases collected here to be evacuated to our dug outs at KRUISSTAAT by hand carriage.	

Instructions regarding War Diaries and Intelligence Summaries are contained in F. S. Regs., Part II. and the Staff Manual respectively. Title pages will be prepared in manuscript.

WAR DIARY
or
INTELLIGENCE SUMMARY.
(Erase heading not required.)

Army Form C. 2118.

Place	Date	Hour	Summary of Events and Information	Remarks and references to Appendices
LABOURSE	18/8/17		Received notice that Captain J.C. Harris RAMC T of this unit had been killed in action while temporarily under the orders of D.M.S. V Army.	
			Sent small party of men to re-inforce A.D.S. staff in connection with carrying parties this evening pursuant to ADMS 46 Div. RAMC. O.O. 112. of 18/8/17.	
			Notified O.C. A.D.S. of probable use by enemy of "yellow cross" gas on this section.	
			Sent up party of bearers to provide ~~against~~ means of evacuation in event of casualties to cylinder carrying party on left subsection of HULLUCH section. Two men were brought down slightly gassed owing to leakage from cylinders	
	19/8/17		Information received from 3rd Australian C.C.S. reveals that Capt. J.C. Harris while attached to that unit was killed by a bomb dropped by aeroplane on 16.8.17.	

A.7092 Wt. W12839/M1293. 750,000. 1/17. D. D & L., Ltd. Forms/C2118/14.

Army Form C. 2118.

Instructions regarding War Diaries and Intelligence Summaries are contained in F. S. Regs., Part II. and the Staff Manual respectively. Title pages will be prepared in manuscript.

WAR DIARY
or
INTELLIGENCE SUMMARY.
(*Erase heading not required.*)

Hour, Date, Place	Summary of Events and Information	Remarks and references to Appendices
July 17 15 Nr POPERINGHE	For Method of collection of wounded from the 46 Division Trenches in the YPRES district See Appendix II	Appendix II
July 19. 15. Nr POPERINGHE.	System of Day & night collection working well. The road is often shelled by day necessitating bearers + their patients taking cover.	
July 20. 15. — do —	Owing to heavy shelling it was impossible to convey rations to the Railway Embankment dugouts + there in MAPLE COPSE.	
July 22. 15 — do —	Sent one Officer + the Tent subdivision of one section to take over the Mill at VLAMERTINGHE at H. 8 a 9.8 No 28 $\frac{1}{20000}$ BELGIUM This to be the Divisional advanced Dressing station from 8 am 23.7.15.	
July 23. 15 — do —	Handed over to 1st N.M F AMB the collecting Posts at KRUISSTAAT H 24(a)4.8 and ZILLEBEKE LAKE I 21(c)6.8	

(9 29 6) W4141—463 100,000 9/14 H W V Forms/C. 2118/10

Instructions regarding War Diaries and Intelligence Summaries are contained in F. S. Regs., Part II. and the Staff Manual respectively. Title pages will be prepared in manuscript.

WAR DIARY
or
~~INTELLIGENCE SUMMARY.~~
(Erase heading not required.)

Army Form C. 2118.

Hour, Date, Place	Summary of Events and Information	Remarks and references to Appendices
20-9-15 (contd)	Railway Section at Embankment dugouts at I21c.7.7 collects from sector of line between I24a and ~~I28~~ I34b. Section at "Bedford House" I26a.8.7 collects from sector of line between I34b and canal in I34.c. by means of Regimental aid posts situated close to canal in I33.a.	
23-9-15	Lt. J. Mavety reported as officer reinforcement.	
25-9-15	Advanced Dressing Station at I21c.7.7 occupied all day: cleared 236 cases wounded of 3rd and 14th divisions in addition to those of 46th division. Arrangements made by Officer in charge Capt. G.T. Haycraft worked very smoothly and were of great service to the divisions on the left in clearing their lines of evacuation.	
29-9-15	Lt. H.W. Greig left the Field Ambulance on being posted to 1/1 N. Mid. Bde RFA vice Capt. Tatlow.	
30-9-15.	Appendices I & II show cases dealt with at ADVANCED DRESSING STATIONS during occupation by the 3rd Field Ambce 46 DIV.	Appendices I & II

H H C Dent Lt Col

Army Form C. 2118.

Instructions regarding War Diaries and Intelligence Summaries are contained in F. S. Regs., Part II. and the Staff Manual respectively. Title Pages will be prepared in manuscript.

WAR DIARY
or
INTELLIGENCE SUMMARY

(Erase heading not required.)

Place	Date	Hour	Summary of Events and Information	Remarks and references to Appendices
LABOURSE	7/8/17		ADMS - visited Field Amb Hospital in afternoon. Arranged routine collection of sick by horsed Amb. from SAILLY-LABOURSE; NOYELLES; MAZINGARBE; NOEUX les MINES.	
			Reported a/S.S.M. Rogers i/c H.T. att'd as inefficient and requested he be dealt with under the provisions of A.A. 183 (2) as extended by A.G. G.H.Q. No B/70 of 7.8.17	
	8/8/17		D.M.S. I Army inspected main dressing station.	
	9/8/17		Captain J. Miller left to act as D.A.D.M.S. during absence on leave of Capt J.R.R. Trist M.C.	
			Held marching order parade of all ranks at Hqrs.	
			S.B.R. drill inspection at A.D.S. - all ranks wearing them for one hour continuously and doing their work in them.	
			Lieut W.B. Jack came to Hdqrs from A.D.S. for duty.	
			Capt E.E. Harga M.C. returned from leave & took command at A.D.S. Lieut W.B. Jack assumes medical charge of main dressing station.	
	11/8/17		Held [illegible] antigas drill all ranks wearing SBR for one hour continuously & carrying on their usual duties.	

2449 Wt. W14957/M90 750,000 1/16 J.B.C. & A. Forms/C.2118/12.

Army Form C. 2118.

WAR DIARY
or
INTELLIGENCE SUMMARY.
(Erase heading not required.)

Instructions regarding War Diaries and Intelligence Summaries are contained in F. S. Regs., Part II. and the Staff Manual respectively. Title pages will be prepared in manuscript.

Place	Date	Hour	Summary of Events and Information	Remarks and references to Appendices
BRUAY	24/4/18		Harassing fire on BRUAY resumed about midnight 23/24. One shell landed beside Ward no 5 which contained 64 patients. wrecked ward completely - no men killed - 2 injured & sent to C.C.S. nine others slightly injured retained. As the crater of the explosion projected into the hut the escape of men sleeping on that side is extraordinary. All officers were quickly on the scene and requisite steps were taken to deal with the emergency. By 2.45 a.m. all were accounted for & tents bedded down except with a lot of men inside them & the staff reduced to normal night proportions. Shelling resumed about 4 am for 4 rounds - visited Hospital & found all quiet, in order. Attended ADMS conference 10 am. With OC 1/1 NMFA inspected camp sites at HESDIGNEUL and in BOIS des DAMES deciding on latter if available. In afternoon with ADMS & Major Bradley visited ADS at GORRE Brewery (Bethune Combined Sheet) serving LOISNES- FESTUBERT section of line and arranged details of relief to take place on 25th. Personnel 2 officers 50 O.R. Posts at LOISNES & TUNING FORK; evacuation via BEUVRY VERQUIN 2 motor Ambs had to go into workshop for repairs leaving only 2 here. Borrowed from other Field Ambs [illegible]	

D. D. & L., London, E.C. (A8604) Wt W3771/M2031 750,000 5/17 Sch. 52 Forms/C2118/14

Confidential

3rd FIELD AMBULANCE
46th DIVISION

Instructions regarding War Diaries and Intelligence Summaries are contained in F. S. Regs., Part II. and the Staff Manual respectively. Title pages will be prepared in manuscript.

WAR DIARY
or
INTELLIGENCE SUMMARY.
(Erase heading not required.)

Army Form C. 2118.

Hour, Date, Place	Summary of Events and Information	Remarks and references to Appendices
7 – 9 – 15	Transport section occupied in making up horse and wagon lines with stone against contingency of continued rain.	
10 – 9 – 15	Lt H. W. Greig RAMC. from 3/1st N. Midland Field Ambulance arrived to replace Lt W. Boyd who is proceeding to Canada by permission of W.O. The daily average of patients in the Rest Station continues to be about 200.	
20 – 9 – 15	Field Ambulance moved its headquarters to field at G21 c.5.6 handing over charge of rest station to 1/1st N. Midland Field Amb. "A" and "B" sections took over collecting stations from 1/2nd N.M. Field Amb at "Bedford House" and "Railway Dug-outs" respectively. The section at latter post is engaged in building an advanced collecting post at I24 c.9.4. till this is completed using dugouts at I24.c.9.1 lent by 138 Infantry Bde.	

(9 29 6) W4141—463 100,000 9/14 H W V Forms/C. 2118/10

Instructions regarding War Diaries and Intelligence Summaries are contained in F. S. Regs., Part II. and the Staff Manual respectively. Title Pages will be prepared in manuscript.

WAR DIARY
or
INTELLIGENCE SUMMARY
(Erase heading not required.)

Army Form C. 2118

Place	Date	Hour	Summary of Events and Information	Remarks and references to Appendices
GAUDIEMPRÉ	18/6/16		Handed over charge of advanced dressing station to OC 1/1 N.M. Fd Amb leaving attached to his command 1 officer Lt D.C. SUTTIE and 62 O.R.	
	19/6/16		Field Coy RE left Hospital which will be completely RAMC.	
	20/6/16		Lt & QM J KING reported for duty from sick leave in U.K.	
	24/6/16		Capt J. Millar — — —	
	25/6/16		Squadrilla of enemy aeroplanes dropped 5 bombs about 200 yards from western side of Hospital – no damage. Capt S.S.B. HARRISON reported for duty from leave.	
	26/6/16		ADMS VII Corps inspected Hospital.	
	27/6/16		Opened duties according to operations time table.	
	29/6/16		Hospital inspected by GOC 46 Div. & DMS IIIrd Army.	

4

Instructions regarding War Diaries and Intelligence Summaries are contained in F. S. Regs., Part II. and the Staff Manual respectively. Title pages will be prepared in manuscript.

WAR DIARY
or
~~INTELLIGENCE~~ SUMMARY.
(Erase heading not required.)

Army Form C. 2118.

1/3 N. M. 7. Ambce RAMC T

Hour, Date, Place	Summary of Events and Information	Remarks and references to Appendices
5 - 5 - 15 BAILLEUL	Carbonate of Soda (No Hypo being available) with instructions to use a 1 in 10 solution of the same -	
	State:- Remained 10 - Admissions 94 Transferred 20 Deaths 1. (gas poisoning) Remaining 73 -	
	Purchased locally 6 beds for seriously wounded -	
	Two nursing sisters reported for duty -	
6 - 5 - 15.	Under orders of II Corps Commander proceeded to HAZEBROUCK to purchase 40 more portable sprays - obtained 5 only - Handed over to II Corps	
	State:- Remained 79 - Admissions 90 Evacuated 84 Deaths 2 - Remaining 83 -	
	No 2337 Sgt T. J. Murray of the unit proceeded to HAZEBROUCK to report to the D.M.S II Army -	
7 - 5 - 15.	Remained 83 - Transferred 30. To Duty 1. Admitted 21. Remaining 73.	

MEDICAL

Instructions regarding War Diaries and Intelligence Summaries are contained in F. S. Regs., Part II. and the Staff Manual respectively. Title Pages will be prepared in manuscript.

WAR DIARY
or
INTELLIGENCE SUMMARY
(Erase heading not required.)

Army Form C. 2118

1/3 N M 7d Amb

Vol 18

Place	Date	Hour	Summary of Events and Information	Remarks and references to Appendices
LA HERLIÈRE	1/8/16		Visited advanced dressing station BERLES au BOIS and also bearer posts (7 amb) and RAPs on centre sector of divisional line in company with ADMS.	
	3/8/16		Visited A.D.S. BERLES to investigate some sanitary arrangements & see method of refuse disposal by Town Majors fatigues. – Found this latter unsatisfactory took steps to effect improvement.	
	4/8/16		Capt. J Miller took over command of Div Sanitary School at BAVINCOURT – vice Major CASTIDSON who left for G.B. to report to W.O. for duty in another command.	
	6/8/16		Prepared "spot-map" of LAHERLIERE showing manure deposits military & civilian – in conjunction with Town Major arranged for civilians to be approached through the Mayor in regard to removal of manure from courtyards to the land and drew up instructions for the Mayor to issue to inhabitants as to this and as to keeping yards cleaner than has been customary.	

Army Form C. 2118.

WAR DIARY
or
INTELLIGENCE SUMMARY.
(*Erase heading not required.*)

Instructions regarding War Diaries and Intelligence Summaries are contained in F. S. Regs., Part II. and the Staff Manual respectively. Title pages will be prepared in manuscript.

Place	Date	Hour	Summary of Events and Information	Remarks and references to Appendices
			motor ambulances through the densely congested mass of traffic on the roads. Many hours were taken by each car in performing the double journey, & at one time in the afternoon when the ADS was full of wounded awaiting removal & there were urgent calls for cars from both car posts no car arrived at ADS for nearly two hours.	
			Constant demands for stretchers from RMO's led to a temporary shortage until fresh ones could be obtained from MDS. This apparently was due to sending German prisoners down carrying stretchers & failing to send RAMC bearers to ADS with them to take a corresponding number of stretchers back to the battalion	
			The numerous prisoners did valuable work in bringing in wounded & greatly relieved the labours of the stretcher bearers	
			MAGNY was shelled intermittently during the day, one shell (a dud) landing in the yard of ADS when it was full of stretcher cases	
			All wounded (British & German) were cleared before midnight. Lieut. F.L. RICHARD RAMC, M.O. att 1/5th. S. Staffs. was wounded early in morning & 1st. Lieut. MORRIS USMC detailed to replace him	ACY

D. D. & L., London, E.C. (A8004) Wt W1771/M2031 750,000 5/17 Sch. 52 Forms/C2118/14

Instructions regarding War Diaries and Intelligence Summaries are contained in F. S. Regs., Part II. and the Staff Manual respectively. Title Pages will be prepared in manuscript.

WAR DIARY
or
INTELLIGENCE SUMMARY
(Erase heading not required.)

Army Form C. 2118

Place	Date	Hour	Summary of Events and Information	Remarks and references to Appendices
MAISON ROLLAND	1/2/16		Field Ambulance - one section - open for reception of SCABIES cases only from all units of Division. Accommodation available for <u>80</u> cases. Bathing facilities created. Remainder of unit occupied with general duties, exercises and construction of sanitary and other improvements.	
	2/2/16		Arrangements made with No. 30 C.C.S. for disinfection of infected clothing as soon as Thresh disinfector arrives there.	
	5/2/16		Inspection of all NCOs & men of unit carried out in accordance with orders - the examinations (3) in the week revealed 2 cases 1 of gonorrhoea and 1 of venereal sore among A.S.C.(HT) attached. The men in question evacuated to Hospital.	
	10/2/16		Submitted report to ADMS on cases of "chronic pyodermia" consequent to SCABIES pointing out that a certain proportion of all SCABIES cases drift into a condition of chronic sepsis of skin and hair follicles in spite of careful treatment in Field Ambulances, including injections of appropriate stock vaccines. These cases improve while in Field Ambulances but relapse in a very short time after discharge to duty - hence the	

1875 Wt. W593/826 1,000,000 4/15 J.B.C. & A. A.D.S.S./Forms/C. 2118.

Army Form C. 2118.

Instructions regarding War Diaries and Intelligence Summaries are contained in F. S. Regs., Part II. and the Staff Manual respectively. Title pages will be prepared in manuscript.

WAR DIARY
or
INTELLIGENCE SUMMARY.
(Erase heading not required.)

Place	Date	Hour	Summary of Events and Information	Remarks and references to Appendices
LABOURSE	16/8/17		Raid from left subsection, HULLUCH section at 11.45 pm by 1/5 Leicesters. Apparently expected by the enemy who were well prepared for it. Casualties approx. between 60 and 70. one third being stretcher cases. Evacuation worked quite smoothly. Practically all cases came down HULLUCH Tunnel to DUMP DRIVE. post, thence over the open to St GEORGES. on trolly man handled ~~from~~ to Halfway House whence mule drawn to PHILOSOPHE. The evacuation from St GEORGES is quite rapid but it is slow from the line to that point: the distance is about 2000 yards and it is hand carriage all the way.	
	17/8/17		Sergeant F.R. Rogers, ASC departed to report to Base ASC depot being supernumerary to Divisional establishment.	
			As result of raid by 1/5 Leicesters 58 wounded were treated in this unit.	
			Visited A.D.S. in afternoon. — work on horse standings resumed.	

A7092 Wt. W12839/M1293 750,000. 1/17. D. D & L., Ltd. Forms/C2118/14.

Army Form C. 2118

Instructions regarding War Diaries and Intelligence Summaries are contained in F. S. Regs., Part II. and the Staff Manual respectively. Title Pages will be prepared in manuscript.

WAR DIARY
or
INTELLIGENCE SUMMARY
(Erase heading not required.)

3RD NORTH MIDLAND FIELD AMBULANCE ROYAL ARMY MEDICAL CORPS

Place	Date	Hour	Summary of Events and Information	Remarks and references to Appendices
FOUQUIERES	29.10.15		Thresh disinfector despatched for use of 12th Division.	
			Instructions received from ADMS re improvement of quarters:	
			Arrangements made with C.R.E. 46th Div. for placing at his disposal portion	
			of lean-to shed at N.E. side of buildings for adaptation as divisional baths.	
			Fitters report pump in laundry a good deal damaged during tenancy	
			of premises by 38th Field Amb. – steps being taken to put it in order again.	
	31/10/15		With exception of 'C' section who are in charge of hospital the men of	
			the unit are being kept fully employed on improvements to quarters	
			on the lines of circular of DDMS XI Corps:	
			The works completed or in hand comprise –	
			Permanent latrines – bucket system	
			Urinal and drainage pit	
			Ablution benches and standings	
			Harness shelter	
			Standings for 58 horses.	
			Kitchen for mens cooks	
			Building of dry paths in all essential directions in the ground.	
			Troughs for watering horses, fed by siphonage from tanks above laundry.	
			A. E. Stodder Major for LIEUT.-COLONEL, COMM'DG 3RD N. MID. FIELD AMB. R.A.M. CORPS.	

1875 Wt. W593/826 1,000,000 4/15 J.B.C. & A. A.D.S.S./Forms/C. 2118.

9

Instructions regarding War Diaries and Intelligence Summaries are contained in F. S. Regs., Part II. and the Staff Manual respectively. Title pages will be prepared in manuscript.

WAR DIARY
or
INTELLIGENCE SUMMARY.
(Erase heading not required.)

Army Form C. 2118.

1/3 N M Fd Amb

Vol 31

Place	Date	Hour	Summary of Events and Information — MEDICAL.	Remarks and references to Appendices
LABOURSE	1/9/17		Visited A.D.S. CAMBRIN and bearer posts in connection therewith and R.A.P. Guys.	
	2/9/17		Capt G.D. FAIRLEY relieved Capt. W.C. GAVIN in medical charge of 8th Notts + Derby Regt, the latter being taken on strength of the Field Ambulance.	
	3/9/17		Lieut Stoman to 8th Notts + Derby Regt temporarily for Capt Fairley while on leave	
			Attended ADMS conference 10 am; arranged details of clerical work while ADSs are evacuating direct, the recording of all battle casualties from divisional front to be done by this Field Ambulance at LABOURSE.	
			Bulk of G.D. privates dispersed to assist other units E.g. 20 to 465 Field Coy RE 20 to 468 " " 20 to Hdqrs R.E. 12 to 453 Coy A.S.C.	
			Visited A.D.S. CAMBRIN in afternoon and arranged for a second motor ambulance to be kept there.	
	5/9/17		Enemy shelled LABOURSE between 12.15pm and 2.15pm in two bouts the first with shells at about 7 minute interval lasting till 1.40pm and the second after 2pm at interval of about 2 minutes. There were no casualties and no useful military end achieved.	

Army Form C. 2118.

Instructions regarding War Diaries and Intelligence Summaries are contained in F. S. Regs., Part II. and the Staff Manual respectively. Title pages will be prepared in manuscript.

WAR DIARY
or
INTELLIGENCE SUMMARY.
(Erase heading not required.)

Place	Date	Hour	Summary of Events and Information	Remarks and references to Appendices
FOUQUIÈRES	10/12/17		Inspection of Field Amb transport complete in column of route by G.O.C. 46 Division. Fault found with small points of appearance, & saluting at march past bad. No fault with vehicles animals or harness.	
	11/12/17		Addressed A section in subject of investment in War savings certificates. Work round "Scabies" hut completed.	
	12/12/17		Addressed A.S.C. after in War savings. Held a combined Whist drive with patients in evening. Work on new harness room & sick bay for horse started & well under way. Days routine varies but little. 16 O.R. returned from temporary duty at 18 C.C.S.	
	13/12/17		Addressed remainder of unit in war savings. Addresses very well received and I think have opened the eyes of many to the probable conditions after the war.	
	14/12/17		Capt E.E. Harga MC returned from leave. Started re-metalling paths at CRS. Extra big admission of 40 today.	

A7092. Wt. W12839/M1293. 750,000. 1/17. D. D & L., Ltd. Forms/C2118/14.

Instructions regarding War Diaries and Intelligence Summaries are contained in F. S. Regs., Part II. and the Staff Manual respectively. Title pages will be prepared in manuscript.

WAR DIARY
or
INTELLIGENCE SUMMARY.
(Erase heading not required.)

Army Form C. 2118.

Hour, Date, Place	Summary of Events and Information	Remarks and references to Appendices
LA HERLIÈRE	they reached at 10.30 pm. In meantime the party of 9 men left in ~~Ravine~~ RAVINE were reinforced by a further party of 8 bearers sent by Capt Harrison from A.D.S.	
	After visiting all posts Capt Harrison remained in vicinity of SB 8 between 91 street and NEVERENDING LANE.	
30/8/16	Gas was liberated at 10 pm – the first gassed case occurred at once owing to a leaky cylinder connection. This was slight & was carried down 91 street to SB 10	
	At 10.20 pm the enemy put up a barrage on the forward end of NEVERENDING LANE so casualties were retained in the trenches till 11 pm when the shelling had stopped. The last gassed case left the trenches at 3 am – this made 7 in all: there were 2 wounded from shell fire.	

(9 29 6) W 4141—463 100,000 9/14 H W V Forms/C. 2118/10

Army Form C. 2118.

WAR DIARY
or
INTELLIGENCE SUMMARY.
(Erase heading not required.)

Instructions regarding War Diaries and Intelligence Summaries are contained in F. S. Regs., Part II. and the Staff Manual respectively. Title pages will be prepared in manuscript.

Place	Date	Hour	Summary of Events and Information	Remarks and references to Appendices
FRESNOY-LE GRAND		13/10/18	Day spent in cleaning up billets & getting the unit into shape again. GGH	
"		14/10/18	Capt MILLAR proceeded on leave. Uneventful day. GGH.	
"		15.10.18	1st Lieut JJ De Vereaux U.S.M.C. reported for duty. Odd shelling of village with H.E. during afternoon & evening. GGH	
"		16.10.18	Uneventful day. Repairs to wagons &c proceeded with. GGH	
		17.10.18	General routine work. During H.E. shelling in morning one RAMC bearer killed. (122469 Pte. ELLIS A.E.) GGH	
"		18.10.18.	The Div^n. being in for an attack. Capt Reid & 56 bearers detailed for duty under orders O.C. 1/2 NMFA & sent to ADS, BOHAIN.	

D. D. & L., London, E.C.
(A8c04) Wt W1771/M2031 750,000 5/17 Sch. 52 Forms/C2118/14

Instructions regarding War Diaries and Intelligence Summaries are contained in F. S. Regs., Part II. and the Staff Manual respectively. Title Pages will be prepared in manuscript.

WAR DIARY
or
INTELLIGENCE SUMMARY

(Erase heading not required.)

Army Form C. 2118

Place	Date	Hour	Summary of Events and Information	Remarks and references to Appendices
GAUDIEMPRÉ	30/4/16		Hospital or Field Ambulance Main Dressing Station practically complete. Consists of 16 standard pattern huts 36' × 16' canvas or tarpaulin roofed with 1 large hut French (Adrian) pattern: in addition 2 standard pattern huts for Pack Store & Q.M. Store and extra buildings for Bath House, Cooks, Latrines: Personnel under canvas and in extemporised shelters and extra canvas available as required for patients. Rough sketch (not to scale) of ground plan of Hospital attached App I. Scheme of procedure - Patients arriving go to Reception (Adrian) hut where they are fed, registered & sorted: from there pass in one or other of Operation Huts where necessary dressing is done: from there pass into one of the evacuation (E) huts & await arrival of MAC to convey them to C.C.S. This procedure refers to wounded casualties: sick after reception are disposed of as circumstances indicate. Water supply - drawn from stand pipes in GAUDIEMPRÉ in water carts & stored in tanks at highest end of ground about 1200 gallons storage. Refuse including excreta burned in suitable incinerator just outside Hospital grounds.	

1875 Wt. W593/826 1,000,000 4/15 J.B.C. & A. A.D.S.S./Forms/C. 2118.

Army Form C. 2118

WAR DIARY
or
INTELLIGENCE SUMMARY
(Erase heading not required.)

Instructions regarding War Diaries and Intelligence Summaries are contained in F. S. Regs., Part II. and the Staff Manual respectively. Title Pages will be prepared in manuscript.

Place	Date	Hour	Summary of Events and Information	Remarks and references to Appendices
	2/7/16		were detained a few hours pending return to their units. In the course of the ~~...~~ period of 36 hours ~~abt~~ 1530 cases were dealt with of whom only 20% were lying cases. Number of deaths in hospital 7 all buried at GAUDIEMPRÉ. In the course of the period hospital was visited by DDMS VII th Corps and DMS 3rd Army who expressed their satisfaction with the way in which all the work was being carried on.	
	3/7/16		Received orders to ~~have~~ ready to move to LAHERLIÈRE & occupy advanced dressing stations at BERLES au BOIS and BAILLEULVAL. One man of the Fd Amb. was killed in the course of his duty & one man slightly wounded.	
	4/7/16		Moved Headquarters to LAHERLIÈRE: accommodation there for about 100 patients in the buildings. Visited advanced dressing stations at BERLES au BOIS and BAILLEULVAL, & the advanced bearer posts in connection with them — also the RAPs along present divisional line. Transferred necessary personnel to carry on ADSs efficiently	

7

Army Form C. 2118.

Instructions regarding War Diaries and Intelligence Summaries are contained in F. S. Regs., Part II. and the Staff Manual respectively. Title pages will be prepared in manuscript.

WAR DIARY
or
INTELLIGENCE SUMMARY.
(Erase heading not required.)

VB 42

Place	Date	Hour	Summary of Events and Information	Remarks and references to Appendices
			Aug. 1918	140/3200.
			SECRET.	
			WAR DIARY	
			of	
			1/3 North Midland Field Ambulance.	
			From 1/8/18 to 31/8/18.	

(A7092). Wt W12839/M1293. 75 ,0 o. 1/17. D. D. & L., Ltd. Forms/C.2118/14.

13

Instructions regarding War Diaries and Intelligence Summaries are contained in F. S. Regs., Part II. and the Staff Manual respectively. Title pages will be prepared in manuscript.

WAR DIARY
or
~~INTELLIGENCE~~ SUMMARY.
(Erase heading not required.)

1/3 Field Ambulance
46 DIVISION

Army Form C. 2118.

Hour, Date, Place	Summary of Events and Information	Remarks and references to Appendices
27-5-15 BAILLEUL	Lt Harrison returned from PARIS having purchased there for II Corps American Cloth, veiling, Cotton waste for 12,000 Masks & waterproof bags -	
28-5-15 BAILLEUL	The unit received no mail this day - Remained 47 Admitted 4 Evacuated 6 To Duty 6 Remaining 39.	
29-5-15 BAILLEUL	Remained 39. Admitted 10 To Duty 5 Remaining 44 One case of Cerebro-spinal Meningitis from the 1/5 North Staffs Regt transferred to the Infectious Hospital St OMER.	
30-5-15 BAILLEUL	Remained 44 Admitted 8 Evacuated 6 Duty 3 Remaining 43	
31-5-15 BAILLEUL	Lt Harrison & the men detailed to assist in the making & issuing of Antigas-Masks have been responsible for the issue of 15,000 to 2nd Corps. That number has already been issued - They are now engaged on another 12,000 -	

(9 29 6) W4141—463 100,000 9/14 H W V Forms/C. 2118/10

Instructions regarding War Diaries and Intelligence Summaries are contained in F. S. Regs., Part II. and the Staff Manual respectively. Title pages will be prepared in manuscript.

WAR DIARY
or
INTELLIGENCE SUMMARY.
(Erase heading not required.)

Army Form C. 2118.

Place	Date	Hour	Summary of Events and Information	Remarks and references to Appendices
BRUAY	18/4/18		Closed up personnel in huts & prepared accommodation for 105 OR. of 1/5 Leicesters suffering from "PUO". These came to be carefully observed with a view to determining the cause of the symptoms. Consulting physician I Army examined men of Monmouths referred to above who all exhibit much the same symptoms viz aphonia (some degree), afebrile or practically so in all cases, with ~~oedema~~ oedema of palate, & pharynx and injection of vocal ~~cords~~ cords: in two cases some superficial ulceration of the latter. Unit standing under 1 hours notice.	App I
	19/4/18		Unit under 4 hours notice – Col. Hume & Douglas AMS visited ambulance & investigated the cases of 1/5 Leicesters referred to above and party of 108 1st Mon. suffering from aphonia. General conclusion arrived at that the latter group owe their symptoms to exposure to gas – probably blue cross – & to a negligeable degree only to infectious epidemic & that the Leicesters group owe condition to infection by some organism of catarrhal group & ~~—~~ negligeably to gas.	
	20/4/18		Further parties of Leicesters arrive for segregation bringing total up to 262: convalescents to number of 80 separated & put in convalescent hut. All cases but one doing well – he evacuated to CCS.	

A7092. Wt. W12839/M1293. 750,000. 1/17. D. D & L., Ltd. Forms/C2118/14.

Instructions regarding War Diaries and Intelligence Summaries are contained in F. S. Regs., Part II. and the Staff Manual respectively. Title pages will be prepared in manuscript.

1

WAR DIARY
or
INTELLIGENCE SUMMARY.
(*Erase heading not required.*)

Army Form C. 2118.

1/3 NM Fd Amb

Vol 32

MEDICAL

Place	Date	Hour	Summary of Events and Information	Remarks and references to Appendices
LABOURSE	1/10/17		Attended conference at ADMS office 10 am. Matters discussed, the month leave for time expired men; the Auxiliary RAMC benevolent fund; details of collection and evacuation of casualties from HULLUCH and LOOS sections and provision of walking wounded collecting posts.	
	2/10/17		Visited Advanced Dressing Stations PHILOSOPHE and FORT GLATZ. going to the latter over the plain from 927 central along old tracks per map. None of these practicable for evacuation of casualties being too much obstructed by old trench systems and wire belts.	
	3/10/17		Capt. J. MILLER returned to duty from ordinary leave. Reported on Q.M.S. Richardson as inefficient - recommended his reduction to sergeant - under KR 183(2) & that he be re-posted for clerical duties only.	
	4/10/17		Routine duties in morning: visited ADS PHILOSOPHE in afternoon made arrangements arising out of RAMC. CO Int. 1 Gas NCO and 20 men report to O/C PHILOSOPHE at 6 pm. daily till further orders. 1 motor cyclist to ADMS office 9 pm daily 1 " " " PHILOSOPHE " " 1 NCO (Gas) and 24 bearers arrived 9 pm as reserve from 1/2 NM Fd Amb.	

Instructions regarding War Diaries and Intelligence Summaries are contained in F. S. Regs., Part II. and the Staff Manual respectively. Title pages will be prepared in manuscript.

WAR DIARY
or
INTELLIGENCE SUMMARY.
(Erase heading not required.)

3RD NORTH MIDLAND FIELD AMBULANCE ROYAL ARMY MEDICAL CORPS

Army Form C. 2118.

Place	Date	Hour	Summary of Events and Information	Remarks and references to Appendices
PREDEFIN (Pas C.)	14/2/18		Physical training and drill carried out by portion of unit remainder draining & cleaning village. The horse-standings are now in much better order and water gets away from them. ~~[illegible]~~	
	15/2/18		Arranged for use of schoolroom & blackboard for lectures on Thursday & Tuesday in afternoon. Visited RE at BOYAVAL to enquire if anything was needed that I could help them with. Sent wagons to draw "gravel" from pit near DENNEBROEUCQ for building up horse standings. On receipt found the gravel valueless not worth the trouble of haulage. Men engaged as yesterday. The "Hospital" is now looking more like a Hospital and is equipped with boiler, 2 baths, good latrines, incinerator etc & may be regarded as a flourishing young concern, one quite worth handing over.	
	16/2/18		Normal day - outdoor training for NCOs & men: map reading for NCOs	

8

Instructions regarding War Diaries and Intelligence Summaries are contained in F. S. Regs., Part II. and the Staff Manual respectively. Title pages will be prepared in manuscript.

WAR DIARY
or
INTELLIGENCE SUMMARY.
(Erase heading not required.)

Army Form C. 2118.

Hour, Date, Place	Summary of Events and Information	Remarks and references to Appendices
24 June 15. BAILLEUL	Remained 82 Admitted 9 Duty 2 Evacuated 5 Remaining 84-	
	B + C sections proceeded to a Field on the POPERINGHE - WESTOUTRE Road 1½ miles due South of the former Town - In the evening	
NEAR POPERINGHE 2¼ miles due South -	myself + Officers went out with 13 Motor Ambce Cars + 40 bearers to a School about 3/4 mile out of YPRES on the MENIN road - collected wounded from the NORTH MIDLAND DIVISION returning 2. AM 25.6.15 These cases were evacuated to the 1 NORTH MIDLAND F AMB who have an ADVANCED D. STATION 3/4 mile due South of our Camp.	
25. June 15.	A. section marched from BAILLEUL to the camp	

(9 29 6) W4141—463 100,000 9/14 H W V Forms/C. 2118/10

Instructions regarding War Diaries and Intelligence Summaries are contained in F. S. Regs., Part II. and the Staff Manual respectively. Title pages will be prepared in manuscript.

WAR DIARY
or
INTELLIGENCE SUMMARY.
(Erase heading not required.)

Army Form C. 2118.

Place	Date	Hour	Summary of Events and Information	Remarks and references to Appendices
LABEUVRIERE	3/4/18		Sent 1 Sgt & 30 men as working party to a R.E. company of Army Troops working on corps line. Number of personnel now on duties detached from Field Amb. 3 officers 53 O.R. Lt Doyle relieved Capt Harrison at 1/5 S. Staffs Regt.	
	4/4/18		Attended conference at ADMS office 10 am. 2nd Amb. team played 337 Amb at soccer & whacked them. Lectured to unit on Industrial re-organisation after the war.	
	5/4/18		DDMS visited the Rest Station – he expressed disapproval of the method adopted for protecting huts against bomb splinters and was not much mollified by learning that the method had been adopted with the concurrence & on the advice of the Field Engineer whom I had consulted before starting. Describes the untidiness of the premises & "not taking into account the fact that most of the departments are in course of repair or alteration & that under these circumstances it is impossible for the place to look like a museum model".	

Instructions regarding War Diaries and Intelligence Summaries are contained in F. S. Regs., Part II. and the Staff Manual respectively. Title pages will be prepared in manuscript.

WAR DIARY
or
INTELLIGENCE SUMMARY.
(Erase heading not required.)

Army Form C. 2118.

Hour, Date, Place	Summary of Events and Information	Remarks and references to Appendices
26-4-15.	At 9.30 convoy of 78 wounded arrived - 3 Decompression operations & one abdominal operation performed - All other cases dressed, several minor operations performed - One man suffering from dyspnoea, cyanosis & oedema of lungs with profuse exudation as a result of "poisonous gas" - 6.30 pm 47 cases evacuated to Hospital Train at BAILLEUL STATION = 18 cases remained from Divisional Rest Station - Total in Hospital (12 noon) 96 = one man died 9.50 pm -	
27-4-15.	At 2.30 am. 35 cases evacuated to Hospital Train. Remaining at 12 noon 14 cases. "B" section of the Field Ambulance took over the Advanced Dressing Station near NEUVE EGLISE. C section took over the STAFFS BRIGADE BATHS in NEUVE EGLISE - At 7.15 pm 28 wounded arrived - All dressed - 3 Trephining Operations & one Amputation performed -	
28-4-15.	At 5. am 28 wounded arrived - Dressed, one Amputation performed - 3.30 pm 34 evacuated to Hosp. Train 20 wounded ~~evacuated~~ 9. am - 20 wounded evacuated 10.15 am - 50 wounded arrived between 9 am & 12 noon -	

Instructions regarding War Diaries and Intelligence Summaries are contained in F. S. Regs., Part II. and the Staff Manual respectively. Title pages will be prepared in manuscript.

WAR DIARY
or
INTELLIGENCE SUMMARY.
(Erase heading not required.)

Army Form C. 2118.

3RD NORTH MIDLAND FIELD AMBULANCE ROYAL ARMY MEDICAL CORPS

Place	Date	Hour	Summary of Events and Information	Remarks and references to Appendices
LABEUVRIERE	8/4/18		Transport Sergt Major left for months probation with a Regt. preparatory to receiving a commission. He is temporarily attached to 1/5 King's Liverpool Rgt.	
	9/4/18		Major E H Bradley went for temporary duty with 1/2 N. M. F. A to assist with a large number of gassed cases received from Lievin, Grenay, Mazingarbe area. Heavy shelling of Bethune & neighbourhood all day and an enemy attack between La BASSEE Canal and ARMENTIERES in which he gained ~~some~~ ground. ~~[illegible]~~ Over 600 German prisoners passed through cage at CHOCQUES. Some shelling of CHOCQUES in night. Lent CRS recreation ground as a park for an A.F.A Bde which had been shelled out of BETHUNE and quartered their men in a vacant hut belonging to CRS.	
	10/4/18		Attended conference at ADMS Office 10 am: principal subject discussed, the measures to be adopted in the event of a withdrawal of Field Ambulances from their present positions consequent on a successful enemy attack in the HULLUCH, LIEVIN sector. Lt Sharp detailed for duty as required in inoculating & vaccinating prisoners at cage at CHOCQUES. On road to [illegible]EMONT passed a large gang of Portuguese doing labour work under armed guards just like P. of W.	

A7092 Wt. W12839/M1293. 750,000. 1/17. D. D. & L. Ltd. Forms/C2118/14.

Instructions regarding War Diaries and Intelligence Summaries are contained in F. S. Regs., Part II. and the Staff Manual respectively. Title pages will be prepared in manuscript.

WAR DIARY
or
INTELLIGENCE SUMMARY.
(Erase heading not required.)

Army Form C. 2118.

Place	Date	Hour	Summary of Events and Information	Remarks and references to Appendices
FOURQUIÈRES	22/12/17		DDMS I Corps visited CRS. Submitted application for increase in fuel allowance for CRS. Attended lecture at 33 CCS at noon given by DDMS Canadian Corps on Medical disposition for the operations culminating in the capture of PASSCHENDAELE. Pontoon Park party gave a concert to patients. About 5pm a squadron of enemy aircraft dropped a number of large bombs on BÉTHUNE causing a considerable number of casualties. Some glass broken at C.R.S. by the concussion of these bombs dropped about 1500 yards away.	
	23/12/17		Capt G D FAIRLEY sent to 1/7 N+D as temp. relief of RMO. Enemy aircraft again dropped a number of bombs on BÉTHUNE about 5pm.	
	24/12/17		1/Lieut T.L. DOYLE M.O.R.C. USA sent to 1/5 Lincolns as temporary relief for RMO proceeding on leave.	

A7092 Wt. W128.9/M1293. 750,000. 1/17. D. D & L., Ltd. Forms/C2118/14.

Instructions regarding War Diaries and Intelligence Summaries are contained in F. S. Regs., Part II. and the Staff Manual respectively. Title pages will be prepared in manuscript.

WAR DIARY
or
INTELLIGENCE SUMMARY.
(Erase heading not required.)

Army Form C. 2118.

Place	Date	Hour	Summary of Events and Information	Remarks and references to Appendices
HESDIGNEUL	17/5/18		Visit by officer to post at FBC 5.9 found all in order and strengthening work in progress: walking wounded boards sent up to be fixed so as to direct wounded clear of the main BETHUNE – BEUVRY Road towards VERQUIN. Received notification from 7 Canadian Gen Hosp. that Pte BURROWS of this unit gassed on 14/5/18 at GORRE had died there on 16th. Rumours also received of two other deaths from the same cause but so far these not confirmed.	
	18/5/18		Visited ADS ESSARS in morning. Normal relief of personnel of F. Amb. on ESSARS section effected: Lt Richard replacing Major Sheya. Capt Reid sent up to ADS GORRE to relieve Capt AU MILLAR MC. Considerable shelling of neighbourhood of GORRE CHATEAU from 10pm 17th onwards with 5.9 HE and Yellow X gas shells. 2 RMOs sent down gassed: 4pm shelling of same type round A.D.S. a fair number of apparently slightly gassed cases have come down & this will probably be increased as the delayed effects in the [illegible] become apparent.	
	19/5/18		The number of gassed cases down from GORRE up to 9am was 57 the majority slight apparently. Completed range of bivouacs capable of accommodating 30 men.	

D. D. & L., London, E.C. (A8co4) Wt W1771/M2031 750,000 5/17 Sch. 52 Forms/C2118/14

Instructions regarding War Diaries and Intelligence Summaries are contained in F. S. Regs., Part II. and the Staff Manual respectively. Title pages will be prepared in manuscript.

WAR DIARY
or
INTELLIGENCE SUMMARY.
(Erase heading not required.)

1/3 N. M. F. Ambce

Army Form C. 2118.

Hour, Date, Place	Summary of Events and Information	Remarks and references to Appendices
31 - 5 - 15 - BAILLEUL	State :- Remained 43 - Admitted 13 - Discharged to Duty 3 Remaining 53. For admissions of Sick & wounded to the Advanced Dressing Station of the unit from the ~~Stat~~ STAFFS INF BRIGADE See Appendix VI	Appendix VI A.H.C.D.
	1500 of the 2nd batch of Respirators issued to III DIVISION ~~Corps~~ - 300 to the 3rd N M R F A.	
	The new pattern respirator bag being made is wallet shaped the flap secured by two "dress" fasteners - 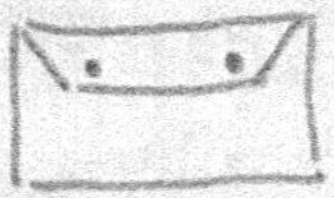 The cotton waste of the Mask is sewn in separate gauze quilted & forms an easily renewable & removable flat-pad. A.H.C.D. Gent LIEUT.-COLONEL, COMM'DG 1/3RD N. MID. FIELD AMB. R.A.M. CORPS.	Improved pattern Mask.

46 Division -

Confidential

Instructions regarding War Diaries and Intelligence Summaries are contained in F. S. Regs., Part II. and the Staff Manual respectively. Title pages will be prepared in manuscript.

WAR DIARY
or
~~INTELLIGENCE~~ SUMMARY.
(Erase heading not required.)

Army Form C. 2118.

3rd N.M F AMB
46 Div

Hour, Date, Place	Summary of Events and Information	Remarks and references to Appendices
Aug 1. 15	Advanced Dressing Stations for the 46 Division at The MILL VLAMERTINGHE + School BRANDHOEC 4 Officers + one section at the former + 3 Officers + 1/2 section at the latter. The acetilene Operating lamps not found sufficient for these Dressing Stations so purchased 4 hand acetilene lamps, 2/- each -	
Aug 7 15	Average number of sick + wounded in 24 hours at both Advanced Dressing Stations 70 - about 15 to 20 being wounded.	
Aug 9. 15	After the attack on HOOGE by the 6th DIVISION at 3.15 am several cases of wounded were treated at No 1 + No 2 Dressing Stations - They began to arrive about 9.15 am	

(9 29 6) W 4141—463 100,000 9/14 H W V Forms/C. 2118/10

Instructions regarding War Diaries and Intelligence Summaries are contained in F. S. Regs., Part II. and the Staff Manual respectively. Title pages will be prepared in manuscript.

WAR DIARY
or
INTELLIGENCE SUMMARY.
(Erase heading not required.)

Army Form C. 2118.

Place	Date	Hour	Summary of Events and Information	Remarks and references to Appendices
VENDELLES	21.9.18		Together with ADMS called on ADMS 4th Australian Division with reference to taking over ADS. ~~[illegible]~~ Went round ADS & car loading posts, & visited ADS at COOKER QUARRY. Capt. T.W RUTTLEDGE departed for duty with 6th. S. Staffs. Regt. & Capt. A.U. MILLAR M.C. returned to this unit. In afternoon Capt. MILLAR, Capt. REID & 25 O.R's proceeded to quarry at R.5.a.8.3 to establish ADS there. Headquarters & transport proceeded by route march to new billets at VENDELLES arriving 8.30 P.M. Twelve more bearers sent to new ADS at midnight. ACY	
	22.9.18		VENDELLES shelled steadily all night; numerous casualties amongst animals of neighbouring units. In morning called on ADMS & arranged for transport to go back to billets at HANCOURT (Q.8.b.5.4). Transport departed at 2 P.M. Headquarters remained at VENDELLES. VENDELLES shelled in afternoon; 3 men killed & 6 wounded, numerous animal casualties in neighbouring units. No RAMC casualties. Together with ADMS visited Left ADS (R.5.a.8.3) In evening called on ADMS to discuss impending operations. ACY	

D. D. & L., London, E.C. (A8co4) Wt W1771/M2031 750,000 5/17 Sch. 52 Forms/C2118/14

Army Form C. 2118.

WAR DIARY
or
INTELLIGENCE SUMMARY.

(Erase heading not required.)

Instructions regarding War Diaries and Intelligence Summaries are contained in F. S. Regs., Part II. and the Staff Manual respectively. Title pages will be prepared in manuscript.

Place	Date	Hour	Summary of Events and Information	Remarks and references to Appendices
BONNAY	14/9/18		Programme of training :- Physical drill, route march, squad drill, + football. ACY.	
	15/9/18		1st. Lieut. T.L. DOYLE MCUSA, sent to 230 Bgde RFA for temporary duty in place of Capt. SHARP evacuated to 41 Gen. Hosp. sick ACY.	
	17/9/18		Capt. A.C REID departed for temporary duty at Corps Walking Wounded Station. ACY	
	18/9/18		Capt. A.C. REID returned from Corps Walking Wounded Station. Transport of unit departed for new area, under Capt. King ACY	
TERTRY	19/9/18		At 3 P.M unit proceeded by route march to HEILLY, and embussed at 4 P.M. Arrived at destination 10.30 P.M. No billets; bivouacked in field between TERTRY & ESTREES-EN-CHAUSSÉE. ACY	
	20/9/18		Called on ADMS & with him went to see ADMS 1st Division re taking over ADS at COOKER QUARRY. (R.11.C.8.9. Sheet 62C) In afternoon Major HARRISON, Capt. BRADLEY, LIEUT. MORRIS, & the whole of C section proceeded in motor ambulances to ADS at COOKER QUARRY which they took over from 2nd. F. Amb. 1st. Div. Capt. A.U. MILLAR M.C. detailed for temporary duty with 6th. S. Staffs. R. Capt. T.W. RUTTLEDGE reported for duty from 5th. Lincoln Regt. ACY	

D. D. & L., London, E.C. (A8604) Wt W1771/M2031 750,000 5/17 Sch. 52 Forms/C2118/14

Instructions regarding War Diaries and Intelligence Summaries are contained in F. S. Regs., Part II. and the Staff Manual respectively. Title Pages will be prepared in manuscript.

WAR DIARY
or
INTELLIGENCE SUMMARY
(Erase heading not required.)

Army Form C. 2118.

Place	Date	Hour	Summary of Events and Information	Remarks and references to Appendices
FOUQUIERRES	9/10/15		Lt GREIG sent to 4th LINCOLNS for 14 days to relieve the MO on leave. same night he returned as relief not necessary –	
	10.10.15		Instituted system of Latrines in which faecal matter is at once burnt in an incinerator within the Latrine enclosure – Urine passed into a separate receptacle + emptied into a urine bucket. Got working the engine in an adjoining steam Laundry – men of the unit repairing the boiler – using the appliances partly as Baths + partly for washing + drying clothes, Hospital Towels etc –	
	12.10.15	10 pm	Received Operation Orders from ADMS to act as Main Dressing Station for Lying cases only to be evacuated from the front held by the 46 Division – Division to attack HOHENZOLLERN REDOUBT + THE DUMP.	
	13.10.15	2 am	Casualties commenced to arrive – Sent 40 Bearers to VERMELLES	
	14.10.15	8 am	Admissions during previous 24 hours wounded Officers 17 O.R. 262 Total 279	
	15.10.15	8 am	" " " " " 16 OR 277. " 293	
	16.10.15	8 am	" " " " " ~~Shaka~~ Officers 5 OR 110 " 115	
	17.10.15	8 am	" " " " " Sick " nil " 26 " 26	

Army Form C[redacted]8.

WAR DIARY
or
INTELLIGENCE SUMMARY.
(Erase heading not required.)

Instructions regarding War Diaries and Intelligence Summ[redacted] are contained in F. S. Regs., Part II. and the Staff Manual respectively. Title pages will be prepared in manuscript.

Place	Date	Hour	Summary of Events and Information	Remarks and references to Appendices
HAYETTES	7.11.18		At 6AM proceeded with ADMS to ~~[illegible]~~ find new billets for unit. Later Hdqrs. of unit moved to HAYETTES (O.8.d.9.2. Sheet 57A). ADS at CARTIGNIES. ACY	
"	8.11.18		Enemy resistance increasing. Visited ADS at CARTIGNIES. During evening large fires seen to eastward, evidently enemy ammunition dumps burning. ACY.	
BOULOGNE SUR HELPE.	9.11.18		Enemy again retreating. Hdqrs. of unit advanced to BOULOGNE SUR HELPE. Good billets in school used by Germans as hospital ACY	
"	11.11.18		Hostilities ceased at 11 AM. an armistice having been signed ACY	
	12.11.18		Called on ADMS. Officers, men & vehicles lent to 1/2nd. N. M. F. Amb returned to this unit, with the exception of Lieut. Stephen who remained with 1/2nd. N. M. F. Amb. ACY	
AVESNES	13.11.18		Unit proceeded by route march to AVESNES. Billets good. ACY	
PREUX	14.11.18		Unit proceeded by route march to PREUX. Billets bad as village has been considerably damaged. ACY	

D. D. & L., London, E.C. (A8co4) Wt W1771/M2031 750,000 5/17 Sch. 52 Forms/C2118/14

Instructions regarding War Diaries and Intelligence Summaries are contained in F. S. Regs., Part II. and the Staff Manual respectively. Title pages will be prepared in manuscript.

WAR DIARY

or

~~INTELLIGENCE SUMMARY.~~

(*Erase heading not required.*)

Army Form C. 2118.

3rd N. M. F. AMB
46 DIV

Hour, Date, Place	Summary of Events and Information	Remarks and references to Appendices
Aug 12. 15	Both Dressing Stations have been quiet since Aug 9. 15.	
Aug 15. 15	Dressing Stations continue to be quiet.	
Aug 18. 15	Received 6 men re-inforcement to complete establishment of sections	
Aug 19. 15	No II Dressing Station at BRANDHOEK evacuated & handed over to III rd Division	
Aug 20. 15	No I Dressing Station at WHITE MILL VLAMERTINGHE evacuated and handed over to 1st N. Midland Field Amb.	
	3rd N Midland Field Amb: replaced 2nd Field Amb, taking over the 46th Divisional Rest Station at WIPPENHOEK FARM.	

Instructions regarding War Diaries and Intelligence Summaries are contained in F. S. Regs., Part II. and the Staff Manual respectively. Title pages will be prepared in manuscript.

WAR DIARY
or
INTELLIGENCE SUMMARY.

(*Erase heading not required.*)

Army Form C. 2118.

Hour, Date, Place	Summary of Events and Information	Remarks and references to Appendices
March 21.15.	Collection of wounded as yesterday -	
" 22.15	- Ditto -	
" 25.15	The Field Ambulance returned from ARMENTIERES to Billets at OULTERSTEENE The system adopted in the unit for the supply of Drugs etc to the unit & the Regimental Medical Officers is as follows - A. Section the Field Ambce & its Equipment is kept as a Head Quarter Section in Reserve - From its Equipment all shortages in drugs etc are supplied to B & C section & the Regimental Officers - A in turn indenting through the ADMS on Advanced Medical Stores - A section also supplies Milk & Medical Comforts to the others & to Regimental Aid Posts -	
" 26.15	Orders ~~[illegible]~~ issued to R.M.O's to apply to the F. Ambce for 6 Haversacs each containing "Shell Dressings" - It being thought that these Haversacs are of more use at Regimental Aid Posts & in the Trenches than with the Bearer Sections F. Ambulance.	

H H C Dent(?)
Lt-Col - OC 1/3 N M F Amblce
RAMC T.

(9 29 6) W4141—463 100,000 9/14 H W V Forms/C. 2118/10

Instructions regarding War Diaries and Intelligence Summaries are contained in F. S. Regs., Part II. and the Staff Manual respectively. Title Pages will be prepared in manuscript.

WAR DIARY
or
INTELLIGENCE SUMMARY
(Erase heading not required.)

Army Form C. 2118

Place	Date	Hour	Summary of Events and Information	Remarks and references to Appendices
			which proceed to AUXRIETZ after dark.	
ECOIVRES	14/3/16		Moved Field Ambulance to quarters in ECOIVRES. and took over communal school buildings for Brigade Hospital. Large quantities of refuse of every kind left in village by outgoing troops. All hands occupied in cleaning up.	
	16/3/16		Visited I.O.M. XVII Corps at SAVY and arranged for repairs to vehicles.	
	17/3/16		Detailed an officer to supervise sanitation in ECOIVRES	
	20/3/16		Visited RAPs and advanced dressing stations with DADMS and Divisional Sanitary officer: Major Stidston men busy improving & increasing accommodation in dugouts at AUXRIETZ.	
	21/3/16		FGCM held on 623 Cpl PALIN. W. 1/3 N.M. F. Amb. for conduct to the prejudice of good order and military discipline — falling out from column in line of march without permission. Prisoner found guilty & sentence to be reduced to the ranks. Sentence confirmed	

3 NM Fd Amb 46

Vol 15

Army Form C. 2118

Instructions regarding War Diaries and Intelligence Summaries are contained in F. S. Regs., Part II. and the Staff Manual respectively. Title Pages will be prepared in manuscript.

WAR DIARY
or
~~INTELLIGENCE SUMMARY~~
(Erase heading not required.)

Place	Date	Hour	Summary of Events and Information	Remarks and references to Appendices
BAILLEUL AUX CORNAILLES U19.b. sheet 36B.	1/5/16		Following 5 officers arrived as reinforcements Capt B.C. Douglas RAMC Lt G.B. Kennedy " " W.E. Frazer " " C.H.H. Coetzee " " D.C. SUTTIE	
	2/5/16		Capt Douglas & Lieut Kennedy sent to 25th Division to replace Capt Harris & Lieut Hartley who returned to this unit. Capt F.G. Bennett returned to 1/1 N.Md Field Amb Capt C.H. Armitage returned from temporary duty with 1/1 Monmouth Regt.	
	3/5/16		~~[illegible]~~ Capt Harrison returned from temporary duty ~~[illegible]~~ at Div Baths & Laundry.	
	4/5/16		'A' section departed via REBREUVIETTE to St AMAND with 137 I.B.	
	5/5/16		DDMS XVII Corps visited hospital. Capt E.W. Strange rejoined from Sick leave in G.B.	

1875 Wt. W593/826 1,000,000 4/15 J.B.C. & A. A.D.S.S./Forms/C. 2118.

Instructions regarding War Diaries and Intelligence Summaries are contained in F. S. Regs., Part II. and the Staff Manual respectively. Title pages will be prepared in manuscript.

WAR DIARY
or
INTELLIGENCE SUMMARY.
(*Erase heading not required.*)

Army Form C. 2118.

Place	Date	Hour	Summary of Events and Information	Remarks and references to Appendices
HESDIGNEUL	12/5/18		Visited emergency dressing station site and found work of strengthening it in progress: obtained assurance from 138 Bde. in occupation next door that no obstacles would be put in the way of RAMC acquiring the premises by them.	
			Went on to ADS GORRE at which work of improvement goes on well. As there are now no posts to be ~~[illegible]~~ manned by RAMC in front of GORRE reduced staff of ADS right section to 1 officer & 24 O.R. 8 of the latter to be relieved every 4th day from Hdqrs.	
			Normal relief of staff of ADS & post L section ESSARS effected today, Major Heiga replacing Lt Richard.	
			From 9pm to midnight 12/13th stood at ½ hours notice: from midnight to 9am 13th at moments notice to staff walking wounded stations.	
	13/5/18		In afternoon & early evening of 12th enemy shelled the area round ~~F13~~ F 13 central for about 4 hours: direct hits were made on all buildings and the premises earmarked as walking wounded post had 3 direct hits & the part above the cellar rendered unserviceable for the purpose.	
			Visited it in morning with ADMS and decided to put up walking wounded collecting post under canvas at or about E 18 d central & to signpost tracks leading from BETHUNE - BEUVRY road thereto. Holding party to remain in cellar at F 13 central meanwhile.	
			Arranged with O.C. 1/2 NMFA to keep wagon loaded with necessary equipment at my Hdqrs to be sent up as and when needed.	

D. D. & L., London, E.C. (A8coi) Wt W1771/M2031 750,000 5/17 Sch. 52 Forms/C2118/14

Instructions regarding War Diaries and Intelligence Summaries are contained in F. S. Regs., Part II. and the Staff Manual respectively. Title pages will be prepared in manuscript.

WAR DIARY
or
INTELLIGENCE SUMMARY.
(Erase heading not required.)

Army Form C. 2118.

Place	Date	Hour	Summary of Events and Information	Remarks and references to Appendices
LABOURSE	31/8/17		Attended funeral of Pte A. Clarke of this unit killed by shell in billet yesterday.	
			Capt Kerr & Lieut Stoman attended lecture by Col. Wallace Consulting Surgeon I Army on Thomas splint.	
			Visited A.D.S. Cambrin in morning with a view to finding further accommodation for RAMC personnel wounded if the need for such should arise	
			Cellars under building used as R.C. Chapel at A19d 6.2. are in good order & would accommodate app. 30 lying. These could be prepared for receiving cases in a couple of hours: there is a suitable standing for 2 motor Ambs. at least on blind side of building.	
			The cellars under the ruined factory about 200 yards east of the above on the main road are very capacious & would hold large numbers: they would however need very thorough propping before putting adequate weight of protection on top and a sloping way would have to be made for stretchers: sand bag rampart protection would be required on an extensive scale also. These changes would entail a great deal of work and a fairly large quantity of material but if properly done the place would make a fine dressing station.	
			Expect Main Dressing Station at LABOURSE will be abolished shortly.	
			A. E. Hodder Lt Col. cdg 1/3 N.M.F. Amb.	

A7092. Wt. W12839/M1293 750,000. 1/17. D. D & L., Ltd. Forms/C2118/14.

Instructions regarding War Diaries and Intelligence Summaries are contained in F. S. Regs., Part II. and the Staff Manual respectively. Title pages will be prepared in manuscript.

WAR DIARY
or
INTELLIGENCE SUMMARY.
(Erase heading not required.)

Army Form C. 2118.

Place	Date	Hour	Summary of Events and Information	Remarks and references to Appendices
FOUQUIERES LES BETHUNE	6.12.17		Capt. V. S. Ullman U.S.M.O.R.C. returned to F. Amb from temporary duty with 1/4 Lincoln Rgt.	
			A.D.V.S. I Corps inspected horses & mules & expressed approval of their condition and of the transport lines. Improvements to station rather in abeyance owing to lack of material	
	8.12.17		1/Lt T. L. Doyle U.S.M.O.R.C and 2 sergeants returned to duty with unit from course at I Army R.A.M.C. school.	
			D.D.M.S. I Corps paid usual weekly visit to Rest Station	

A7092 Wt W12839/M1293 750,000 1/17. D. D & L., Ltd. Forms/C2118/14.

Instructions regarding War Diaries and Intelligence Summaries are contained in F. S. Regs., Part II. and the Staff Manual respectively. Title pages will be prepared in manuscript.

WAR DIARY
or
INTELLIGENCE SUMMARY.
(Erase heading not required.)

Army Form C. 2118.

Place	Date	Hour	Summary of Events and Information	Remarks and references to Appendices
HESDIGNEUL	4/6/18		Inspection of Transport 10am by G.O.C. 46 Division. He was evidently in a vile temper as he condemned everything and said the drivers could not ride or drive and did not know how to put on harness & equipment and that the mules were in bad condition and the wagons dropping to pieces from neglect. This was difficult to reconcile with the commendation of the Corps Commander on the occasion of the inspection of the Corps when he saw them unofficially and on 31st May the report of the Divisional Veterinary Officer of a recent date which gave the state of the animals "very good throughout". "What is truth" and "where shall wisdom be found"? 21 O.R. from ADS GORRE and posts relieved this morning by train. AH	
	5/6/18		Attended conference 10am at ADMS. Consulted with OC Div. Train on transport question and arranged for him to inspect H.T. on 6th the parade to be identical with that seen by G.O.C. Two more gas doors put up in cellar at ADS. GORRE and some strengthening effected at Dummy Fork post: some ropes put across canal to assist and cable with trolley in prospect of creation.	

D. D. & L., London, E.C. (A8c04) Wt. W1771/M2031 750,000 5/17 Sch. 52 Forms/C2118/14

Instructions regarding War Diaries and Intelligence Summaries are contained in F. S. Regs., Part II. and the Staff Manual respectively. Title pages will be prepared in manuscript.

WAR DIARY
or
INTELLIGENCE SUMMARY.
(Erase heading not required.)

Army Form C. 2118.

Place	Date	Hour	Summary of Events and Information	Remarks and references to Appendices
HESDIGNEUL	4/5/18		Two more men from GORRE sent down with eye symptoms - all slight + they will be retained with unit. Lt Doyle rejoins unit and is excused duty pro tem.	
			Visited ADS ESSARS opat - protection of cover + propping almost completed. No further communication from R.E. as to Elephant tubing for A.D.S.: reconnoitring of roads + tracks being carried out by Officer i/c.	
			Orderly from GORRE ADS made journey down by freight train from LEQUESNOY to LA PIERRETTE sidings K2 a 84. in evening + reported favourably of the smoothness of running: journey by freight train takes 2 hours at present, largely occupied by shunting operations at various sidings.	
			Submitted to ADMS for approval recirculation completed scheme of medical arrangements in event of heavy enemy attack + to OC ADS GORRE programme for the evacuation of casualties by light railway service.	
			Received 5 o.r. reinforcements from Base.	
	5/5/18		Visited Hdqrs 137 I.B. and afterwards examined premises of BETHUNE SOUTH laundry at E23 b 1.8 with a view to their serviceability as dressing station in case of need. Approaches & ways out are good, it is remote from other buildings and q[uiet] (relatively) and the space available is ample. The engine house is fairly substantial: there are no cellars: only one dugout giving sleeping accommodation for 14 men.	
			Officers gassed who are now at CRS are making good progress.	

D. D. & L., London, E.C. (A8co4) Wt W1771/M2031 750,000 5/17 Sch. 52 Forms/C2118/14

Army Form C. 2118.

Instructions regarding War Diaries and Intelligence Summaries are contained in F. S. Regs., Part II. and the Staff Manual respectively. Title Pages will be prepared in manuscript.

WAR DIARY
or
~~INTELLIGENCE SUMMARY~~
(Erase heading not required.)

Place	Date	Hour	Summary of Events and Information	Remarks and references to Appendices
FOUQUIÈRES	2/11/15		Lt. J.L. MAVETY sent to 2nd Bde RFA for duty vice M.O. invalided	
	5 Nov		Moved with 137 Inf. Bde via HINGES to CROIX DE MARMUSE. On arrival found all billets occupied by Infantry: when this had been adjusted Staff Capt. DEHRA DUN Bde arrived and claimed them for his men who were being relieved in trenches. In consequence ordered by ADMS to return to FOUQUIÈRES.	
			Capt. G.F. Haycraft sent to 1/5 N. Staffs Regt for duty.	
ZELOBES	7 Nov.		2 Sections (B & C) of unit occupied billets at Cx de MARMUSE. A section & Transport billets at ZELOBES, the former taking over premises from 129th Indian Field Amb. These premises were left in a dirty condition, the outgoing unit having taken no steps to ~~[illegible]~~ clean the quarters prior to departure. A small detachment under Major Stidston occupied Advanced Dressing station at KINGS ROAD – X 11.b. (BETHUNE Combined Sheet 1/40000)	

Instructions regarding War Diaries and Intelligence Summaries are contained in F. S. Regs., Part II. and the Staff Manual respectively. Title pages will be prepared in manuscript.

WAR DIARY
or
INTELLIGENCE SUMMARY.
(Erase heading not required.)

Army Form C. 2118.

Place	Date	Hour	Summary of Events and Information	Remarks and references to Appendices
LABOURSE	16/10/17		Visited advanced dressing stations PHILOSOPHE & FORTGLATZ in morning. Some enemy shelling of Battery positions behind Crassier at the former: one short landed on foot-path just outside ADS No damage done. Good progress being made with false roof for carrying off rain water. Received recommendation of CRE re heating at PHILOSOPHE and indented for stoves (Canadian) he recommended. Question of steam heating put up to ADMS 1 Army: who will endeavour to get it carried forward.	
	17/10/17		Received from BRCS 2 doz I.R. hot water bottles, sufficient to supply RMOs of 2 Brigades: Requested OC 1/1 NMFA to supply remaining units. Attended ADMS conference 10 am. Scheme discussed for overtaking arrears in the case of men long overdue for months leave on reengaging, and approved by which the whole allotment of leave for O.R. for one month will be devoted to these. This will clear off 26 of the most pressing: the remainder will be inserted in the ordinary leaves in proportion of one to 7 or 8 approximately. Took over responsibility for Baths at NOYELLES and PHILOSOPHE unsupervised former. Pte ACKERLEY appointed unpaid a/Cpl. for purposes of discipline while in charge of former.	

A 692 Wt W12539/M1293 750,000 1/17 D. D. & L., Ltd. Forms/C2118/14.

9

Instructions regarding War Diaries and Intelligence Summaries are contained in F. S. Regs., Part II. and the Staff Manual respectively. Title pages will be prepared in manuscript.

WAR DIARY
or
INTELLIGENCE SUMMARY.
(Erase heading not required.)

Army Form C. 2118.

Hour, Date, Place	Summary of Events and Information	Remarks and references to Appendices
25 - 6 - 15	taken by the rest of the unit = at 8 pm sent out 12 cars 4 Officers + 40 NCOs + men to collect from trenches held by the N. Mid or 46 Div - No casualties =	
FARM 1½ miles South of POPERINGHE	Camp water obtained from an Artesian well at POPERINGHE. No washing water here. A few tents erected for sick of the unit. Marching in strength, 3 over strength :— Collecting of wounded in the night	
26 - 6 - 15	Collection of wounded - 14 cases - Evacuated to ADV. DRESSING STATION at Sheet 28. G26 2.3.	
27 - 6 - 15.	Operation Orders received from ADMS 46th Div on method of collecting + evacuating - Collecting of wounded during the evening - on	

Army Form C. 2118

WAR DIARY
or
INTELLIGENCE SUMMARY
(Erase heading not required.)

Instructions regarding War Diaries and Intelligence Summaries are contained in F. S. Regs., Part II. and the Staff Manual respectively. Title Pages will be prepared in manuscript.

Place	Date	Hour	Summary of Events and Information	Remarks and references to Appendices
LA HERLIERE	27/8/16		Received 6 reinforcements three of whom were men of unit who had gone down to Base previously.	
	28/8/16		Lean-to shed at back of Hospital Barn fell down this afternoon apparently – the immediate cause was a distant explosion – the ~~usual~~ occupant – the tinsmith having left it a few minutes previously no one was hurt. 1 Farrier reinforcement arrived.	
	29/8/16		Pte W. B. Everitt RAMCT reported to unit from 233 Bde RFA where he had been doing water duty & was taken on the strength.	
	30/8/16	8.0pm	Message received from ADMS "Mails will be delivered 10pm". Sent up bearers in motor ambulances to BERLES in accordance with previous arrangements to report to Capt. S S B Harrison who was in charge of RAMC party. This officer with 3 NCOs and 17 men left ADS for trenches at 8.20 pm. By 9.30pm these bearers were disposed in the front line posts ~~Newark~~ (NEWARK St to 91 St) less 2 men left in large dugout (SB 10) with restoratives. Lt Robertson party of 19 men from HQrs reached BERLES 9.45pm & proceeded to Ravine: 10 of these were put into SB 10 which they	

1875 Wt. W593/826 1,000,000 4/15 J.B.C. & A. A.D.S.S./Forms/C. 2118.

2

Instructions regarding War Diaries and Intelligence Summaries are contained in F. S. Regs., Part II. and the Staff Manual respectively. Title pages will be prepared in manuscript.

WAR DIARY
or
INTELLIGENCE SUMMARY.
(Erase heading not required.)

Army Form C. 2118.

Hour, Date, Place	Summary of Events and Information	Remarks and references to Appendices
7 - 6 - 15 BAILLEUL	State :- Remained 71. Admitted 9 Duty 11 Evacuated 20 Remaining 49.	
8 - 6 - 15 BAILLEUL	State : Remained 49. Admitted 12 Duty 3. Evacuated 3 Remaining 55 -	
9 - 6 - 15 BAILLEUL	State of Rest Stn - Remained 55 - Admitted 3 Evacuated 2. Remaining 56.	
10 - 6 - 15	State. Remained 56. Admitted 21 Duty 2 Transfers 5 Remaining 70	
11 - 6 - 15	" Remained 70. Admitted 12 Duty 8 Transfers 6 Remaining 68 One wheeled stretcher carrier of the fixed frame pattern received - Sent to Adv Dressing Station NEUVE EGLISE.	

(9 29 6) W 4141—463 100,000 9/14 H W V Forms/C. 2118/10

Army Form C. 2118.

Instructions regarding War Diaries and Intelligence Summaries are contained in F. S. Regs., Part II. and the Staff Manual respectively. Title pages will be prepared in manuscript.

WAR DIARY
or
INTELLIGENCE SUMMARY.
(Erase heading not required.)

Hour, Date, Place	Summary of Events and Information	Remarks and references to Appendices
Aug 25 15	Lt Col. H.H.C DENT O.C 3rd Field Ambce was temporarily attached to No 10 C.C Stn near POPERINGHE for surgical work. = The efficiency of the Rest Station is very seriously hampered by water shortage. Practically all water for drinking & washing for the personnel & patients (500) has to be carried 3 miles. H H C Dent Lt Col	

1

Instructions regarding War Diaries and Intelligence Summaries are contained in F. S. Regs., Part II. and the Staff Manual respectively. Title pages will be prepared in manuscript.

WAR DIARY
or
~~INTELLIGENCE~~ ~~SUMMARY~~.
(Erase heading not required.)

1/3 FIELD AMBULANCE
46 DIVISION

Army Form C. 2118.

Hour, Date, Place	Summary of Events and Information	Remarks and references to Appendices
June 1st 1915 BAILLEUL	State of Rest Station :- Remained 53, Admitted 23, Duty 6, Evacuated 6 - Remaining 64.	
II nd VI 15. BAILLEUL	Remained 64. Admitted 17. To Duty 5. Evacuated 2 Remaining 74.	
3rd June 15 BAILLEUL	Remained 74 Admitted 5. To Duty 3 Evacuated 2 Remaining 74 -	
4 June 15. BAILLEUL	Examined specimen of water for the DDMS Lt Col Stevens came round Field Ambulance — Examined specimen of Drinking water for DDMS State :- Remained 74 Admitted 11 To Duty 6 Evacuated 3 Remaining 76.	
5. June 15 BAILLEUL	Remained 76 - Admitted 7 To Duty 20 Remaining 63 -	
6. June 15 BAILLEUL	Remained 63 - Admitted 11 To Duty 3 Remaining 71.	

Army Form C. 2118.

Instructions regarding War Diaries and Intelligence Summaries are contained in F. S. Regs., Part II. and the Staff Manual respectively. Title Pages will be prepared in manuscript.

WAR DIARY
or
INTELLIGENCE SUMMARY
(Erase heading not required.)

Place	Date	Hour	Summary of Events and Information	Remarks and references to Appendices
LABEUVRIERE	16		Lieut PHIBBS reported to ADMS for duty with 231 Bde. RFA. Detailed two motor ambulances to convey patients from ALLOUAGNE to MERVILLE. Capt. E.E. HERGA reported from duty from 231 Bde. RFA	
	17		General routine. C.E service 2-30. p.m. Nonconformist parade service 11.30. a.m.	
	18		Attended Conference ADMS office. Received initial operation order that A.D.S. MAROC was being taken over by 6th Division to be complete by nov 20th	
	19		Wrote to Capt. Miller with regard to various details of relief and ordered two distinguishing flags to be made for bearer post (which will now become ADS) at PONT GRENAY.	
	20	3.0 a.m.	Received wire ADMS telling me to send 24 bearers to report 7. AM to 1/2 N.M. F. Amb. and to hold all horse & motor ambs. in readiness and all available officers and other ranks. Replied that beyond 24 I had no available bearers.	

2449 Wt. W14957/M90 750,000 1/16 J.B.C. & A. Forms/C.2118/12.

Instructions regarding War Diaries and Intelligence Summaries are contained in F. S. Regs., Part II. and the Staff Manual respectively. Title pages will be prepared in manuscript.

WAR DIARY
or
INTELLIGENCE SUMMARY.
(Erase heading not required.)

Army Form C. 2118.

Place	Date	Hour	Summary of Events and Information	Remarks and references to Appendices
HESDIGNEUL	20/5/18		Started on protection of tentage occupants against bombs dropped from E.A. The whole tent to be sunk to a depth of 18" and the earth excavated to be built up as a ramp round the outside. Bethune is on fire in several places as a result of shelling with incendiary shells and a fair breeze is fanning the flames. Houses are being blown up to limit the fire. – cui bono? 38 reinforcements arrived.	
	21/5/18		Continued sinking tents – Battn Stage meanwhile Brewery GORRE but is not in any way restricting the ADS accommodation. Lt Richard takes charge of new draft for all purposes having replaced at ADS by Lieut Doyle. Quality of draft good.	
	22/5/18		In night 21/22 many E.A. over. One man of new draft killed by enemy M.G. bullet as he lay in his tent. One man of draft with large spleen acquired in E. Africa on service developed temperature of 103° after exercise was sent to Hospital ?malaria. Pushing on tentage protection at rate of 3 per day: protection of horse standings to follow. Heavy enemy gas shelling of GORRE-TUNING FORK area from 10pm 22nd – 4am 22nd. A large number of casualties 137 Bde – approx 450 gassed men and 17 officers passing through ADS GORRE. Relieved portion of ADS staff in running	

D. D. & L., London, E.C. (A8co4) Wt W1771/M2031 750,000 5/17 Sch. 52 Forms/C2118/14

8

Instructions regarding War Diaries and Intelligence Summaries are contained in F. S. Regs., Part II. and the Staff Manual respectively. Title pages will be prepared in manuscript.

WAR DIARY
or
~~INTELLIGENCE SUMMARY~~.
(Erase heading not required.)

1/3 N M. 7. Amb

Army Form C. 2118.

Hour, Date, Place	Summary of Events and Information	Remarks and references to Appendices
May 12 - 1915 BAILLEUL	State :- Remained 79 - Admitted 4 Transferred 73 Returned to Duty 2 Deaths 1. Remaining 7.	
	=	
May 13 - 1915. BAILLEUL	A letter to the ADMS N.M Division from Lt Col Evans D.A.D.M.S. MAC G.H.Q forwarded to the OC 1/3 N M FIELD Amb. stating that the B. RED CROSS have offered to have 6 of the MILLER-JAMES Stretcher Carriers made - Sgt James asked for the address of the makers & specifications of improvements that have been suggested - These (furnished by him) sent to G.H.Q -	
	State :- Remained 7. Admitted (3 officers 3 men) 6 To duty 1. Remained 12.	
May 14 - 1915.	Paid the NCOs + Men 10 Francs each.	
	State :- Remained 12 - Admitted 126 - Evacuated 111 To Duty 1 - Remaining 26	

Army Form C. 2118.

Instructions regarding War Diaries and Intelligence Summaries are contained in F. S. Regs., Part II. and the Staff Manual respectively. Title pages will be prepared in manuscript.

WAR DIARY
or
INTELLIGENCE SUMMARY.
(Erase heading not required.)

Hour, Date, Place	Summary of Events and Information	Remarks and references to Appendices
Near POPERINGHE July 2 - 15	water from well - Collection of wounded carried out South of YPRES the bearers following the TRANSPORT along the N.W corner of ZILLEBEKE LAKE.	
— do — July 3. 15	Gen Allenbury V Corps inspected the Camping Ground 6 pm - Collection of wounded	
July 4. 15	Collection of wounded	
July 5. 15	Collection of wounded -	
July 6 - 15	— do —	
July 7. 15	Went with ADMS 46. DIVISION to KRUISSTAAT to inspect Dugouts at H 24 (a) 4·8 No 28 1/40,000. BELGIUM - Found them not yet roofed over =	
July 8. 15	Sent 1 officer 6 men + 3 horsed Ambulances to the half finished dugouts by orders of ADMS 46 Division at H 24 (a) 4·8 - Sheet 28 BELGIUM.	

(9 29 6) W 4141—463 100,000 9/14 H W V Forms/C. 2118/10

Instructions regarding War Diaries and Intelligence Summaries are contained in F. S. Regs., Part II. and the Staff Manual respectively. Title Pages will be prepared in manuscript.

WAR DIARY
or
INTELLIGENCE SUMMARY
(Erase heading not required.)

Army Form C. 2118

Place	Date	Hour	Summary of Events and Information	Remarks and references to Appendices
BUSNES – ST VENANT RD	26/12/15		Owing to increase in number of patients at Dressing Station at ISBERGUES, increased personnel there up to one section complete with Transport.	
	27/12/15		Removed all scabies cases from ISBERGUES and ~~acco~~ accommodated them in barns close to Field Amb. Headquarters. – Lt H W Greig departed for temporary duty with 4th N.M. Bde R.F.A.	
	30/12/15		Field Ambulance Headquarters moved to ISBERGUES O 10 central [Sheet 36A Belgium] – men accommodated in good billets and very good lines secured for Transport Section. – Scabies cases accommodated in empty house.	
	31/12/15		Capt G. F. Haycraft departed on temporary duty with 1/5 Notts & Derby Rgt.	

A E Hodder Major
Cdg 1/3 N.M. F Amb. RAMC (TF)

1875 Wt. W593/826 1,000,000 4/15 J.B.C. & A. A.D.S.S./Forms/C. 2118.

Instructions regarding War Diaries and Intelligence Summaries are contained in F. S. Regs., Part II. and the Staff Manual respectively. Title Pages will be prepared in manuscript.

WAR DIARY
or
INTELLIGENCE SUMMARY
(Erase heading not required.)

Army Form C. 2118

Place	Date	Hour	Summary of Events and Information	Remarks and references to Appendices
LA HERLIÈRE	3/9/16		Had orders to carry out Evacuation service from BIENVILLERS and POMMIER so established 1 motor ambulance permanently at latter place to be available on demand from NCO i/c A.D.S. BIENVILLERS and ordered a daily round of a horsed ambulance wagon to leave LA HERLIÈRE at 10am calling at BIENVILLERS and POMMIER to bring sick to Hosp. also ~~I~~ notified 138 I.B. of arrangements made.	
		3/pm	On receipt of notice of ~~[illegible]~~ raiding operation impending on BERLES sector of line, I reinforced bearer party at A.D.S. by 12 bearers and transport by 5 motor ambs. at 10 pm. These with the existing bearers at ADS were found sufficient for the purpose.	
	4/9/16		Pursuant to instructions visited BAILLEULMONT & arranged for daily sick of No 16 A.A. battery to be seen by M.O. 230 Bde RFA.	

1875 Wt. W593/826 1,000,000 4/15 J.B.C. & A. A.D.S.S./Forms/C. 2118.

Army Form C. 2118.

WAR DIARY
or
INTELLIGENCE SUMMARY.
(Erase heading not required.)

Instructions regarding War Diaries and Intelligence Summaries are contained in F. S. Regs., Part II. and the Staff Manual respectively. Title pages will be prepared in manuscript.

Place	Date	Hour	Summary of Events and Information	Remarks and references to Appendices
COOKER QUARRY	29/9/18		At 5.45 AM the 46th Division attacked the ST QUENTIN CANAL & HINDENBURG LINE, the 137th Brigade leading on a three battalion front, the 138th & 139th Brigades following, each on a one battalion front, the 32nd Division in support. Dense fog prevailed until 11 AM. making it practically impossible to find or bring down wounded or for motor ambulances to move along roads. The fog cleared suddenly at 11 AM & after that the work of evacuation proceeded smoothly & rapidly the only difficulty experienced being that of getting the motor ambulances through the densely congested mass of traffic on the roads. At NOON Major Graham M.C. was sent forward & opened an ADS in the open at M.2.d.8.6. In the afternoon Captain Bradley & in the evening Major Lane M.C. reconnoitred the village of BELLENGLISE; both reported that it was being so heavily shelled that it was impossible to get wounded through it. Casualties were therefore evacuated by a route to the North of the village, a collecting post being established at G.34.a.0.5. in	

D. D. & L., London, E.C. (A8c04) Wt W1771/M2031 750,000 5/17 Sch. 52 Forms/C2118/14

Army Form C. 2118.

Instructions regarding War Diaries and Intelligence Summaries are contained in F. S. Regs., Part II. and the Staff Manual respectively. Title pages will be prepared in manuscript.

WAR DIARY
or
INTELLIGENCE SUMMARY.
(Erase heading not required.)

Place	Date	Hour	Summary of Events and Information	Remarks and references to Appendices
COOKER QUARRY	4.10.18		At 8.45 A.M received information that ADS at MAGNY had been gassed. Proceeded thither together with ADMS & found that during the night a gas shell had burst in the doorway of ADS.	
			The following officers were suffering from the effects of gas:– Major HARRISON M.C., Capt. MILLAR M.C., Capt. SPRAWSON (1/1st. N.M. F. Amb) 1st. Lieut. DOYLE USMC., 1st. Lieut. McCORMICK USMC., Major GRAHAM MC (1/2nd. N.M. F. Amb.). About thirty other ranks were more or less affected.	
			Visited Major LANE M.C at SWISS COTTAGE & found several French civilians liberated from RAMICOURT in the previous days fighting, in his charge. Arranged for the transport to MAGNY of those unable to walk. Visited RAP's 5th & 8th. Sherwoods.	
			1st. Lieut. DOYLE USMC. & fifteen other ranks evacuated to CCS suffering from shell gas (W)	
			In evening car post at SWISS COTTAGE handed over to 6th. Australian Field Ambulance.	ACY.
	5.10.18		Together with ADMS called on ADMS 6th. Division re impending relief. Major HARRISON M.C. evacuated to CCS suffering from shell gas (W).	

Instructions regarding War Diaries and Intelligence Summaries are contained in F. S. Regs., Part II. and the Staff Manual respectively. Title pages will be prepared in manuscript.

WAR DIARY
or
INTELLIGENCE SUMMARY.
(Erase heading not required.)

Army Form C. 2118.

Place	Date	Hour	Summary of Events and Information	Remarks and references to Appendices
HESDIGNEUL	3/5/18		At ADS itself it could no longer be smelt but there is still some apparently hanging about in parts of the cellars: gave requisite instructions as to clearing this part and as to further protection against similar shelling in future. Arranged for staff at ADS to be reduced to the bare minimum the surplus to be returned to Hdqrs from whence relief will be furnished as needed. Officer i/c Capt A.V. Miller MC shows signs of slight conjunctivitis as also a Corporal. The latter to be sent up to Hdqrs at once. On return journey examined light railway track from GREEN SPUR F8 b.7.8 and road marked as running from that point to F8 c.4.1. The latter is quite impracticable for transport but the line of the track might be used for walking wounded continued journey along line of track to siding at K2a.9.4 Once across the main BETHUNE-BEUVRY road the journey should be a comfortable one but from LE QUESNOY to that point may be rather rough & perhaps exciting. Thence to Headquarters. – Sent in recommendation for M.M. of an NCO orderly who had performed conspicuously good service during the shelling. Situation report from O/c ADS ESSARS reports a few gas shells in neighbourhood of ADS in evening 2nd but no ill effects. Strengthening of cellars at ADS & post at LE HAMEL continues. Water supply at latter post is failing and drinking water must be sent up from ESSARS in tins. Engineers examined ADS with a view to putting in an elephant tube.	

D. D. & L., London, E.C.
(A8004) Wt W1771/M2031 750,000 5/17 Sch. 52 Forms/C2118/14

19

Army Form C. 2118.

Instructions regarding War Diaries and Intelligence Summaries are contained in F. S. Regs., Part II. and the Staff Manual respectively. Title pages will be prepared in manuscript.

WAR DIARY
or
INTELLIGENCE SUMMARY.
(Erase heading not required.)

1/3 NM Fd Amb
Vol 33

MEDICAL.

Place	Date	Hour	Summary of Events and Information	Remarks and references to Appendices
LABOURSE	1/11/17		Capt G.S. BROWN RAMC (TC) from 57 C.C.S and 1/Lt T.L. DOYLE MORC. USA reported for duty & were taken on strength. Routine day.	
	2/11/17		Capt BROWN to FORT GLATZ : Capt J.S. ULLMAN to PHILOSOPHE Capt STEEL to Headquarters for duty. Inspection of personnel in marching order and general kit inspection.	
	3/11/17		Visited A.D.S. ~~PH~~ PHILOSOPHE in morning and found all in order - also inspected baths at same village: these are running smoothly and the disinfestation & drying chamber in process of construction should be completed in a week. L/Cpl R E Potter RAMCT returned from period of probation of 1 month with 1/5 S. Staffs as an applicant for a commission in Infantry. Submitted weekly report on working of Foden Thresh to ADMS. Total for week disinfected equivalent of 5100 blankets. Total hours working 38. Average disinfected per hour 140 blankets or the equivalent.	
	4/11/17		Raid on Hill 70 section by 2 companies 1/6 N&D. Regt. Evacuation of casualties (17 wounded) proceeded smoothly & quickly & all cases arrived at MDS in good condition.	

A7092 Wt. W12839/M1293. 750,000. 1/17. D. D & L., Ltd. Forms/C2118/14.

Instructions regarding War Diaries and Intelligence Summaries are contained in F. S. Regs., Part II. and the Staff Manual respectively. Title Pages will be prepared in manuscript.

WAR DIARY
or
INTELLIGENCE SUMMARY
(Erase heading not required.)

Army Form C. 2118

Place	Date	Hour	Summary of Events and Information	Remarks and references to Appendices
LAHOUSSOYE	27/8/16		bursting a gas cylinder in our trenches. - Of these 16 - one died at A.D.S. and one at main dressing station of Field Ambulance. Postmortem examination of the case which died at A.D.S. was made 23.8.16: This showed the following features.	
			Heart - dilated particularly on right side and heart muscle rather flabby - There was an old pericardial adhesion near apex of L ventricle	
			Lungs - Mucosa of bronchi engorged & in many cases submucous ecchymoses. All bronchi filled with frothy fluid. ~~lung~~ Lung tissue oedematous & engorged with blood & presenting almost appearance of liver.	
			Spleen - Enlarged due to engorgement with blood	
			Kidneys - Also engorged with blood: glomeruli showing up very vividly.	
			Stomach - ~~Gastric mucosa~~ Interior showed submucous ecchymoses in places, with general hyperaemia.	
			The appearances were those generally of right heart failure plus those of direct irritant to mucous membrane.	

1875 Wt. W593/826 1,000,000 4/15 J.B.C. & A. A.D.S.S./Forms/C. 2118.

Instructions regarding War Diaries and Intelligence Summaries are contained in F. S. Regs., Part II. and the Staff Manual respectively. Title Pages will be prepared in manuscript.

WAR DIARY
or
INTELLIGENCE SUMMARY
(Erase heading not required.)

Army Form C. 2118

Place	Date	Hour	Summary of Events and Information	Remarks and references to Appendices
AIX-NOULETTE	5/5/17		DMS I Army inspected Hospital AIX-NOULETTE. Capt J. MILLER returned to duty from short leave.	
	7/5/17		Visited A.D.S. and bearer posts: arranged to take over from 1/1 N.M.F.Amb two bearer posts in LIÈVIN held by them at M22 a 9.4 and M22 b. 8 9. A Staff Sergeant RAMC(TF) sent up as reinforcement vice S.Sgt. Hidans G. killed in action who has practically no Field Ambulance experience, has only been in France 2½ months at Base depot, and is therefore as far as 1st line ~~medical~~ RAMC work is concerned at the mercy of experienced privates. Submitted special report to ADMS on the subject pointing out that a former experienced S.Sgt. of this unit is at Base depot waiting & anxious to rejoin his unit.	
	8/5/17		Enemy shelled LIÈVIN with mixed H.E. and gas shells from 8pm 7th to about 4am 8th: between 10.30 pm + 12.30 am about 50 gas shells fell in close proximity to A.D.S. the cellars becoming quickly full of gas: S.B.R. were worn by all ranks & patients and one was gassed in the A.D.S.: the gas was cleared by fires and fans the process having to be repeated 3 times.	

1875 Wt. W593/826 1,000,000 4/15 J.B.C. & A. A.D.S.S./Forms/C. 2118.

Instructions regarding War Diaries and Intelligence Summaries are contained in F. S. Regs., Part II. and the Staff Manual respectively. Title pages will be prepared in manuscript.

WAR DIARY
or
INTELLIGENCE SUMMARY.
(Erase heading not required.)

Army Form C. 2118.

Place	Date	Hour	Summary of Events and Information	Remarks and references to Appendices
FOUQUIÈRES	29/11/17		DDMS 1 Corps visited C.R.S.	
	30/11/17		Capt. John Miller appointed to command 1/2 N.M.F. Amb.	
			" A.W.D. Steel " DADMS. 46 Div. & struck off strength.	
			Capt G.D. Fairley despatched to duty 21 Division by order from DDMS. 1 Corps. On arrival there orders cancelled & he returned to the unit.	
			Held smoking concert for F Amb personnel in evening.	
			A Rick fire occurred close to the hospital but the wind was setting away & no government property was damaged. Posted guards round the fire as requisite & reported to Town Major HESDIGNEUL. Handed over to his police at 10 pm. & withdrew guard.	
			Summary of changes month of Nov. –	
			Officers on 3	
			Officers off 3.	
			O.R. off 3	
			A E Hodder Lieut Col. cdg 1/3 N M F Amb	

A3092. Wt. W12839/M1293. 750,000. 1/17. D. D & L., Ltd. Forms/C2118/14.

Army Form C. 2118.

WAR DIARY
or
INTELLIGENCE SUMMARY.

(*Erase heading not required.*)

Instructions regarding War Diaries and Intelligence Summaries are contained in F. S. Regs., Part II. and the Staff Manual respectively. Title pages will be prepared in manuscript.

Place	Date	Hour	Summary of Events and Information	Remarks and references to Appendices
HESDIGNEUL	27/4/18		In morning inspected Field Amb. advanced dressing stations and regimental aid posts. posts & also visited ... had been effected since Found very great improvement ... was clean and orderly and taking over — every place the work of strengthening the buildings and cellars was being pushed on with energy. Road from LOISNE to LE HAMEL not recommended for carriage of casualties as it is under observation and a good deal sniped. I explored track to across the fields from LOISNE direct to ESSARS and found them quite practicable but the going would be heavy in wet weather and the distance is considerable (2000 yards) but as an alternative might be very useful. Direct evacuation through BETHUNE to HESDIGNEUL is feasible at most times and more speedy than going round the town. The route to be adopted is left to the discretion of the M.T. drivers on the spot. — Paid all ranks at routine rates.	
	28/4/18		Visited detachment at BRUAY in morning. Found everything going on well. Numbers in Hospital reduced to 90 by evening. Also visited 1/2 N M F A at LABEUVRIERE and arranged some details affecting both units. Heavy shelling of BETHUNE in afternoon, the general activity of artillery increasing towards evening.	

D. D. & L., London, E.C.
(A8co4) Wt W1771/M2031 750,000 5/17 Sch. 52 Forms/C2118/14

Army Form C. 2118.

Instructions regarding War Diaries and Intelligence Summaries are contained in F. S. Regs., Part II. and the Staff Manual respectively. Title pages will be prepared in manuscript.

WAR DIARY
or
INTELLIGENCE SUMMARY.
(Erase heading not required.)

Place	Date	Hour	Summary of Events and Information	Remarks and references to Appendices
PREUX	15.11.18		1st. Lieut. J. J. DE VEREAUX evacuated to CCS sick. Capt. D. GILLIES & 11 O.R's returned from IX Corps MDS. ACY	
"	17.11.18		Capt. A.C. REID proceeded to England on special leave. ACY	
"	18.11.18		This division to clear country east of devastated area, commencing with present billetting area. Area allotted to this unit to be cleared. Called on B.G.C. 137th. Inf. Bgde. to discuss scheme of work. ACY	
	19.11.18		Work commenced, filling shell holes & trenches, salving equipment, ammunition etc. Each section assigned an area & working under the section officer. Each section accompanied by party of RE's to destroy duds etc. & by a limber to convey salvage to central dump near orderly room. ACY	
	21.11.18		Capt. E.J BRADLEY M.C. reported for duty from base. ACY	
	22.11.18		Inspection of transport by ADMS. ACY	
	24.11.18		Capt. & QMR KING proceeded on leave. ACY	
	25.11.18		1st. Lieut. E.M MORRIS USMC proceeded on leave to PARIS. ACY	
	26.11.18		Inspection of transport by GOC; result satisfactory. ACY	

A C [signature]
LIEUT.-COL. COMMDG.
2/3rd N. MID. FIELD AMB.,
R.A.M.C.

D. D. & L., London, E.C.
(A8c04) Wt W1771/M2031 750,000 5/17 Sch. 52 Forms/C2118/14

Army Form C. 2118.

Instructions regarding War Diaries and Intelligence Summaries are contained in F. S. Regs., Part II. and the Staff Manual respectively. Title pages will be prepared in manuscript.

WAR DIARY
or
INTELLIGENCE SUMMARY.
(Erase heading not required.)

Place	Date	Hour	Summary of Events and Information	Remarks and references to Appendices
FOUQUIÈRES 1/23 BÉTHUNE	12/8		Visited Field Ambulance position at ANNEZIN in view of expected change of station and also C.R.S. LABEUVRIÈRE with same object. Huts 4 and 5 inspected by Field Engineer I Corps at my request: No 4 condemned as dangerous for occupation and in need of taking down & re building. No 5 not dangerous but in need of bracing. Notified DDMS of the verdict & that accommodation at the C.R.S. will be reduced to 276 pending the rebuilding of No 4. All patients removed from this hut to others & the hut equipment stored.	
	14/8		Pursuant to orders from ADMS 46 Div. visited 3/4 Fd Amb. and arranged details of taking over from them. Met OC 33 F Amb. by appointment & arranged details of handing over C.R.S. to that unit. Carried out examination & classification of personnel of No 11 Ammunition Sub Park and also of ASC personnel attached to this unit.	

A/092 Wt. W1289/M1293. 750,000. 1/17. D. D & L., Ltd. Forms/C2118/14.

Instructions regarding War Diaries and Intelligence Summaries are contained in F. S. Regs., Part II. and the Staff Manual respectively. Title pages will be prepared in manuscript.

WAR DIARY
or
INTELLIGENCE SUMMARY.
(Erase heading not required.)

Army Form C. 2118.

Place	Date	Hour	Summary of Events and Information	Remarks and references to Appendices
COOKER QUARRY.	5.10.18		ADS at MAGNY handed over to 6th Division (17th F. Amb). ACY	
	6.10.18		Men resting, & cleaning up. Many suffering slightly from effects of gas. ACY.	
	7.10.18		O.C. 1/3 N.M.F.A controlling evacuation of wounded &c. SHH	
COOKER QUARRY	8.10.18		Col Turner proceeded on leave. Major Hengs Cdg Capt Bradley evacuated to C.C.S suffering from Pleurisy Seven men evacuated to C.C.S suffering from effects of Shell Gas (W) A number of other men suffering slightly from shell gas resting. Capt Reid + 24 other ranks detailed for advanced 138 Bde + 8 O.R. to each of the battns in 137 Bde. SHH	
MAGNY LA FOSSE	9.10.18		Moved to Trenches near MAGNY-LA-FOSSE - LEHAUCOURT, - Capt Millar - Lt RICHARD + 30 O.R. suffering from gas carried on ambulances. Advised of Major Harrison's death from Gas Shell (W). SHH	

D. D. & L., London, E.C.
(A8co4) Wt W1771/M2031 750,000 5/17 Sch. 52 Forms/C2118/14

Instructions regarding War Diaries and Intelligence Summaries are contained in F. S. Regs., Part II. and the Staff Manual respectively. Title pages will be prepared in manuscript.

WAR DIARY
or
INTELLIGENCE SUMMARY.
(Erase heading not required.)

Army Form C. 2118.

Place	Date	Hour	Summary of Events and Information	Remarks and references to Appendices
BETHUNE	14/3/18		With Major Bradley located positions where French civilians unable to travel should be collected by Motor Ambulance if circumstances should make this necessary.	
			Horse line work proceeding satisfactorily.	
"	15/3/18		Lt Jack RAMC admitted to F.A. for skin treatment + also for duty when required	
			Lt Sharp relieved Capt Lang - on leave - with 231 Bde R.F.A.	
"	16/3/18		Usual routine work. Lt A.C. Reid returned from attached duty at 18 C.C.S.	
"	17/3/18		Lt. Doyle returned from leave, late owing to delay in Paris + Amiens.	
			Major Bradley left for Cambrin A.D.S. to investigate present system at A.D.S.	
"	18/3/18		Rev Harper C.F. transferred to M.G. Battn - 46 Divn. Rev Mason C.F. transferred to 1/3 NMFA from 1/5 S. Staffs Battn.	

A7092 Wt. W12839/M1293. 750,000. 1/17. D. D & L., Ltd. Forms/C2118/14.

Instructions regarding War Diaries and Intelligence Summaries are contained in F. S. Regs., Part II. and the Staff Manual respectively. Title pages will be prepared in manuscript.

WAR DIARY
or
INTELLIGENCE SUMMARY.
(Erase heading not required.)

Army Form C. 2118.

Place	Date	Hour	Summary of Events and Information	Remarks and references to Appendices
HESDIGNEUL	9/5/18		Attended special conference at ADMS office in connection with expected enemy attack. Took steps, arising out of the discussion, to deal with evacuation of casualties on normal lines, separating walking from lying cases & disposing transport at suitable spots & also reserve bearers. At 10 pm. RAMC disposed as follows. [Map. Ref. BETHUNE Combined sheet] Right section ADS. GORRE BREWERY F3c.6.4. Bearer post LOISNE X28a.4.7. Motor Amb rendezvous E24 d.3.1.	
			Left section ADS - ESSARS W30 d.2.5 : forward post LE HAMEL X20 c.8.5.	
			Car rendezvous at MDS HESDIGNEUL	
			Walking wounded collecting post F13c.5.9 : to which reports should be sent to OC 1/3 NMFA i/c of operations.	
			Reserve bearers Tobacco factory E17 b.8.8.	
			Horsed Amb at F13.c.5.9 and evacuation also arranged for by light railway from F13 central to LA PIERRETTE K2 a 8.5 and thence to MDS by Horsed Amb or other vehicle.	
	10/5/18		"Stood to" till 5 am when orders to resume normal situation were received.	
			LCpl Connolly W.J. and Pte Morris C awarded a Military Medal by G.O.C. I Corps C.R.O. 2539 of 8.5.18	

D. D. & L., London, E.C. (A8c04) Wt W1771/M2031 750,000 5/17 Sch. 52 Forms/C2118/14

3

Instructions regarding War Diaries and Intelligence Summaries are contained in F. S. Regs., Part II. and the Staff Manual respectively. Title pages will be prepared in manuscript.

WAR DIARY
or
INTELLIGENCE SUMMARY.
(Erase heading not required.)

Army Form C. 2118.

Hour, Date, Place	Summary of Events and Information	Remarks and references to Appendices
12-6-15 BAILLEUL	State:- Remained 68 - Admitted 12 Remaining ~~68~~ 74 Duty 6	
13-6-15 BAILLEUL	" Remained 74 Admitted 5 Duty 4 Remaining 75	
14-6-15 BAILLEUL	" Remained 75 Admitted 8 Duty 2 Transferred 1. Remaining 80	
15-6-15 BAILLEUL	" Remained 80 Admitted 4 Duty 16 Transferred 3 Remaining 65.	
	At NEUVE EGLISE the following Camp improvements have been carried out by MAJOR HODDER + the Carpenters of the Unit:- On 1-6-15 a Messing Hut for the Transport Section was constructed.	

Instructions regarding War Diaries and Intelligence Summaries are contained in F. S. Regs., Part II. and the Staff Manual respectively. Title pages will be prepared in manuscript.

WAR DIARY
or
INTELLIGENCE SUMMARY.
(*Erase heading not required.*)

Army Form C. 2118.

Place	Date	Hour	Summary of Events and Information	Remarks and references to Appendices
HESDIGNEUL	7/6/18		DDMS I Army visited the Field Ambulance.	
			Sent 1 limber load of sand to ADS ESSARS for concreting.	
			Lieut Chaundy went up to ADS for training.	
			Cutch stained 1 Operating tent.	
			Started making new mounting boards for wagon of biscuit tin stamped.	
			Party of 10 men from 1/5 S. Staffs arrived for instruction as stretcher bearers.	AH
	8/6/18		Lieut E.D. McCREA. RAMC reported for duty & taken on strength (Supernumerary). This officer is a bacteriologist & has been seconded for past 6 months for work in Biochemical Laboratory at Cambridge University.	
			Lectured to unit on Flies in relation to disease.	
			Submitted an application for my transfer to a unit C.C.S. or Stationary Hospital in order to be in touch again with clinical medicine.	AH
	9/6/18		Visited ADS ESSARS with ADMS: the departure of the artillery from here has increased the accommodation considerably & has enabled my men to make great improvements to the ADS. Strengthening is going on all the time and a great part of the ADS would survive a few 5.9 HE. I think	AH

D. D. & L., London, E.C. (A8004) Wt W1771/M2031 750,000 5/17 Sch. 52 Forms/C2118/14.

Instructions regarding War Diaries and Intelligence Summaries are contained in F. S. Regs., Part II. and the Staff Manual respectively. Title Pages will be prepared in manuscript.

WAR DIARY
or
INTELLIGENCE SUMMARY
(Erase heading not required.)

Army Form C. 2118

11

Place	Date	Hour	Summary of Events and Information	Remarks and references to Appendices
ISBERGUE	1/1/16		Major Hodder returned from ordinary leave. Ordinary patients in Dressing station averaging 40 per day Scabies " — — — — — 30 " " Stall used as hospital not well suited for the purpose; the floor being close to the ground is constantly damp & in some places rotten.	
	3/1/16		Took over charge of transport personnel & animals of 1/1st + 1/2nd N.M.F. Ambs. Appointed fixed sanitary cadre for the unit & Capt J. Miller to take charge of sanitary matters. Major A.E. Hodder promoted Temp'y Lt Col as from 26/11/15.	
	6/1/16		Post mortem examination by Major C.A. Stidston on body of L/Cpl Stone 1/5 Sherwood Foresters who died suddenly in night of 5th-6th Jan.	
	7/1/16		Warned for entraining on 9/1/16 – Major C.A. Stidston remaining behind with certain details as Senior Medical Officer – Capt Haycraft and Lieut Greig remain to assist him – Lt Armitage to accompany details of 2nd N.M. Bde R.F.A. – Carried out arrangements for accommodation of sick in trains; each train having one van reserved for sick under care of RAMC personnel: each such van supplied with medical comforts and washing and latrine accommodation	

Instructions regarding War Diaries and Intelligence Summaries are contained in F. S. Regs., Part II. and the Staff Manual respectively. Title pages will be prepared in manuscript.

WAR DIARY
or
INTELLIGENCE SUMMARY.
(Erase heading not required.)

Army Form C. 2118.

Place	Date	Hour	Summary of Events and Information	Remarks and references to Appendices
BÉTHUNE	5/3/18		Put working party on to build protective ramps of earth round horse standings: and the necessary fatigue parties for cleaning up generally.	
			Furnish 2 G.S. wagons daily to Town Major, one for drawing rations one for scavenging duties.	
			Fixed up routine collection of sick by Horsed Ambce daily from villages occupied by 46 (NM) divisional troops. This duty will be performed on alternate days by vehicles of this unit & 1/2 NMFA.	
			Received draft of 30 RAMC reinforcements – a poor lot – all class B2 on account of various disabilities.	
			Selected 10 of these for this unit: 5 went to 1/2 NMFA & remainder for 1/1 NMFA.	
			A "female impersonator" from the Palladium is included in the draft. Officer i/c I Corps Concert party was down here by 6 pm inquiring for him & obviously wants him badly. O/C Whizz Bangs – the 46 Div. Troupe also wants him. The Judgement of Solomon is again required. He doesn't look as if he would make a good bearer.	
			Capt AV MILLAR MC returned from ordinary leave.	

A7092 Wt. W12839/M1293. 750,000. 1/17. D. D & L., Ltd. Forms/C2118/14.

Instructions regarding War Diaries and Intelligence Summaries are contained in F. S. Regs., Part II. and the Staff Manual respectively. Title Pages will be prepared in manuscript.

WAR DIARY
or
~~INTELLIGENCE SUMMARY~~
(Erase heading not required.)

Army Form C. 2118

Place	Date	Hour	Summary of Events and Information	Remarks and references to Appendices
GAUDIEMPRÉ	17/3/16		Visited advanced dressing station and afterwards explored evacuation trench fully. Find it in worse repair than appeared on former examination: estimate that about 1000 yards of new trench will be required to be dug in addition to putting the existing one in repair – with 150 RAMC men at work on it consider that 3 weeks would be the least time that it would be ready in its whole length for evacuation of patients.	
			Large dugouts at A.D.S. being strengthened & improved by increasing thickness of earth on top & putting on an exploding layer of iron & timber – gas traps being fitted everywhere and ~~arrangements for~~ sanitary arrangements being improved.	
			Capt. Harris supervising sanitation of FONQUEVILLERS working through Town Major and R.M.O.s.	

Army Form C. 2118.

WAR DIARY
or
INTELLIGENCE SUMMARY.
(Erase heading not required.)

Instructions regarding War Diaries and Intelligence Summaries are contained in F. S. Regs., Part II. and the Staff Manual respectively. Title pages will be prepared in manuscript.

Place	Date	Hour	Summary of Events and Information	Remarks and references to Appendices
HESDIGNEUL	5/5/18		A great deal of annoyance is caused and attention drawn to ADS ESSARS by the action of artillery belonging to the battery in rear – in full light with enemy planes over & balloons up they bring G.S. Wagons & teams with ammunition etc into the yard of the dressing station and on other occasions collect salvage with wagons in daylight. Behaviour of this kind will probably result in the ADS being obliterated by heavy shelling. O.C. ADS ESSARS reports a burst of gas shelling ~~last~~ about 9am lasting 15 minutes. 3 shells dropped in the yard but there were no casualties.	
	6/5/18		Ordinary routine day fairly fine – relief of O.R. personnel on L. Brigade section ADS & post.	
	7/5/18		Visited ADSs ESSARS & GORRE: some corrugated sheet lining (quasi-elephant) & 1000 sandbags have been supplied by R.E. the latter erected in dressing room. Strengthening and supporting of latter to be pushed. At ADS GORRE a good deal of improvement has been effected outdoors but much more remains to be done. All cellars to be completely emptied of civilian stuff: Roof propped as requisite, gas blanketing	

D. D. & L., London, E.C. (A8c04) Wt W1771/M2031 750,000 5/17 Sch. 52 Forms/C2118/14

Instructions regarding War Diaries and Intelligence Summaries are contained in F. S. Regs., Part II. and the Staff Manual respectively. Title Pages will be prepared in manuscript.

WAR DIARY
or
~~INTELLIGENCE SUMMARY~~
(Erase heading not required.)

Army Form C. 2118

Place	Date	Hour	Summary of Events and Information	Remarks and references to Appendices
GAUDIEMPRÉ	10/6/16		With ADMS reconnoitred means of evacuation from FONQUEVILLERS in morning – the only trench available is badly out of repair but if repaired and made fit to take a wheeled stretcher carrier should be very useful in case of a "show" when the only road would probably be barraged. In afternoon inspected LA BAZÈQUE with a view to taking it for dressing station: regard it as suitable and with a little work would accommodate in existing barns about 300 patients on stretchers. Reported to above effect to ADMS.	
	11/6/16		Visited BAZÈQUE with ADMS & Div Sanitary Officer who agree as to its eligibility. Received a W.O. from Div Train to take in charge of Horse Transport.	

Army Form C. 2118.

Instructions regarding War Diaries and Intelligence Summaries are contained in F. S. Regs., Part II. and the Staff Manual respectively. Title pages will be prepared in manuscript.

WAR DIARY
or
INTELLIGENCE SUMMARY.

(Erase heading not required.)

MEDICAL

Place	Date	Hour	Summary of Events and Information	Remarks and references to Appendices
HESDIGNEUL.	1/8/18		Finishing touches for D. Horse Show to wagons &c. SSH	
	2/8/18		Divl. Horse Show. This unit secured 1st prize for Motor Ambulance; 2nd — — Ambulance Turnout; 2nd — — N.C.Os high jumping. SSH	
	3/8/18		Visited A.D.S. ESSARS + bearer posts in that sector to increase accommodation at A.D.S. have asked for R.E. officer to report on suitability for concreted Elephant tube shelter there. SSH	
	4/8/18		R.E. officer visited A.D.S. ESSARS + scheme of Elephant tubing approved + preliminary work commenced. Visited A.D.S. GORRE + R.A.P. 1/4 LEICs — Reinforcing work continued here. SSH	
	5/8/18		ESSARS normal relief. General camp work carried on at H.Qrs. — Capt Reid returned from 1/4 LEIC. Regt. SSH	

D. D. & L., London, E.C.
(A8004) Wt W1771/M2031 750,000 5/17 Sch. 52 Forms/C2118/14

Instructions regarding War Diaries and Intelligence Summaries are contained in F. S. Regs., Part II. and the Staff Manual respectively. Title pages will be prepared in manuscript.

WAR DIARY
or
INTELLIGENCE SUMMARY.
(Erase heading not required.)

Army Form C. 2118.

Place	Date	Hour	Summary of Events and Information	Remarks and references to Appendices
BRUAY	24/4/18		Collected sick from units of 137 I.B. and despatched Horsed Ambs to follow them in move to FOUQUIÈRES area. Arranged move of residue of Field Amb to HESDIGNEUL on 25th. Personnel to be under canvas.	
HESDIGNEUL	25/4/18		Moved Headquarters to HESDIGNEUL [D30c.5.0] 10 am. Left 1 officer and 30 O.R. to look after patients remaining at BRUAY: sent 2 officers & 50 O.R. to take over ADS at GORRE Brewery ~~& subsidiary~~ posts – relief completed 5.30 pm. Major Haig reported in person in afternoon on the conditions in left subsection ADS & posts. Work started to improve ADS there & clean up generally. Heavy thunderstorm in afternoon after the tents had been pitched fortunately.	
	26/4/18		Fairly quiet night – visited ADMS, CRS and hospital at BRUAY: numbers at last named being steadily reduced but it will have to be kept going for some time probably as an overflow annexe to CRS LABEUVRIÈRE. Employed wagons drawing shale for roads at ADS. & Horsed Amb for routine sick collection from FOUQUIÈRES and GOSNAY.	

D. D. & L., London, E.C.
(A8c04) Wt W1771/M2031 750,000 5/17 Sch. 52 Forms/C2118/14

Instructions regarding War Diaries and Intelligence Summaries are contained in F. S. Regs., Part II. and the Staff Manual respectively. Title pages will be prepared in manuscript.

WAR DIARY
or
INTELLIGENCE SUMMARY.
(Erase heading not required.)

Army Form C. 2118.

MEDICAL

Place	Date	Hour	Summary of Events and Information	Remarks and references to Appendices
HESDIGNEUL	1/7/18		Toured A. D. Stations, bearer posts & RAPs of both Brigades in the line with DDMS XIII Corp & ADMS 46 Div. "Everything very satisfactory"	
			Lt Col A.E. Hodder DSO. returned to command - from No 6 C.C.S.	
			a/S.S.M. IRVING A.S.C. from 457 Coy posted to Field Amb. as S.M. for M.T. section. AEH	
	2/7/18		Lieut Chamley posted to 1/5 Notts & Derby Rgt. struck off strength. Capt A Florian MRC. U.S.A. ~~returned~~ from 1/5 N & D. Rgt. taken on strength. AEH	
	3/7/18		Visited A.D.S. ESSARS and forward post LE HAMEL. Between 11.30 pm & midnight enemy aircraft dropped six bombs in close proximity to camp & ~~[illegible]~~s. Several casualties among personnel and patients of Main dressing station but none of this unit. Several tents were however torn by fragments. All of Asc 1/2 NMFA returned to their unit and numbers of them attached here reduced to 20. AEH	
	4/7/18		DDMS XIII corps inspected camp. 30 O.R. returned to unit from Corps Scabies Camp ALLOUAGNE. Total of Transport section down with PUO (influenza) 18. AEH	

D. D. & L., London, E.C. (A8co4) Wt. W1771/M2031 750,000 5/17 Sch. 52 Forms/C2118/14

Instructions regarding War Diaries and Intelligence Summaries are contained in F. S. Regs., Part II. and the Staff Manual respectively. Title pages will be prepared in manuscript.

Army Form C. 2118.

WAR DIARY
or
INTELLIGENCE SUMMARY.
(*Erase heading not required.*)

Place	Date	Hour	Summary of Events and Information	Remarks and references to Appendices
HESDIGNEUL	5/6/18		About 1am a quarter hour of shelling of F.A. post at LE HAMEL: one NCO severely wounded and one Motor Amb driver less so. The latter in spite of his right leg being useless & bleeding from the wounds was only concerned for his dangerously wounded comrade and drove him to ADS ESSARS himself though the road was being shelled at the time. Recommended him for recognition (Military Medal). Extension of Tramways Light Railway to ESSARS has rendered forward post less comfortable as the terminus is only about 100 yards from the post, and it will inevitably attract shelling. There is however no alternative ~~[illegible]~~ position. ALH	
	6/6/18		Capt Rutledge to 1/8 N.S.D. for temporary duty. Inspection of H.T. in detail by OC Div. Train. Various minor defects pointed out particularly in setting up of small parts of harness. ~~[illegible]~~ Maltese cart condemned as unserviceable & not susceptible of repair: repairs necessary to wagons are much delayed owing to scarcity of suitable [illegible]. Opinion expressed that transport was on the whole good and certainly eminently serviceable. ALH	

D. D. & L., London, E.C. (A8c04) Wt. W1771/M2031 750,000 5/17 Sch. 52 Forms/C2118/14

Instructions regarding War Diaries and Intelligence Summaries are contained in F. S. Regs., Part II and the Staff Manual respectively. Title Pages will be prepared in manuscript.

Army Form C. 2118

WAR DIARY
or
INTELLIGENCE SUMMARY
(Erase heading not required.)

Place	Date	Hour	Summary of Events and Information	Remarks and references to Appendices
MON PLAISIR near HEM	2/3/16		"B" section closed on Headquarters having disposed of patients and shut down hospital at LONGVILLERS.	
Ref. LENS 11.	3.3.16		Lieut A.V. MILLAR RAMC from 46 D.A.C. joined and was taken on the strength.	
	4.3.16		Capt H.W. GREIG sent on regimental duty to 1/5th N. Staff Rgt.	
	5.3.16		Issued "FIRE ORDERS" for Field Ambulance - ~~Appx~~	Appx 1
CANETTE-MONT. (LENS.11)	6.3.16		Field Ambulance moved quarters to CANETTEMONT. distance about 12 miles via NEUVILETTE and BOCQUEMAISON and REBREUVIETTE. No casualties on march: Lt J.N.J. HARTLEY taken on strength of unit.	
	9.3.16		Field Ambulance moved to MAGNICOURT - distance 3 miles.	
MAGNICOURT.	10/3/16		Inspected prospective billets at ACQ and ECOIVRES [F13. Sheet 51c 1/40000] and arranged to take over quarters at latter place when vacated by French Groupe des Brancardiers.	
	11/3/16		Field Ambulance moved to ACQ. [E12c sheet 51c] - march 6 hours accomplished without incident.	

1875 Wt. W593/826 1,000,000 4/15 J.B.C. & A. A.D.S.S./Forms/C. 2118.

Instructions regarding War Diaries and Intelligence Summaries are contained in F. S. Regs., Part II. and the Staff Manual respectively. Title pages will be prepared in manuscript.

WAR DIARY
or
INTELLIGENCE SUMMARY.
(*Erase heading not required.*)

Army Form C. 2118.

Place	Date	Hour	Summary of Events and Information	Remarks and references to Appendices
HESDIGNEUL	15/5/18		A quiet day apart from above. Routine duties at Hdqrs and physical exercises for and drill for O.R. in afternoon. Morning occupied with fatigues. Lt Doyle visited RAMC post at F13 central & found all in order. All movement rear (North) of the building prohibited in daylight & to be restricted as much as possible during the day in the whole surrounding area.	
	16/5/18		Relief of one third of ADS party GORRE Brewery effected. Despatched limber to HERLIES to which place Divisional Dump has been removed to withdraw some needed stores. A long journey 30 miles each way; incidentally no notice was circulated by Divisional Q that dump had been removed. Received notice from OC ADS ESSARS that the ADS was shelled with 4.2 Blue Cross HE gas shells about 1pm but no material damage was done.	
	17/5/18		A couple of enemy aircraft over the camp about 11pm 16th. Numerous search lights round about endeavoured to locate them and A.A. and Lewis guns were busy but apparently without much result. Normal quiet day. OC ADS GORRE reported continuation of strengthening work on ADS and applied for a working party to assist him. 1 NCO & 7 men sent up 6pm. [illegible] of 45 reinforcements being en route to Division from Base.	

(A8c94) Wt. W1771/M2031 750,000 5/17 Sch. 52 Forms/C2118/14 D. D. & L., London, E.C.

Instructions regarding War Diaries and Intelligence Summaries are contained in F. S. Regs., Part II. and the Staff Manual respectively. Title Pages will be prepared in manuscript.

WAR DIARY
or
INTELLIGENCE SUMMARY
(Erase heading not required.)

Army Form C. 2118

Place	Date	Hour	Summary of Events and Information	Remarks and references to Appendices
LA HERLIERE	14/8/16		In conjunction with O.C. "P" Coy special Brigade RE i/c Gas operations Capt S.S.B. HARRISON has made the following dispositions.	
			1 Bearer Posts are established in saps behind the Bays in front line trenches & are numbered from north to South: the position being marked by an indicator board at entrance of sap with the number of the post on it – Thus [SB – 4]	

Positions of posts

No	Trench	Bay	Stretcher bearers
1	93	11	4
2	93	6	2
3	93	4	4
4	92	9	2
5	92	6	4
6	92	5	2
7	92	1	2
8	92	14	6 + 1 M.O.

9 . Shelter for 2 bearers 30 yards down 91 street on southern side

~~91 street~~

10 Bearer dugout at junction of NEVERENDING LANE with support line – 1 M.O. and 20 Mm.

Numbers 8 & 10 to be supplied with gas restoratives

WAR DIARY
or
INTELLIGENCE SUMMARY.
(*Erase heading not required.*)

Army Form C. 2118.

Instructions regarding War Diaries and Intelligence Summaries are contained in F. S. Regs., Part II. and the Staff Manual respectively. Title pages will be prepared in manuscript.

Place	Date	Hour	Summary of Events and Information	Remarks and references to Appendices
LABOURSE	7/10/17		Lieut W.B. Jack and Capt J.S. Ullman exchanged duties. Issued instructions to certain Regimental Medical Officers how to obtain medical & other stores as there appeared to be a good deal of ignorance of how to do so & consequent delay & annoyance.	
	9/10/17		In company with ADMS. visited ADS PHILOSOPHE & post and RAP PONT STREET. The recent heavy rains have put a good deal of water into parts of the cellars at ADS and it will be necessary to put a false roof up inside the shell of the building to carry off the rain water. Bearer Post at PONT St. is in need of ventilation by an upcast shaft if possible. Capt Harga attended FGCM at LILLERS on a case of S.I. wound. Major General cdg 46 Div. inspected Main Dressing Station & Transport lines in afternoon – no adverse comments.	
	10/10/17		Attended conference at ADMS Office 10am. Detailed officers for inspection of baths at PHILOSOPHE, NOYELLES and MAZINGARBE and inspection for scabies of Regimental Transport personnel quartered in LABOURSE. Arranged for further instruction of Capt Ullman U.S.M.R.C. (attd) in duties of Regimental Medical Officer.	

A7092. Wt. W12839/M1293. 750,000. 1/17. D. D & L., Ltd. Forms/C2118/14.

13 N M F A

Army Form C. 2118.

51

Instructions regarding War Diaries and Intelligence Summaries are contained in F. S. Regs., Part II. and the Staff Manual respectively. Title pages will be prepared in manuscript.

WAR DIARY
or
INTELLIGENCE SUMMARY.
(Erase heading not required.)

Place	Date	Hour	Summary of Events and Information	Remarks and references to Appendices
TROISVILLES	4/5/19		1 Serg + 2 Pte ASC MT left unit for demobilisation	
			1 Dr ASC HT left unit for demobilisation	
"	5/5/19		1 Cpl + 1 Pte ASC MT left unit for demobilisation	
"	7/5/19		2 Dr ASC HT left unit on leave to U.K.	
			1 Dr ASC HT left unit on leave to U.K.	
"	12/5/19		2 Ptes RAMC left unit on leave to U.K	
"	13/5/19		4 O R RAMC left unit for demobilisation	
"	14/5/19		3 O R ASC HT left unit for demobilisation	
			1 Pte RAMC left unit on leave to U.K	
"	19/5/19		1 Pte RAMC left unit on leave to U.K.	
"	21/5/19		1 Pte RAMC left unit on leave to U.K	
"	22/5/19		1 Pte RAMC left unit on leave to U.K.	
"	24/5/19		1 Pte RAMC + 1 Pte ASC MT left unit on leave to U.K	
"	26/5/19		1 Pte ASC HT left for demobilisation	
			1 Dr ASC HT left unit for demobilisation	
"	30/5/19		2 O.R. ASC HT left unit for demobilisation	

G. Bransfield
R. Lt.

D. D. & L., London, E.C.
(20349) W1 W5300/P713 750,000 3/18 E 2588 Forms C/2118/16.

Army Form C. 2118.

Instructions regarding War Diaries and Intelligence Summaries are contained in F. S. Regs., Part II. and the Staff Manual respectively. Title pages will be prepared in manuscript.

WAR DIARY
or
INTELLIGENCE SUMMARY.
(Erase heading not required.)

Place	Date	Hour	Summary of Events and Information	Remarks and references to Appendices
HESDIGNEUL	22/5/18		including Capt Reid whose eyes were becoming affected again. Some bursts of shelling in course of day round ADS - ESSARS a direct hit in the building being made. No casualties but some slight damage done to motor ambulances. Capt T.W. Ruttledge RAMC(T) joined from Base.	
	23/5/18		~~Visited ADS~~ Visited ADS GORRE and took Capt Ruttledge there to remain & learn the working. G.O.C 46 Division expressed to me his satisfaction with the work of the ADS evacuation on 22nd. Routine train service for evacuation of casualties from GORRE inaugurated today. Trains leave GORRE 5.30 am and 6.30 pm daily arriving Hospital siding on road between HESDIGNEUL and VAUDRICOURT about 1 1/4 hours later. Accommodation normally 2 trucks carrying 12 stretcher & 30 sitting cases: further accommodation of 12 stretcher and unlimited sitting ~~…~~ available if needed and in case of heavy casualties ~~…~~ a 2 hourly service may be maintained.	
	24/5/18		Heavy rain on 23rd made a considerable mess of the camp. Men occupied for some time in draining and drying tents. Extension of protective ramps for [illegible]. Normal day at ADSs but reliefs carried out at both.	

D. D. & L., London, E.C. (A8c04) Wt W1771/M2031 750,000 5/17 Sch. 52 Forms/C2118/14

Instructions regarding War Diaries and Intelligence Summaries are contained in F. S. Regs., Part II. and the Staff Manual respectively. Title pages will be prepared in manuscript.

WAR DIARY
or
INTELLIGENCE SUMMARY.
(Erase heading not required.)

Army Form C. 2118.

Place	Date	Hour	Summary of Events and Information	Remarks and references to Appendices
HESDIGNEUL	28 5/18		On representation from O.C. ADS GORRE arranged with C.L.R.O. for evening ambulance train service to be suspended for the present and for trains to load at point where light railway crosses GORRE–LE QUESNOY Road in future beginning with 5.30 am train 29th. also for trains to be supplied as needed on demand direct to control post ESSARS JUNCTION in F.8. – some shelling of HESDIGNEUL	
	29 5/18		Relief of personnel of Right ADS GORRE effected by train and completed 7.10 am. Some shelling of HESDIGNEUL again. Lowering of floors of all tents occupied by personnel completed with exception of guard tent. One inter-horse line revetted bank completed and a second marked out ready for piling and placing. Interpreter Leblanc reported on return from leave. 4.30 pm report from ADS – GORRE : states situation quiet. 10 yellow cross gassed cases from 1/5 Leicesters received & evacuated. 55th Division have evacuated Batt'n Hqrs. & RAP in Tuning Fork South & Field Amb. bearers have re-occupied RAP.	
	30 5/18		Enemy 395 I. Regt. about 50 storm troops in strength attacked Route A Keep in early morning & were repulsed leaving one wounded prisoner in our hands & about 30 dead on wire. Our casualties 3 killed 11 wounded. These were evacuated with others by light railway: 3 lying & 27 sitting cases being sent down. Train service satisfactory.	

D. D. & L., London, E.C.
(A8c04) Wt W1771/M2031 750,000 5/17 Sch. 52 Forms/C2118/14

Instructions regarding War Diaries and Intelligence Summaries are contained in F. S. Regs., Part II. and the Staff Manual respectively. Title pages will be prepared in manuscript.

WAR DIARY
or
INTELLIGENCE SUMMARY.
(Erase heading not required.)

Army Form C. 2118.

Place	Date	Hour	Summary of Events and Information MEDICAL	Remarks and references to Appendices
COOKER QUARRY R.11.a.9.7 Sheet 62c	1/10/18		New ADS established in cellar at MAGNY LA FOSSE under Major Lane MC. Capt. Reid remaining at BELLENGLISE. Numerous casualties of 32nd Division treated. ACY	
	2.10.18		Visited both ADS's & also called on H.Q. 137th & 139th Bgdes. & 8th Sherwoods. Hdqrs. of unit & transport moved to COOKER QUARRY. Samples of water from ST QUENTIN CANAL & from BELLENGLISE tunnel taken for testing. ACY	
	3.10.18		At 2 AM received notice of impending attack. Proceeded to ADS at MAGNY, bearers & equipment following under Major HERGA M.C. Major LANE M.C. was detailed to act as bearer officer for the Left Sector; fifty bearers & two motor ambulances were assigned to him & he was instructed to establish car posts as far forward as possible along the JONCOURT Road. Capt. MILLAR with fifty bearers & four motor ambulances was detailed to evacuate cases in a similar manner along the LEVERGIES Road; as the road from LEVERGIES to ADS was hopelessly blocked by a derelict tank he was instructed to clear wounded straight to MDS without passing through ADS. Three horsed ambulance waggons were detailed to work as far as possible	

D. D. & L., London, E.C. (A8cog) Wt W1771/M2031 750,000 5/17 Sch. 52 Forms/C2118/14

Instructions regarding War Diaries and Intelligence Summaries are contained in F. S. Regs., Part II. and the Staff Manual respectively. Title pages will be prepared in manuscript.

WAR DIARY
or
INTELLIGENCE SUMMARY.
(*Erase heading not required.*)

Army Form C. 2118.

Place	Date	Hour	Summary of Events and Information	Remarks and references to Appendices
PRÉDEFIN	11/2/18		Visited all units of Brigade Group (137) and arranged for sick parade for 137 MG Coy & Bde Hqrs EQUIRRE and for RE Field Coy at BOYAVAL & for routine collection of sick by Horsed Ambulance covering Brigade Area. Men of unit employed in clearing & cleaning billets & cleaning own equipment.	
	12/2/18		Visited 452 & 453 Coys ASC on leaving their location and arranged for an officer of Field Ambulance to visit them daily to see sick & make necessary inspections. Men of unit engaged fully in cleaning stables, draining roads & cleaning the village of refuse & filling up old latrines. The village had been left in a bad state by previous occupants and 2 wagon loads of salvage mainly ammunition were collected from the various billets.	
	13/2/18		Attended lecture on Social Reconstruction after the War, at Church Hut LAIRES. Men carrying on with general sanitary improvements. C.O. visited ADMS Hdqrs for usual weekly conference. Very wet day: inspected billets & work in village in afternoon.	

A7092 Wt. W12859/M1293 750,000. 1/17. D. D & L., Ltd. Forms/C2118/14.

Instructions regarding War Diaries and Intelligence Summaries are contained in F. S. Regs., Part II. and the Staff Manual respectively. Title pages will be prepared in manuscript.

WAR DIARY
or
INTELLIGENCE SUMMARY.
(Erase heading not required.)

Army Form C. 2118.

Hour, Date, Place	Summary of Events and Information	Remarks and references to Appendices
March 9. 15.	On march the two Motor Ambulances presented to the unit were picked up - At BORRE 3. Sunbeam Motor Ambulances + a FORD Motor Ambulance joined. The springs of the 3. Motor Ambulances (12-16 Sunbeams) are not equal to the loads + the bad roads - One car has a broken spring + another much strained in the Dumb Iron -	
March 10. 15.	Maps drawn from Divisional HQuarters - Ordered to be ready to move at 1 hours notice -	
March 11. 15.	Marched from BORRE at 1.50 pm via PRADELLES - STRAZELLE - MERRIS - BLEU - Road angle SOUTH of the D in DOULIEU + 2nd A in TROU BAYARD - Reached billets situated at Road Junction 1/4 mile N.E. of the E in COURANT DE LE METEREN + North of ESTAIRES	
March 13. 15.	Sent 3 officers of the unit to help the 21st Field Ambulance in ESTAIRES - who had a large number of Casualties coming in.	

(9 29 6) W4141—463 100,000 9/14 H W V Forms/C. 2118/10

Instructions regarding War Diaries and Intelligence Summaries are contained in F. S. Regs., Part II. and the Staff Manual respectively. Title pages will be prepared in manuscript.

WAR DIARY
or
INTELLIGENCE SUMMARY.
(Erase heading not required.)

Army Form C. 2118.

NORTH MIDLAND FIELD AMBULANCE ROYAL ARMY

Place	Date	Hour	Summary of Events and Information	Remarks and references to Appendices
		14/7/17	Capt. Chamberlain F W. post as M.O first Monmouth Regt. and struck off the strength of this unit.	
			Capt. L W. D. Steel MC taken on strength of unit.	
			9 RAMC reinforcements received.	
		16/7/17	attended conference at ADMS office. DDMS visited Hospital.	
		17/7/17	Lieut. Jack to temporary duty at 1st Corps Schools	
		18/7/17	Lieut Col AE HODDER. DSO. reported on arrival from Base and assumed command.	
		19/7/17	Attended conference at ADMS office 9.30 am Afterwards visited Main Dressing Station LA BOURSE and A.D.S. PHILOSOPHE and arranged details of relief of No 18 Field Amb as present holding these posts. In afternoon inspected Rest Station and Transport lines	
		20/7/17	Received RAMC Operation order from ADMS relative to move to new area.	

(A7092). Wt. W12839/M1293 750,000. 1/17. D. D. & L., Ltd. Forms/C.2118/14.

11

Instructions regarding War Diaries and Intelligence Summaries are contained in F. S. Regs., Part II. and the Staff Manual respectively. Title pages will be prepared in manuscript.

WAR DIARY
or
INTELLIGENCE SUMMARY.
(Erase heading not required.)

Army Form C. 2118.

3RD NORTH MIDLAND FIELD AMBULANCE ROYAL ARMY MEDICAL CORPS

1/3 N M Fd Amb

Vol 38

Place	Date	Hour	MEDICAL Summary of Events and Information	Remarks and references to Appendices
LABEUVRIÈRE	1/4/18		Very fine day. – wagons busy drawing shale from BRUAY for road making. Tarring Bath house started & cement floor for extension to kitchen. Wash house in connection with Bath House well forward. Sent 3 corporals for duty as Bath directors to Divisional Headquarters.	
	2/4/18		Lieut G.R. Sharp reported from duty with 230 Bde R.F.A. Roadmaking going on steadily: work on ablution house delayed for lack of materials indented for particularly cement. This and wire netting badly needed. Bath house disinfestation chamber working well.	
	3/4/18		Recreation Theatre of the rest station having been lent to the "Balmorals" the troupe of a Highland Division, engagements of other concert parties which had been fixed for the entertainment of patients have had to be scratched. This is some hardship to the patients as admission to the Balmorals show is not free. Post patients personnel	

A5092 Wt W12839/M1293 750,000. 1/17. D. D. & L. Ltd. Forms/C2118/14.

Instructions regarding War Diaries and Intelligence Summaries are contained in F. S. Regs., Part II. and the Staff Manual respectively. Title pages will be prepared in manuscript.

WAR DIARY
or
INTELLIGENCE SUMMARY.
(*Erase heading not required.*)

Army Form C. 2118.

Place	Date	Hour	Summary of Events and Information	Remarks and references to Appendices
HESDIGNEUL	21/7/18		Uneventful day SIBH.	
	22/7/18		Nothing of interest SIBH	
	23/7/18		Quiet day SIBH	
	24/7/18		Visited CORRE + ESSARS – Very heavy weather SIBH. Lt Col AE HODDER rejoined 10pm from temporary duty as acting ADMS. AEH	
	25/7/18		Attended at ADMS office 2pm to discuss with him points that had arisen during his absence on leave. O.C. 453 Coy A.S.C. inspected wagons & harness in reference to Divisional Horse Show Exhibits. Attended 46 Div R.F.A. horse show in afternoon. The wagons all very beautiful but a monument of misdirected energy and extravagance in paint etc. Excellent in peace time but hardly helping on the war. AEH	
	26/7/18		Major Hartley A.V.C. inspected L.D. horses and mules with a view to picking these for exhibition. New oven for kitchen in camp begun, but progress delayed by rain. About 15 HV shells – probably 120mm – fell in the valley on Northern side of camp about midnight. Some progress made with protection of horse standings and with a drainage system for camp ground. AEH	

D. D. & L., London, E.C.
(A8004) Wt W1771/M2031 750,000 5/17 Sch. 52 Forms/C2118/14

Instructions regarding War Diaries and Intelligence Summaries are contained in F. S. Regs., Part II. and the Staff Manual respectively. Title pages will be prepared in manuscript.

WAR DIARY
or
INTELLIGENCE SUMMARY.
(Erase heading not required.)

Army Form C. 2118.

Place	Date	Hour	Summary of Events and Information	Remarks and references to Appendices
VENDELLES	27.9.18		Visited Left ADS. Called on ADMS & O.C. No 1 F. Amb. re arrangements at VADENCOURT. ACY	
COOKER QUARRY.	28.9.18		At 5 P.M. Hdqrs. moved to ADS at COOKER QUARRY. At 8 PM Left ADS was handed over to 32nd Division & personnel & equipment transferred to COOKER QUARRY. Sixteen RAMC bearers were attached to each battalion of 137th Brigade; eight RAMC bearers were attached to each battalion of 138th & 139th Brigades. One hundred bearers (Concert troupe, Labour Coy. & 139th Bgde. Band) were supplied by Division. Beaners were disposed as follows:- One hundred attached to battalions, forty at COOKER QUARRY, one hundred at VENDELLES, eighty at HANCOURT. Three limbers, each loaded with the necessary equipment for an ADS & accompanied by the requisite personnel were provided by 1/1st. & 1/2nd. N. M. F. Ambs. One of these was stationed at VADENCOURT & two at VENDELLES. Two motor ambulances were stationed at COOKER QUARRY & two at VADENCOURT; the remainder were pooled at POEUILLY. ACY	

D. D. & L., London, E.C. (A8co4) Wt W1771/M2031 750,000 5/17 Sch. 52 Forms/C2118/14

Instructions regarding War Diaries and Intelligence Summaries are contained in F. S. Regs., Part II. and the Staff Manual respectively. Title Pages will be prepared in manuscript.

3RD NORTH MIDLAND FIELD AMBULANCE ROYAL ARMY MEDICAL CORPS

WAR DIARY
or
INTELLIGENCE SUMMARY
(Erase heading not required.)

Army Form C. 2118

Place	Date	Hour	Summary of Events and Information	Remarks and references to Appendices
LA HERLIÈRE	10/9/16		Reinforced bearer post in RAVINE and large dugout near junction of Support line with NEVERENDING St in view of transport of Gas cylinders tonight & succeeding nights & supplied additional transport at BERLES.	
	11/9/16		Accommodation of Hospital here increased by provision of 1 more hut holding 24 beds.	
	13/9/16		Visited S.B. posts & dugouts in BERLES sector in view of "Gas Operations" & made provisional arrangements.	
	14/9/16		Gas operations Stand to ordered 6.55 pm. – washed out 2am	
	15/9/16		" " " " 7.30 " – " "	
	16/9/16		Evacuated 66 patients on receipt of orders to clear all who would not be fit for duty in a week.	

Army Form C. 2118.

WAR DIARY
or
INTELLIGENCE SUMMARY.
(*Erase heading not required.*)

Instructions regarding War Diaries and Intelligence Summaries are contained in F. S. Regs., Part II. and the Staff Manual respectively. Title pages will be prepared in manuscript.

Place	Date	Hour	Summary of Events and Information	Remarks and references to Appendices
LABEUVRIERE	6/4/18		Subscriptions for RAMC prisoners of war fund are coming in fairly well. A separate list is being maintained for ASC prisoners of war. Despatched 5. O.R. for water point duty under 240 Employment Coy at LES BREBIS. Total personnel now away on detached duty 60. Obtained consent of DDMS to conducting an experiment in the treatment of scabies without parasiticides & arranged for 15 scabies cases to be sent here direct from division. Major E.L. Hega will carry out the experiment under careful supervision.	
	7/4/18		Amount subscribed to P of W Fund 430 francs RAMC & 67 francs ASC. Celebration of Holy Communion at 9am & Evening Service 6pm. The latter was badly attended owing to the counter attraction of a Pierrot show in the Recreation theatre by the Balmorals.	

A5092 Wt. W12839/M1293. 750,000. 1/17. D. D & L., Ltd. Forms/C2118/14.

12

Instructions regarding War Diaries and Intelligence Summaries are contained in F. S. Regs., Part II. and the Staff Manual respectively. Title pages will be prepared in manuscript.

WAR DIARY

or

~~INTELLIGENCE SUMMARY.~~ 1/3 N M 7 Ambce

(Erase heading not required.)

Army Form C. 2118.

Hour, Date, Place	Summary of Events and Information	Remarks and references to Appendices
25 - 5 - 15. BAILLEUL	Lt Harrison 1/3 Field Ambce 46 Division sent to PARIS in a Motor Ambulance to purchase material for Anti gas masks & Container bags - Remained 55 Admitted 88 To Duty 4 Died 1 Evacuated 50 Remaining 88	
26 - 5 - 15 BAILLEUL	Remained 88 Admitted 4. Evacuated 33 Died 1 To Duty 5 Remaining 53.	
27 - 5 - 15	Sgt Murray of the unit tested the action of "Hypo" Sodium Carbonate the chemicals used in the Anti-Gas Masks on elastic + found that it was not affected by the same =. He also tested a sample of water for the ADMS collected near the ground occupied by the 1st Battery 4th Howitzer Brigade 46 Division reported it free from Arsenic & Soluble Cyanide Remained 53 - Admitted 9. Discharged to duty 6 Transferred 9 Remaining 47 -	

(9 29 6) W 4141—463 100,000 9/14 H W V Forms/C. 2118/10

Army Form C. 2118

Instructions regarding War Diaries and Intelligence Summaries are contained in F. S. Regs., Part II. and the Staff Manual respectively. Title Pages will be prepared in manuscript.

WAR DIARY
or
~~INTELLIGENCE SUMMARY~~
(Erase heading not required.)

Place	Date	Hour	Summary of Events and Information	Remarks and references to Appendices
GAUDIEMPRE	14/5/16		Visited Hqrs 233 Bde RFA to inquire into working of the arrangements for collection of sick & supply of medical stores.	
	15/5/16		Reconnoitred proposed trench for evacuation of casualties from A.D.S. – Capt Starns & party working at improvements to ADS but are hampered by lack of RE material.	
	17/5/16		Visited 137 Bde Hqrs & arranged transport to reserve area of men unfit to march.	
	20/5/16		Sent 45 men of 'C' section to A.D.S. for digging & similar work on evacuation trench.	
	21/5/16		Went over line of proposed trench with RE Officer & decided to make a switch of new trench which will go round existing Battery positions – applied to 1/1 and 1/2 N.M. Field Amb for 50 men from each to assist in the digging	
	22/5/16		100 men asked for arrived under command of Capt Yates	

1875 Wt. W593/826 1,000,000 4/15 J.B.C. & A. A.D.S.S./Forms/C. 2118.

Instructions regarding War Diaries and Intelligence Summaries are contained in F. S. Regs., Part II. and the Staff Manual respectively. Title pages will be prepared in manuscript.

WAR DIARY
or
INTELLIGENCE SUMMARY.
(Erase heading not required.)

Army Form C. 2118.

Place	Date	Hour	Summary of Events and Information	Remarks and references to Appendices
LABEOVRIÈRE	24 3 18		C.O. attended conference at ADMS office relating to expected enemy activity.	
			Took the following steps pursuant to orders	
			Sent 1 officer 4 NCOs 48 bearers for duty under OC 1/2 NMFA as reserve: also 2 Motor Ambulance & Motor cyclist and 100 blankets & 6 Thomas splints & M.J. wheeled carriers.	
			Sent 3 Horsed Ambulances to 1/1 NM F Amb. for carriage of lightly wounded if required. & am holding 4 G.S.W. in readiness for same purpose on demand.	
			Took steps to obtain a collective expression of opinion from the unit on the question of remaining with division or becoming Corps or Army Troops.	
			D.C.G. held service 6pm in dining hall.	
			All leave stopped: Enemy shelled CHOCQUES and got direct hit on station.	
			From 11pm onwards enemy aeroplanes busy all over vicinity observing & dropping bombs. This continued till 2.30 am 25th	

A7092. Wt. W12839/M1293. 750,000. 1/17. D. D & L., Ltd. Forms/C2118/14.

Army Form C. 2118

WAR DIARY
or
INTELLIGENCE SUMMARY
(Erase heading not required.)

Instructions regarding War Diaries and Intelligence Summaries are contained in F. S. Regs., Part II. and the Staff Manual respectively. Title Pages will be prepared in manuscript.

Place	Date	Hour	Summary of Events and Information	Remarks and references to Appendices
MARSEILLE	18/1/16		Capt S.S.B Harrison & 1 NCO departed on detached duty i/c convoy of convalescent invalids and sick to LE HAVRE.	
			1 NCO & 1 pte reported on return from detached duty with 46 D.S.C.	
	19/1/16		All Chaplains attached ~~at~~ embarked on S.S. ARONDA	
	20/1/16		Lieut G.C.R. CHESTER RAMC from 36th Div. reported for duty as Quartermaster & was taken on the strength.	
			1 Corporal detached for water duty with 1/3 N.M. Bde R.F.A. to replace ~~sa~~ a casualty.	
	23/1/16		Capt S.S.B Harrison & 1 NCO reported on return from duty with sick convoy.	
	25/1/16		Capt J. Miller detached for medical duty on Div. Hqrs train and duties on arrival in new area.	
			Capt Harrison c̄ "B" section took over Camp Hospital at SANTI Camp from 1/1 N.M. Field Amb.	

Instructions regarding War Diaries and Intelligence Summaries are contained in F. S. Regs., Part II. and the Staff Manual respectively. Title pages will be prepared in manuscript.

WAR DIARY
or
INTELLIGENCE SUMMARY.
(Erase heading not required.)

Army Form C. 2118.

Place	Date	Hour	Summary of Events and Information	Remarks and references to Appendices
HESDIGNEUL	6/8/18		General routine work. LT Morris relieved Capt Miller at ESSARS - normal relief. GGH	
	7/8/18		Visited A.D.S. GORRE + ESSARS - also 1/1 NMFA post at BETHUNE &c with D.M.S. V Army + retinue. Very satisfactory throughout. GGH	
	8/8/18		visited A.D.S. ESSARS ref to new Elephant shelter. This is erected but concrete difficult to obtain. GGH	
	9/8/18		GORRE A.D.S. shelled 60 rounds 8" + 200 rounds 5.9" + 4.2" - Damage done to cellars nil but top part of building looks wormeaten. No casualties. Visited the A.D.S. + started off the work of clearing up, new bathhouse - new chlorine chamber &c. GGH	
	10/8/18		Capt REID relieved LT DOYLE at GORRE - men at posts + A.D.S. changed about. GGH	

D. D. & L., London, E.C.
(A8094) Wt W1771/M2031 750,000 5/17 Sch. 52 Forms/C2118/14

Instructions regarding War Diaries and Intelligence Summaries are contained in F. S. Regs., Part II. and the Staff Manual respectively. Title Pages will be prepared in manuscript.

WAR DIARY
or
INTELLIGENCE SUMMARY
(Erase heading not required.)

Army Form C. 2118

Place	Date	Hour	Summary of Events and Information	Remarks and references to Appendices
Aix Noulette ~~21-5-17~~ ~~(contd)~~	21.5.17		The transport billet (at the time unoccupied) was blown in & much clothing & equipment destroyed.	
Aix Noulette	22/5/17		Went to A D M S Office. In the afternoon returned to Aix Noulette with O C 1/2 N. Mid Fd Amb who inspected all the premises with a view to taking over. Arranged all details of ~~relief~~ exchange to take place on May 24th	
"	23/5/17		Capt. J. Miller, Lieut Jack & 1 Sergt. proceeded to A.D.S. Maroc to take over from 1/2 N. Mid Field Amb. O R 29 proceeded later in the day with complete horse transport (less horse ambulance)	
			Major Turner & Lieut Dowling of 1/2 N. Mid Field Amb with O R 14 arrived 9.30 a.m at Main Dressing Station. Major Turner with 8 men proceeded to A D S Lievin	
			Capt Gavin, Capt Harris 1 Sergt O R 8 came down from Lievin in the afternoon	
			2nd Lieut & Q M J. King proceeded to A section I Corps Rest Station	

Instructions regarding War Diaries and Intelligence Summaries are contained in F. S. Regs., Part II. and the Staff Manual respectively. Title pages will be prepared in manuscript.

WAR DIARY
or
INTELLIGENCE SUMMARY.
(Erase heading not required.)

Army Form C. 2118.

Place	Date	Hour	Summary of Events and Information	Remarks and references to Appendices
ANNEZIN	25/1/18		Spent day in settling unit in arranging programme of work & training. Owing to number of extraneous duties to be furnished the number of men available for field training will be limited to about <u>60</u>.	
	26/1/18		Inspected sanitation of billets occupied by 1/6 N. Staffs in FOUQUIÈRES at request of O.C. Forwarded recommendations to Sub-area Cdt. and copy to ADMS. Detailed 1 Officer to see sick daily & conduct Scabies inspection of 137 M.G. Coy at VENDIN lez BÉTHUNE. Started on earth ramp to protect horse standings from aerial bombing attacks.	
	28/1/18		Earth Ramp completed as far as possible till revetting material becomes available. Inspected sanitation of billets occupied in FOUQUIÈRES by 230 Bde R.F.A. at request of M.O. & advised as to remedies. Extensive enemy bombing raid in vicinity of station at FOUQUEREUIL and railway line. No military casualties caused but 13 civilian railway operatives were brought to Field Amb. badly wounded, of whom 2 died and 6 others were killed outright. Cases were attended to and sent to No I C.C.S. forthwith. Interpreter reported as requisite to Local French Authorities. ADMS 46 Div. visited Field Ambulance station.	

Instructions regarding War Diaries and Intelligence Summaries are contained in F. S. Regs., Part II. and the Staff Manual respectively. Title Pages will be prepared in manuscript.

WAR DIARY
or
INTELLIGENCE SUMMARY
(Erase heading not required.)

Army Form C. 2118

Place	Date	Hour	Summary of Events and Information	Remarks and references to Appendices
ACQ	12/3/16		Changed billets at ACQ in order to adjust Brigade area. Visited advanced dressing stations in NEUVILLE ST VAAST and AUX RIETZ — [A8b 79 and A8c 45 respectively sheet 57 b]: established personnel of officers and O.R. in these: Major Stidston in charge.	
	13/3/16		Visited with Major Stidston Regimental Aid Posts of the sector occupied by 137 Brigade. There are two in number. At A3a 8.10 fair accommodation in large deep dugout with good route for evacuation of cases by Boyau CHASSERY to adv. dressing station at A8b 79. At A3d 5.3. dugout for RMO fairly good but entrance bad: it is not suited for reception of wounded which would have to be dressed in the communication trench and carried at once via Boyau DENIS LARROQUE to advanced dressing station as above or to AUX RIETZ. Accommodation will need to be improved at this aid post as soon as possible. Method of evacuation — Sick and wounded brought from RAPs are retained during day at one or other of the advanced dressing stations & cleared by motor ambulances	

1875 Wt. W593/826 1,000,000 4/15 J.B.C. & A. A.D.S.S./Forms/C. 2118.

11

1/3 N M Fd Amb

Vol 39

WAR DIARY
or
INTELLIGENCE SUMMARY.
(Erase heading not required.)

Army Form C. 2118.

Instructions regarding War Diaries and Intelligence Summaries are contained in F. S. Regs., Part II. and the Staff Manual respectively. Title pages will be prepared in manuscript.

Place	Date	Hour	Summary of Events and Information	Remarks and references to Appendices
			MEDICAL.	
HESDIGNEUL	1/5/18		Attended weekly conference at ADMS - 10 am. Topic discussed, medical arrangements for Division in event of successful enemy attack. Inspected detachment & patients at BRUAY and arranged for part of personnel to rejoin H.Qrs. In afternoon with Major Hega and Capt Steel DADMS reconnoitred routes of evacuation and sites for dressing stations in the event of enemy advance - also saw Corps Light Railway officer and made preliminary arrangements for establishment of a train service for casualties from GORRE - actually Green Spur LEQUESNOY (F86.7.8) to sidings at K2a 8.5 where ambulances would meet them and convey them to main dressing station at HESDIGNEUL. Suggested service of 2 ambulance trucks attached to train leaving GREEN SPUR 12.30 pm and 6.45 pm thus conforming to existing service from PHILOSOPHE and VERMELLES to RUITZ. This is convenient however if these times are quite suitable as the accommodation at ADS GORRE is limited to a few cases only and it may be necessary to run an independent service. Heavy shelling of GORRE from 3.45 am for 4 or 5 hours with mustard gas shells. Casualties in ADS personnel replaced as they came down. Lt Doyle USA relieved Major Bradley & Lieut REID till evening when RAMC who were both suffering from gas. Further RAMC O.R. came down in evening making total casualties in Field Ambulance of 31 O.R. plus 2 officers. All O.R. evacuated to C.C.S. Officers retained in Main dressing Station pending transfer to Corps Rest Station. In evening Major Hega who was exposed to phosgene gas on evening of 28th at ESSARS exhibited signs of delayed poisoning in headache, dizziness & pain and shortness of breath so arranged for him to be taken in at C.R.S.	

D. D. & L., London, E.C.
(A8604) Wt W1771/M2031 750,000 5/17 Sch. 52 Forms/C2118/14

46

3 NM Fd Amb
Vol 16

Army Form C. 2118

WAR DIARY
or
INTELLIGENCE SUMMARY
(Erase heading not required.)

Instructions regarding War Diaries and Intelligence Summaries are contained in F. S. Regs., Part II. and the Staff Manual respectively. Title Pages will be prepared in manuscript.

Place	Date	Hour	Summary of Events and Information	Remarks and references to Appendices
GAUDIEMPRÉ	1/6/16		Lieut. B. Graves RAMC reported for duty & to be given opportunity if possible of investigating ocular conditions in cases of shell shock.	
	2/6/16		Inspected Advanced Dressing Station & structural alterations being made at ~~new~~ dugouts at N. end of FONCQUEVILLERS to convert them to A.D.S. purposes. Switch trench cut through from ADS to old evacuation trench except where road crosses it - this piece awaits assistance of RE for bridging.	
	3/6/16		Visited Field Ambulance of 48th & 56th Divisions at COUIN to inspect system of water storage. Capt E.S. DIXON RAMC reported for duty. Major CA Stidston RAMCT returned from temporary duty with 4th Divn.	
	4/6/16		Capt E.S. DIXON transferred to 1/2nd N. Mid Field Amb.	

1875 Wt. W593/826 1,000,000 4/15 J.B.C. & A. A.D.S.S./Forms/C. 2118.

Instructions regarding War Diaries and Intelligence Summ[illegible] are contained in F. S. Regs., Part II. and the Staff Manual respectively. Title pages will be prepared in manuscript.

WAR DIARY
or
INTELLIGENCE SUMMARY.
(Erase heading not required.)

Army Form C. [illegible]8.

MEDICAL

Place	Date	Hour	Summary of Events and Information	Remarks and references to Appendices
BUSIGNY	1.11.18		Called on ADMS to discuss impending operations. ACY.	
	2.11.18		Proceeded to reconnoitre roads in forward area. ACY.	
	4.11.18		At 6.30 AM. 1st Division attacked line of SAMBRE canal, the 46th Division being in support. At 6AM all horsed & motor ambulances of unit proceeded to ARBRE de GUISE where they were placed under orders of O.C. 1/2nd. N.M. F. Amb. Two limbers each packed with material for an ADS, two water carts, one GS waggon & all available bearers also proceeded to ARBRE de GUISE. In afternoon 46th. Division crossed canal & relieved 1st Division. In evening ADS established at CATILLON under Major Herga M.C. & another at LA LAURETTE under Lieut. Richard. Very few casualties. ACY.	
CATILLON	5.11.18.		ADS advanced from CATILLON to MEZIERES; dressing station at LA LAURETTE closed. One Ford car got over canal with great difficulty; subsequent attempts to get horsed waggons over failed, the approaches to pontoons being crowded with vehicles & deep in mud. Enemy retreating rapidly. Very few casualties. Hdqrs. of unit moved from BUSIGNY to CATILLON. ACY.	
	6.11.18		Bridge over canal at CATILLON repaired. Enemy still retiring. ADS advanced to N.19.a.4.6. ACY	

D. D. & L., London, E.C. (A8c04) Wt W1771/M2031 750,000 5/17 Sch. 52 Forms/C2118/14

Instructions regarding War Diaries and Intelligence Summaries are contained in F. S. Regs., Part II. and the Staff Manual respectively. Title pages will be prepared in manuscript.

WAR DIARY
or
INTELLIGENCE SUMMARY.
(Erase heading not required.)

Army Form C. 2118.

Place	Date	Hour	Summary of Events and Information	Remarks and references to Appendices
BURBURE	6/9/18		At 2 P.M. unit left BRUAY & proceeded by route march to BURBURE arriving at 4.30 P.M. Billets satisfactory. ACY.	
	7/8/18		Physical training, route march. & squad drill. ACY	
	9/8/18			
	10/9/18		Capt. E.J. BRADLEY RAMC (SR) reported for duty from Base ACY	
	11/9/18		Attended ADMS conference. Capt. A.U. MILLAR RAMC (TC) reported for duty from No 2 CCS. ACY	
IN THE TRAIN	12/9/18		Waggons packed in morning. At 9.30 AM Transport & loading party proceeded to LILLERS, remainder of unit following at 11 AM. Train due to leave 1.41 P.M. arrived at 1.45 P.M Entraining completed by 3 P.M. Train departed 4 P.M ACY.	
BONNAY	13/9/18		Train arrived at HEILLY 1.45 A.M. Started detraining at 6.45 A.M. Completed by 8 AM. Unit proceeded to billets at BONNAY arriving 8.40 AM. Billets satisfactory. Called on ADMS & Hdqrs. 137th. Bgde. Hospital opened in barn, accommodation 30 patients ACY.	

D. D. & L., London, E.C. (A8c04) Wt W1771/M2031 750,000 5/17 Sch. 52 Forms/C2118/14

Instructions regarding War Diaries and Intelligence Summaries are contained in F. S. Regs., Part II. and the Staff Manual respectively. Title Pages will be prepared in manuscript.

WAR DIARY
or
INTELLIGENCE SUMMARY
(Erase heading not required.)

Army Form C. 2118

3RD NORTH MIDLAND FIELD AMBULANCE ROYAL ARMY MEDICAL CORPS

Place	Date	Hour	Summary of Events and Information	Remarks and references to Appendices
	6/12/16		Moved off 7.30 am arrived St AMAND 12.15 pm: very hilly road for first half of journey but transport came along in good order	
St AMAND			and without losing ground. Hdqrs opened opposite church.	
			Sent further parties opened to ADS ~~Bienvillers~~ BIENVILLERS	
			Visited advanced dressing stations at both places.	
	7/12/16		Inspected bearer posts along line of evacuation from left & centre sectors: principal defect of these posts & also of dressing station at E 8 a 4.4 is lack of protection against gas. This being remedied as rapidly as possible.	
			Positions of Dressing Stations for left and centre sectors as follows.	
			E 2 d 2.5. / E 8 a 4.4 } BIENVILLERS. under Lt Waterhouse	
			Bearer posts E 16 a 4.3 / E 9 d 8.7 / E 4 d 5.3 / E 9 b 3.4 } 4 men at each place to furnish relays of bearers for carriage of wounded. all under O/C ADS BIENVILLERS.	
			Dressing stations for Right sector	
			E 27 a 2.5 / E 21 d 0.7 } FONQUEVILLERS.	

MEDICAL

Instructions regarding War Diaries and Intelligence Summaries are contained in F. S. Regs., Part II. and the Staff Manual respectively. Title Pages will be prepared in manuscript.

WAR DIARY
or
INTELLIGENCE SUMMARY
(Erase heading not required.)

Army Form C. 2118

3 NM Fd Amb 46/6

Vol 17

Place	Date	Hour	Summary of Events and Information	Remarks and references to Appendices
GAUDIEMPRÉ	1/7/16		Increased activity on Division front began about midnight 31st-1st. 7.15 am despatched all available motor and horsed transport of all three Field Ambulances to rendezvous at cross roads 1 Km. west of SOUASTRE on SOUASTRE-HÉNU Road. From 9 am onwards casualties were brought in easily & rapidly by the transport available, - motor ambulances being able to run right up to dressing stations at FONCQUEVILLERS. About 1pm ~~[illegible]~~ there was some congestion in the reception hut as the clearing of the trenches of wounded was being effected more rapidly than they could be recorded and dressed here. At 3pm started to comb out the waiting cases, sending off to C.C.S. direct all that needed no dressing immediately, after giving 300 units A.T.S. These cases went straight to Ambulance Train. This effected a great clearance and no further congestion occurred. By 10pm the back of the rush was broken & from then onwards the work diminished. By 12 noon 2/7/16 the hospital was empty save for casual cases coming in & the patients very slightly injured who were	

Instructions regarding War Diaries and Intelligence Summaries are contained in F. S. Regs., Part II. and the Staff Manual respectively. Title pages will be prepared in manuscript.

WAR DIARY
or
INTELLIGENCE SUMMARY.
(Erase heading not required.)

Army Form C. 2118.

MEDICAL

Place	Date	Hour	Summary of Events and Information	Remarks and references to Appendices
HESDIGNEUL	1/6/18		An exceptionally quiet day as regards gun fire. Very little H.V. harassing fire on the back area. Received notification of Inspection of transport by G.O.C. 46 Div on Tuesday June 4th 10 am. ACH	
	2/6/18		a/S. S. M. Ridgson departed for 1 Batt HAC - GHQ troops preparatory to embarking for England to take up permanent commission in Infantry. Forwarded to ADMS for action a report by O/C ADS GORRE complaining of storage of ammunition and mobile charges of explosive in cellars and sheds of Brewery, and requesting the building of a small pontoon bridge to carry stretcher bearers across the canal close to Brewery, as it is not proposed to have any motor ambulances on N side of canal during active hostility. Held an inspection of horsed transport in afternoon: G.O.C. [illegible] Corps who was near by, inspected them unofficially and complimented Sergt [illegible] on the excellent turn out. ACH	
	3/6/18		Capt A.C. Reid proceeded on 14 days contract leave. Ammunition and explosives removed from GORRE brewery. Started on construction of bivouacs to hold another 40 men. Went down 4 am by light railway with intention of visiting GORRE but found track had been blown out by a shell just previously about 2/3 of the way there: so was unable to continue journey. ACH	

D. D. & L., London, E.C. (A8004) Wt W1771/M2031 750,000 5/17 Sch. 52 Forms/C2118/14

Army Form C. 2118

WAR DIARY
or
INTELLIGENCE SUMMARY
(Erase heading not required.)

Instructions regarding War Diaries and Intelligence Summaries are contained in F. S. Regs., Part II. and the Staff Manual respectively. Title Pages will be prepared in manuscript.

Place	Date	Hour	Summary of Events and Information	Remarks and references to Appendices
LA HERLIERE	6/8/16		Measures advised (1) Removal on to the land of when possible of all manure collection in yards. (2) When this is not possible collection of the manure into compact heaps, fresh being kept apart from old so as to facilitate watering with cresol solution. This watering to be done daily for all heaps in the village by Sanitary squad of Field Ambulance.	
	9/8/16		Capt H. GREY RAMC (TC) reported for duty.	
			Visited ADS BERLES in afternoon to inspect gas traps + gas locks in dug outs of RAMC.	
	10/8/16		Received 8 reinforcements of good quality	
	11/8/16		Took preliminary steps in connection with para (2) RAMC OO no 70. of ADMS 46 Div. conduct of the ~~op~~ RAMC operation on the spot to be in the hands of Capt S.S.B Harrison.	

Instructions regarding War Diaries and Intelligence Summaries are contained in F. S. Regs., Part II. and the Staff Manual respectively. Title Pages will be prepared in manuscript.

WAR DIARY
or
INTELLIGENCE SUMMARY
(Erase heading not required.)

Army Form C. 2118

Place	Date	Hour	Summary of Events and Information	Remarks and references to Appendices
GAPENNES	8/11/16		Met ADMS by appointment and reconnoitred training area to find suitable parade ground for inspection of Field Ambulances by G.O.C. 46 Div. Heavy Rain nearly all day.	
FROYELLES.	11/11/16		Moved unit to FROYELLES (map ref as before) - Good quarters for men & officers: received 1 large I.P. marquee for patients. Started to erect vapour bath so as to deal with cases of scabies from the division.	
	12/11/16		Recd warning to prepare to take over quarters at Presbytery DOMVAST occupied by 1/2 N.M. Field Amb. for a scabies hospital.	
	13/11/16		Inspection by G.O.C. of all three Field Ambulances - ground was difficult & too small to admit of effective display: turn out on the whole fairly good & not severely criticised. March past in column of route satisfactory but in line very bad - conditions very difficult as ground was heavy & sloped from left to right flank.	

Instructions regarding War Diaries and Intelligence Summaries are contained in F. S. Regs., Part II. and the Staff Manual respectively. Title pages will be prepared in manuscript.

WAR DIARY
or
INTELLIGENCE SUMMARY.
(Erase heading not required.)

Army Form C. 2118.

Place	Date	Hour	Summary of Events and Information	Remarks and references to Appendices
FOUQUIÈRES	25.12.17		Xmas dinner for patients 12 noon: for personnel 3pm. All well fed & contented. Entertainment for personnel in evening.	
	26.12.17		Entertainment for patients in evening. All work in the way of improvements to Camp held up still on account of frost & snow.	
	28.12.17		DDMS I Corps visited CRS and warned me that it would be necessary to find accommodation for scabies cases.	
	29.12.17		Scabies cases began to arrive & were accommodated in Hut 11.	
	30.12.17		Capt Beard RAMC(TC) attd temporarily under command of OC 1/2 NMFA for instruction in A.D.S. duties. The "VERY LIGHTS" a I Corps Entertainment troupe gave a show at C.R.S. A collection in aid of St Dunstan's Hostel for the blind realised 140 fr. 90 cen.	
	31.12.17		Summary of changes of personnel for month Dec.	
			Officers struck off strength 4	
			" taken on " 4	
			OR struck off " 2	
			" taken on " 2	
			A E Hodder Lt Col cdg 1/3 N.M.F.A.	

A7092. Wt. W12839/M1293. 750,000. 1/17. D. D & L., Ltd. Forms/C2118/14.

Instructions regarding War Diaries and Intelligence Summaries are contained in F. S. Regs., Part II. and the Staff Manual respectively. Title Pages will be prepared in manuscript.

WAR DIARY
or
INTELLIGENCE SUMMARY
(Erase heading not required.)

Army Form C. 2118

Place	Date	Hour	Summary of Events and Information	Remarks and references to Appendices
GRAND DIEMPRE	30/6/16		Bath house – consists of 3 chambers – one for dressing room one for steam chamber & one shower bath chamber. These communicate suitably. Steam & shower chambers concrete floored & drained suitably. Capacity – about 250 men per day. Annexes to Bath house provide covered ablution place for patients & RAMC personnel separately. All water from Bath & wash places passes through soap trap & is delivered almost soap free into main drain running along East side of ground. Greasy water from Kitchens passes through grease traps & is similarly discharged grease free into main drain. Cooks department consists of Building for storage & preparing and external Roasting & boiling furnaces. Capacity for roasting or baking 16 dishes at one time " " boiling 12 Kettles " " " " In addition SOYERS stoves available for hot water. Latrines Officers, OR patients & RAMC personnel separated: Bucket system – excreta burnt. Fixed urinal – urine discharges into main drain after passing through suitable box in which oxidation is effected.	

1875 Wt. W593/826 1,000,000 4/15 J.B.C. & A. A.D.S.S./Forms/C. 2118.

3rd NORTH MIDLAND FIELD AMB
46 DIVISION

Army Form C. 21[illegible]

WAR DIARY
or
INTELLIGENCE SUMMARY
(Erase heading not required.)

Instructions regarding War Diaries and Intelligence Summaries are contained in F. S. Regs., Part II. and the Staff Manual respectively. Title Pages will be prepared in manuscript.

3RD NORTH MIDLAND FIELD AMBULANCE ROYAL ARMY MEDICAL CORPS

Place	Date	Hour	Summary of Events and Information	Remarks and references to Appendices
Near POPERINGHE	2/10/1915	P.M. 1.10	Left camp on the POPERINGHE - RENINGHELST Road BELGIUM in Motor Busses - Personnel + Motor Ambulances billetted at CENSE LA VALLEE near GONNEHEM - Horse Transport left 7. pm by road + billetted at VIEUX BERQUIN.	
	4.10.15	3 am	Transport joined the unit at above billets.	
	6.10.15	12.15	Left Billets at CENSE LA VALLEE being held up for one hour by blocked roads the XXVIII DIVISION passing the 137 Brigade + causing delay.	
	"	5 pm	arrived at large school Building near FOUQUIERES E15.C 3.3. 1/40000 36 36a 36b 36C. Proceeded to convert into a main Dressing station + Field Hospital. The building consists of (1) a main House capable of billetting one section of a F Ambce with room for 20 sick officers (2). A school capable of holding 60 sick (3) Two wooden rooms in the grounds capable of taking 120 sick - Total capacity 200 - capable of expansion to 300 - Remainder of personnel put into a loft + into tents.	

1875 Wt. W593/826 1,000,000 4/15 J.B.C. & A. A.D.S.S./Forms/C. 2118.

Army Form C. 2118.

Instructions regarding War Diaries and Intelligence Summaries are contained in F. S. Regs., Part II. and the Staff Manual respectively. Title pages will be prepared in manuscript.

WAR DIARY
or
INTELLIGENCE SUMMARY.
(Erase heading not required.)

Place	Date	Hour	Summary of Events and Information	Remarks and references to Appendices
FRESNOY	29.10.18		Received orders to be prepared to move to BOHAIN area. ACY.	
BUSIGNY	31.10.18		No billets being available in BOHAIN unit proceeded by route march to BUSIGNY at 1 PM arriving at 4 PM. Billets satisfactory Hospital at FRESNOY handed over to 18th F. Amb.	
			A. C. Turner Lt Col	
			COMM'DG. 1/3rd N. MID FIELD AMB. R. A. M. CORPS	
			1. 11. 18	

D. D. & L., London, E.C.
(A8co4) Wt W1771/M2031 750,000 5/17 Sch. 52 Forms/C2118/14

Instructions regarding War Diaries and Intelligence Summaries are contained in F. S. Regs., Part II. and the Staff Manual respectively. Title pages will be prepared in manuscript.

WAR DIARY
or
INTELLIGENCE SUMMARY.
(Erase heading not required.)

Army Form C. 2118.

Place	Date	Hour	Summary of Events and Information	Remarks and references to Appendices
~~10/7/~~ HESDIGNEUL	10/7/18		Lt Col A.E. Hodder D.S.O. acting temporarily as A.D.M.S. Divn, owing to absence on leave of A.D.M.S. SBH	
	11/7/18		Visited A.D.Ss. at GORRE + ESSARS – Nil to report SBH	
	12/7/18		Uneventful day. SBH	
	13/7/18		Visited A.D.S. at ESSARS. Four men under a N.C.O. installed in the cellars at the Civil + Military Hospital in BETHUNE, to open as a RELAY POST if necessary. Major HERC A M C. left for ENGLAND on Leave. SJDH	
	14/7/18		Nothing of note. Visited GORRE A.D.S and Posts. SJDH	
	15/7/18		Visited ESSARS and Civil + Military Hospital in BETHUNE. SJDH	
	16/7/18		Nothing of note. SJDH	
	17/7/18		uneventful day. SJDH	
	18/7/18		Visited ESSARS. SJDH	
	19/7/18		Civil + Military Hospital taken over by 1st N.M. Fd Amb. SJDH	
	20/7/18		Visited GORRE. SJDH	

D. D. & L., London, E.C.
(A8c04) Wt W1771/M2031 750,000 5/17 Sch. 52 Forms/C2118/14

Instructions regarding War Diaries and Intelligence Summaries are contained in F. S. Regs., Part II. and the Staff Manual respectively. Title pages will be prepared in manuscript.

WAR DIARY
or
INTELLIGENCE SUMMARY.
(Erase heading not required.)

Army Form C. 2118.

Place	Date	Hour	Summary of Events and Information	Remarks and references to Appendices
HESDIGNEUL	30/4/18		Summary of changes in personnel for month of April	
			Officers – on 1, off 2, net decrease 1	
			OR – on 5, off 12, net decrease 7	
			Appendix attd. giving analysis of cases of 1/5 Leicester Rgt. admitted for observation.	
			A. E. Hodder Lt Col cdg 1/3 N. Mid. Fd Amb	

D. D. & L., London, E.C.
(A8c04) Wt W1771/M2031 750,000 5/17 Sch. 52 Forms/C2118/14

Army Form C. 2118.

WAR DIARY
or
INTELLIGENCE SUMMARY.
(Erase heading not required.)

Instructions regarding War Diaries and Intelligence Summaries are contained in F. S. Regs., Part II. and the Staff Manual respectively. Title pages will be prepared in manuscript.

Place	Date	Hour	Summary of Events and Information	Remarks and references to Appendices
HESDIGNEUL	1/5/18		Wrote to next of kin of all the casualties in Other Ranks notifying them of the casualty. Arranged for remainder of C section to be relieved by A section on 2.5.18.	
	2/5/18		Further mustard gas casualties continue to come in from GORRE ADS. bringing the total of casualties in Field Ambulance personnel up to 33 plus 3 officers. Steps being taken to get all gas out of cellars and buildings. 3 officers suffering from gas poisoning transferred to I Corps Rest Station. Relief of staff of ADS post effected in evening; the Hospital at BRUAY having been cleared in morning and staff withdrawn to Headquarters HESDIGNEUL.	
	3/5/18		Lt Doyle from ADS GORRE and 12 OR sent down to Main Dressing Station suffering from Gas poisoning. 9 of these were evacuated to CCS the officer & 3 OR being retained as symptoms were entirely limited to the eyes. Total casualties RAMC now 42 OR and 4 officers. Visited C.L.R.O. and got further information re light railway truck service from GORRE and fixed times ~~of~~ regular service for 5.30 am and 6.45 pm: with the opportunity of using the ordinary ration train service in addition on notice by phone being sent from ADS to C.L.R.O. who will attach ~~trucks~~ the necessary trucks. On going to ADS GORRE the smell of mustard gas was distinctly perceptible in LE QUESNOY and on N.W. side of BEUVRY	

D. D. & L., London, E.C. (A8c04) Wt W1771/M2031 750,000 5/17 Sch. 52 Forms/C2118/14

Instructions regarding War Diaries and Intelligence Summaries are contained in F. S. Regs., Part II. and the Staff Manual respectively. Title Pages will be prepared in manuscript.

WAR DIARY
or
INTELLIGENCE SUMMARY
(Erase heading not required.)

Army Form C. 2118

Place	Date	Hour	Summary of Events and Information	Remarks and references to Appendices
FOUQUIERES	17.10.15	8.30	Double Thresh Disinfector received from XI Corps started disinfecting clothing - 60 men in 1¼ hours. Blankets done first - men then remove all clothes & put on great coats & wrap in their blankets - Trousers pants, shirts, socks, then wrapped in the same & put through. CRE XI Corps visited the unit - also CRE 46 Division - The former suggested building Baths adjoining the Laundry - storage in latter place for about 6000 galls of water fed by the Engine there from a well below.	
"	20.10.15	10. Am	Marched via CHOQUES to ALLOUAGNE - Opened Hospital at the Schools there	
ALLOUAGNE	21.10.15	10.30 Am	Inspected by G.O.C at LABEUVRIÈRE.	
	27.10.15	10 am	Unit returned via LABEUVRIÈRE to no 2 area, taking up former quarters at ORPHANAGE - FOUQUIÈRES. — Thresh disinfector received for use of Division. Selected party of NCOs and men, 15 in all told off to form part of Division RAMC company ~~under~~ attended rehearsal of parade for inspection by H.M. The KING	
	28.10.15		Inspection by H.M. The KING.	

1875 Wt. W593/826 1,000,000 4/15 J.B.C. & A. A.D.S.S./Forms/C. 2118.

4

Instructions regarding War Diaries and Intelligence Summaries are contained in F. S. Regs., Part II. and the Staff Manual respectively. Title pages will be prepared in manuscript.

WAR DIARY
or
INTELLIGENCE SUMMARY.
(Erase heading not required.)

Army Form C. 2118.

Hour, Date, Place	Summary of Events and Information	Remarks and references to Appendices
NEUVE EGLISE	On 7.6.15 - A cistern was dug in the lower part of the field + a continuous spring tapped - capacity 400 gallons - The overflow was turned into a horse trough + is now used for watering horses - Water for drinking is obtained from this cistern - Ablution benches made near + tubs for baths provided - but the waste from the benches flows away from this supply - Washing water is obtained from another pit some distance away - The drinking water has been examined + was found quite sound -	
	4 large incinerators have been constructed + all manure is burnt along with all other rubbish	

Appendix I War Diary.

Medical Arrangements for Evacuations from Front for which this Field Ambulance is responsible.

Map References 36.C.,N.W.3,and S.W.1-1/10,000.
Northern limit of front VENDIN ALLEY(H.19.a.3.3)approx.
Southern limit " " NOGGIN ALLEY(Approx:N.2.b.6.7).

Front divided into two sections Northern or HULLUCH,and SOUTHERN or LOOS. draining respectively to Advanced Dressing Stations PHILOSOPHE(G.20.a. 5.2)and FORT GLATZ(G.35.b.2.7).
Of these the LOOS Sector is by far the larger and FORT GLATZ receives casualties from front covered by one Brigade plus half a battalion. PHILOSOPHE and its Bearer Posts in connection HALF-WAY HOUSE(G.22.b.2.3) ST:GEORGES(G.23.b.6.8)and PONT St:(G.24.a.1.2)receive casualties from half a battalion only.
Bearer Posts in connection with LOOS Sector NAVAL POST(H.31.b.1.1) in connection with R.A.P.,Right Battalion,
TUNNELL POST(H.31.c.6.2)and SOLENT POST(G.36.d.2.2)~~draining to~~chain leading to FORT GLATZ.

CHALK PIT ALLEY Post in connection with R.A.P.serving Right Half Battalion Centre Brigade.
v TOSH KEEP Bearer Post in connection with combined R.A.P's,Left and Support Battions Right Brigade.
Both these draining similarly to FORT GLATZ.

Evacuation from FORT GLATZ and PHILOSOPHE by Motor Ambulance along main LENS-BETHUNE Road to Main Dressing Station,LABOURSE.

From the above summary it will be seen that the Dressing Station, PHILOSOPHE,and Posts in connection therewith are very much more than is needed at the present time to cope with casualties from the small length of front that they drain;while the Dressing Station FORT GLATZ and the five Bearer Posts dependant on it are perhaps inadequate for the LOOS Sector in any but quiet periods.
It is very desireable that an alternative to the evacuation from FORT GLATZ should be provided but a careful examination of the ground points to this not being feasible at the present time,and until there is a fresh grouping of troops on the Divisional Front the Medical Arrangements for the evacuation of casualties must,of necessity,be ill balanced.

A E Hodder.
Lt Col cmdg 1/3 N-Mid. Fd. Amb.

1/3RD NORTH MIDLAND FIELD AMBULANCE
ROYAL ARMY MEDICAL CORPS.

30/9/1917.

Appendise II

EVACUATION OF CASUALTIES.

Method of evacuation of Casualties from the line held by the 46th:Division:- Reference sheet 28, 1/40,000.The line held extends roughly from I.18d 10.10 to I.34b 9.9.

1.The line to I.30 evacuates its sick,and wounded to an Advanced Aid Post where the Field Ambulance have 1 N.C.O.,and 8 men in a dug-out at I.24a2.2.

2.The line south of this evacuates to two Advanced Aid Posts to which the bearers of the Field Ambulance go to collect at I.29 c 3.7,and I.27 b 5.5.The Artillery Batteries send to the ~~same~~ NEAREST Post.

Two main Advanced Dressing Stations are established at H.24 a 7.9 and I.21 c 8.8.At H.24 a 7.9,there are two very large dug-outs and one smaller dug-out.The largest acts as a Dressing Station where the equipment of the Medical Store Cart is set out.The other dug-outs house 30 N.C.O's,and men ,and 2 Officers.
Transport is parked at H.23 b 4.8.Two Motor Ambulances are kept here always.
Casualties reporting at Maple Copse I.24 a 2.2,are sent down singly to near the N.W.corner of Zillebeke Lake.The N.C.O. telephoning to H.24 a 7.9 that they have started.Bearers with wheeled stretchers start from H.24 a 7.9 to meet them and go by Bridge 14,and then almost due East to the N.W.corner of Zillebeke Lake.At this point bearers change and return to original starting points.On arrival at Dressing Station at H.24 a 7.9 cases are dressed and evacuated to the Dressing Station by Motor Ambulance at G.26 c 3.3.As the Motor Ambulance passes the Headquarters of the collecting Field Ambulance at G.20 c 4.8 another Motor Ambulance goes to H.24 a 7.9.This evacuation goes on all through the day.
At night two or three Horsed Ambulances go up to Maple Copse,and arrive about 10.p.m.load up with sick,and wounded and return at once.Six to eight Motor Cars go to H.23 b 3.8,arriving about 10.p.m.for the evacuation of these cases and cases from the Southern Section.
The second Advanced Dressing Station is in dug-outs in the North bank of the Railway Embankment at I.21 c 8.8.Two Medical Officers, and 50 bearers with the equipment of one Medical Store Cart are stationed here.
During the day walking cases only can be sent down from the R.A.P. at I.29 c 3.7 as the communication trench will not admit of stretchers being used.Stretcher cases from here are collected by night.
Two R.A.P's exist at I.28 d 2.3,and I.34 a 8.8,from which the Regimental Stretcher Bearers convey cases during the day,and night to BLAUWEPOORT FARM in I.27 b 5.5,and the Field Ambulance Bearers take over from them here.
Cases from these places are then conveyed to a large dug-out in the Railway Embankment and dressed if necessary.
From these dug-outs a cyclist orderly proceeds to the Motor Ambulance Park at H.23 b 4.8,and a car proceeds to the Loading Station at I.20 a 5.3.The wounded are conveyed by wheeled stretchers to this point along the North side of the Railway Embankment,and transferred to the Motor Ambulances there.
A Motor Ambulance remains at this point from 10.p.m. to 3.a.m. each night.
Rations are sent up to Maple Copse,and to the Railway Embankment dug-outs by night only.
Water Supply.One Water cart at H.24 a 7.9 which fills early morning from Dickebusch.
Petrol Tins taken up on Supply Wagon at night for Railway dug-outs or better a water cart kept concealed near.

July 17 15.

H H C Dent
LIEUT.-COLONEL,
COMM'DG 3RD N. MID. FIELD AMB. R.A.M. CORPS.

Instructions regarding War Diaries and Intelligence Summaries are contained in F. S. Regs., Part II. and the Staff Manual respectively. Title Pages will be prepared in manuscript.

WAR DIARY
or
INTELLIGENCE SUMMARY
(Erase heading not required.)

Army Form C. 2118

Place	Date	Hour	Summary of Events and Information	Remarks and references to Appendices
MAISON ROLLAND	15/7/16		Under authority from DADOS purchased in ABBEVILLE, chain, spring shackles and rings for making 32 mule chains.	
	19/7/16		Sent "B" section in pursuance of orders from ADMS to occupy derelict house at LONGVILLERS and prepare it for reception of patients. House in question will accommodate about 100 patients when put in repair - adjacent barn-loft will accommodate 30 more. The whole structure is in very bad repair, the roof and windows needing particular attention & also the approach to the door.	
	20/7/16		Sent Billeting party to MESNIL-DOMQUEUR to arrange for reception of Field Ambulance.	
	21/7/16		Transferred all patients from MAISON ROLLAND to Hosp. at LONGVILLERS and "C" section to MESNIL. Met DADMS and O.C. Pioneer Battn who has charge of necessary repairs & improvements to Hosp. at LONGVILLERS and decided on minimum amount of work to be done at once.	
	22/7/16		Transferred patients back to MAISON ROLLAND for convenience of workmen at Hospital.	
	23/7/16		Under orders from ADMS, transferred patients back to LONGVILLERS sending all Scabies cases to 1/1 N.M. Field Amb. BERNEUIL. Prepared for move of whole unit to FORCEVILLE via VAL DE MAISON.	

Instructions regarding War Diaries and Intelligence Summaries are contained in F. S. Regs., Part II. and the Staff Manual respectively. Title Pages will be prepared in manuscript.

WAR DIARY
or
INTELLIGENCE SUMMARY
(Erase heading not required.)

Army Form C. 2118

Place	Date	Hour	Summary of Events and Information	Remarks and references to Appendices
AIX-NOULETTE	8/5/17		A number of patients arrived at Main Dressing Station: 78 in all. One case died in the Field Amb. The symptoms exhibited by the patients were of the usual type: the effect of the lacrimator component of the gas was very persistent. The majority of these cases were slight. In addition 41 men were sent for observation in whom the gassing was very doubtful: these were detained in F Amb for early return to duty. Took over from 1/1 NMF Amb the two bearer posts referred to on 7/7/15.	
	9/5/17		Visited ADS & bearer posts in LIEVIN and put in hand various structural improvements including the digging of sloping entrance to White Chateau from roadway, on blind side and a sap connecting two of the cellars at relay post ROLLENCOURT also at the latter further propping of cellar roof to take the weight of the house walls which I propose to pull down on top to afford further cover. The communication between the 3 dugouts at M22d 8.4. to be opened up and the dugouts repaired so as to accommodate a large body of bearers if needed.	

1875 Wt. W593/826 1,000,000 4/15 J.B.C. & A. A.D.S.S./Forms/C. 2118.

Instructions regarding War Diaries and Intelligence Summaries are contained in F. S. Regs., Part II. and the Staff Manual respectively. Title Pages will be prepared in manuscript.

WAR DIARY
or
INTELLIGENCE SUMMARY
(Erase heading not required.)

Army Form C. 2118

Place	Date	Hour	Summary of Events and Information	Remarks and references to Appendices
LA HERLIÈRE	29/10/16		A section under Capt S. Miller moved as advance party to LE SOUICH taking over quarters of 96 Fd. Amb.	
			Advance party of 97 Field Amb. moved in to LA HERLIÈRE and took over Advanced Dressing Stations at BERLES and BIENVILLERS.	
			Capt S.S.B. Harrison left for permanent duty with 1/5 S. Staffs. Regt.	
	30/10/16		Field Amb. moved to quarters at BREVILLERS on completion of relief by 97 Field Amb. Heavy rain on march for about 2/3 of the journey.	

A E Hodder
Lt Col cdg 1/3 N. Mid Fd Amb.

Instructions regarding War Diaries and Intelligence Summaries are contained in F. S. Regs., Part II. and the Staff Manual respectively. Title Pages will be prepared in manuscript.

WAR DIARY
or
INTELLIGENCE SUMMARY
(Erase heading not required.)

Army Form C. 211

Place	Date	Hour	Summary of Events and Information	Remarks and references to Appendices
LABEUVRIERE	21/7/17		Captain E.E. HERGA and 40 O.R. left 9am to take over advanced dressing station PHILOSOPHE G20 a.4.2 and bearer posts at St GEORGES G23 b.8.8 ; G22 b 2.2 and G22 a.0.3 [Map sheet 36C. 1/40000] from No 18 Field Amb VI Division.	
			O.C. no 16 Field Amb. visited C.R.S. in reference to relieving this unit at an early date.	
	22/7/17		ADMS VI Division went round C.R.S. preparatory to ~~[illegible]~~ a unit of his division taking over.	
			Horsed Amb. despatched to act under orders 139 I.B. for line of march.	
	23/7/17		DDMS I Corps inspected C.R.S.	
			Advance party 1 officer + 9 OR. arrived 11am to take over.	
			Organised athletic sports in evening for personnel.	
	24/7/17		Capt. J Miller and A section less certain details left 9am to relieve No 18 Field Amb at main dressing station LABOURSE.	
			Head Quarters Field Amb moved 2pm after handing over C.R.S. to no 16 Field Amb and arrived LABOURSE 5pm.	

Instructions regarding War Diaries and Intelligence Summaries are contained in F. S. Regs., Part II. and the Staff Manual respectively. Title pages will be prepared in manuscript.

WAR DIARY
or
INTELLIGENCE SUMMARY.
(Erase heading not required.)

Army Form C. 2118.

Place	Date	Hour	Summary of Events and Information	Remarks and references to Appendices
HESDIGNEUL	12/6/18		Second party of 20 O.R. arrived from 1/2 NM Fa as reserve bearers. ALH	
	13/6/18		Sent party of 10 OR 1/2 NMFa to ADS Gorre and 2 OR to ADS ESSARS for instruction & to learn the ground. Rigid inspection of unit for pediculosis with remedial steps following. ALH	
	14/6/18		"First" blanket collected for return to railhead; started to enlarge bivouac accommodation so as to accommodate a party of stretcher bearers [illegible] for instruction constantly. Made arrangements with O.C. ADS ESSARS to supply green forage each night for the present. Lt McCREA returned from ADS. ALH	
	15/6/18		O.C. 453 Coy Div. Train inspected wagons and draughts [?] and arranged for further repair to be carried out. ALH	
	16/6/18		Lt McCREA admitted to 1/1 NMF Amb. – PUO (Trench Fever) ALH	
	17/6/18		Lieut Colonel Hodder today left for 14 days instruction, at No 6 C.C.S. Pernes, in C.C.S. administration. Normal relief Essars section bearers. ALH	

Instructions regarding War Diaries and Intelligence Summaries are contained in F. S. Regs., Part II. and the Staff Manual respectively. Title Pages will be prepared in manuscript.

WAR DIARY
or
INTELLIGENCE SUMMARY
(Erase heading not required.)

Army Form C. 2118

Place	Date	Hour	Summary of Events and Information	Remarks and references to Appendices
MAISON ROLLAND	10/2/16 (continued)		the same men come in as patients time after time. It is evident that the resistance of these men to certain forms of pyogenic cocci is seriously lowered, and that something more is required than temporary raising of their immunity before they can be regarded as efficient for duty: recommended that such cases should be evacuated through C.C.S. with a report in detail and sent to convalescent camp preferably at sea side where there would be available in addition to specific vaccine treatment the best facilities for bathing, frequent changes of clothing and abundant fresh vegetable food.	
	12/2/16		Submitted report to ADMS on structural and sanitary improvements effected by the Field Ambulance during its occupancy of these quarters.	Copy of report App. I
			Lt C.A. ARMITAGE and 1 orderly RAMC reported on return from detached duty.	
	15/2/16		Average daily number of cases in hospital – Scabies & Pyodermia – 35.	

Instructions regarding War Diaries and Intelligence Summaries are contained in F. S. Regs., Part II. and the Staff Manual respectively. Title pages will be prepared in manuscript.

WAR DIARY
or
INTELLIGENCE SUMMARY.
(Erase heading not required.)

Army Form C. 2118.

Place	Date	Hour	Summary of Events and Information	Remarks and references to Appendices
BRUAY	23/8/18		Line practically stationary. On ESSARS subsector both right & left RAP's returned to old positions at LE HAMEL. Bearer posts established at X.15.c. central & at X.15.d.2.0. ACY.	
	24/8/18		First Lieut. E.M. MORRIS detailed for temporary duty with 1/1st N.M.F.A. ACY	
	25/8/18		C section relieved B section at GORRE. GORRE heavily shelled in morning; two motor ambulances damaged. Major E.E. HERGA M.C relieved Capt. A.U. MILLAR M.C. at ESSARS. Capt. A.U MILLAR M.C. proceeded to no. 2 CCS for temporary duty. ACY	
	26/8/18		Capt. P.B. BELANGER M.C. RAMC reported from 1/2nd. N.M.F. Amb for temporary duty. Visited ADS. GORRE & support RAP. ACY.	
	28/8/18		Attended ADMS conference. Visited ADS ESSARS. ACY	
	30/8/18		Visited ADS GORRE & Tuning Fork bearer post. Enemy retiring; LACOUTURE occupied by our troops. RAP of forward battalion ESSARS subsector advanced to X.15.b.1.8. ACY	

D. D. & L., London, E.C. (A8c04) Wt W1771/M2031 750,000 5/17 Sch. 52 Forms/C2118/14

Army Form C. 2118.

WAR DIARY
or
INTELLIGENCE SUMMARY.
(Erase heading not required.)

Instructions regarding War Diaries and Intelligence Summaries are contained in F. S. Regs., Part II. and the Staff Manual respectively. Title pages will be prepared in manuscript.

Place	Date	Hour	Summary of Events and Information	Remarks and references to Appendices
			up the valley between the JONCOURT & LEVERGIES Roads, to meet any stretcher squads using that route & to convey wounded to A.D.S.	
			At 6.15 AM the 46th. Division attacked enemy lines, the 137th. Bgde. on right, 139th. Bgde. on left, 138th. Bgde. in support. Car posts were established in the first place at H.15.a.4.9 on left sector & at H.33.b.7.9. on right sector. In the afternoon the left car post was advanced to SWISS COTTAGE H.10.b.2.9.	
			Twenty bearers from 1/1st. N.M.F. Amb., & forty bearers & three horsed ambulance waggons from 1/2nd. N.M.F. Amb. arrived at MAGNY during the morning. The horsed ambulances were used to evacuate the less seriously wounded cases.	
			Walking wounded were directed to the Walking Wounded Collecting Post in MAGNY LA FOSSE which was staffed by the 1/2nd. N. Mid. F. Amb. & from which wounded were evacuated by lorries to CCS.	
			Evacuation proceeded smoothly & fairly rapidly, the only serious difficulty being that of getting	

D. D. & L., London, E.C.
(A8c04) Wt W1771/M2031 750,000 5/17 Sch. 52 Forms/C2118/14

Instructions regarding War Diaries and Intelligence Summaries are contained in F. S. Regs., Part II. and the Staff Manual respectively. Title pages will be prepared in manuscript.

Army Form C. 2118.

WAR DIARY
or
INTELLIGENCE SUMMARY.
(Erase heading not required.)

Place	Date	Hour	Summary of Events and Information	Remarks and references to Appendices
LABEUVRIÈRE	29/3/18		Grouping of patients into three categories completed as follows. 1) All on admission go to A block and after bathing, hair cutting etc are put to bed. 2) On 4th day - normally - they are transferred to C Block where they come on to ordinary diet and are available for fatigues, gardening & other work up to 4 hours daily. 3) On 8th day after admission they pass to "B" block where their kits & rifles are issued to them from pack store and they undergo training of a more military character viz physical exercises, marching, anti gas drill in addition to fatigues as needed about their own range of buildings. In C & B blocks patients are exclusively responsible for the cleanliness & maintenance of ablution places, latrines, & wards & are under their own NCOs for discipline except that the wardmasters of these blocks act as provost sergeants. There must necessarily be some overlapping of days according to the medical condition of the patients but the essentials are that all patients who are at all ill & require other than ordinary diet are in A block & are not	

A7092. Wt W12839/M1293. 750,000. 1/17. D. D & L. Ltd. Forms/C2118/14.

Instructions regarding War Diaries and Intelligence Summaries are contained in F. S. Regs., Part II. and the Staff Manual respectively. Title pages will be prepared in manuscript.

Army Form C. 2118.

WAR DIARY
or
INTELLIGENCE SUMMARY.
(Erase heading not required.)

Place	Date	Hour	Summary of Events and Information	Remarks and references to Appendices
FRESNOY LE GRAND	3.1.19		Capt. A.U. MILLAR M.C. detailed for temporary duty with 1/1st N.M.F. Amb. ACY	
	8.1.19		Capt. A.U. MILLAR M.C. detailed for duty with 231 Bgde. R.F.A. in relief of Capt. D. GILLIES who returned to this unit. Extract from London Gazette 6.1.19. Capt. E.J. BRADLEY M.C. awarded bar to Military Cross. Capt. A.U. MILLAR M.C. to be Major from 20.10.18 to 23.11.18 Capt. E.J. BRADLEY M.C. to be Major from 7.12.18. ACY	
"	12.1.19.		DDMS XIII th Corps called & inspected hospital. ACY.	
	17.1.19		Major E.E. HERGA M.C. departed on leave. ACY	
	20.1.19		Inspected cookhouses, water carts & latrines of 1/5th S. Staff. Regt. ACY.	
	22.1.19		Inspected cookhouses, water carts & latrines of 1/6th. S. Staff. Regt. ACY	
	24.1.19		Inspected cookhouses, water carts & latrines of 1/6th. N. Staff. Regt. Capt. D. GILLIES proceeded on leave to BRUSSELS. ACY.	
	27.1.19		G.O.C. & B.G.C. called & inspected hospital. ACY	

A C Turner
LIEUT.-COL. COMMDG.
2/3rd N. MID. FIELD AMB.
R. A. M. C.

D. D. & L., London, E.C.
(A8co4) Wt W1771/M2031 750,000 5/17 Sch. 52 Forms/C2118/14

24

Instructions regarding War Diaries and Intelligence Summaries are contained in F. S. Regs., Part II. and the Staff Manual respectively. Title Pages will be prepared in manuscript.

WAR DIARY
or
INTELLIGENCE SUMMARY
(Erase heading not required.)

Army Form C. 2118.

Vol 28

Place	Date	Hour	Summary of Events and Information	Remarks and references to Appendices
			WAR DIARY of MAJOR T. A. BARRON O.C. 1/3 N. M. F. AMB. 1st JUNE to 30th JUNE 1917	

2449 Wt. W14957/M90 750,000 1/16 J.B.C. & A. Forms/C.2118/12.

Instructions regarding War Diaries and Intelligence Summaries are contained in F. S. Regs., Part II. and the Staff Manual respectively. Title pages will be prepared in manuscript.

WAR DIARY
or
INTELLIGENCE SUMMARY.
(*Erase heading not required.*)

Army Form C. 2118.

Hour, Date, Place	Summary of Events and Information	Remarks and references to Appendices
March 14. 15.	Sent 3 more Officers to the 21st Field Ambulance to assist in the work of receiving Casualties - these Officers worked from 9. pm the previous night until 5 am in the morning in each case - Church parade 10.30 am	
" 15 - 15.	Received orders to march to new Billetts at MERRIS - started 10.5 am but ordered to return to Billets	
" 16 - 15	Marched in rear of the STAFFS INF BRIGADE to OULTERSTEENE - Starting point at 9.50 am Road junction 1/4 mile NW of the church at SAILLY SUR LA LYS -	
" 19 - 15.	The Field Ambce marched to ARMENTIERS in rear of the Staffs Inf Brigade via BAILLEUL and NIEPPE. attached there to the 17. BRIGADE FIELD AMB.ce In the evening men + Officers went out with the 3 Ambce wagons + collected wounded	
" 20 - 15.	Collection of wounded as yesterday -	

Instructions regarding War Diaries and Intelligence Summaries are contained in F. S. Regs., Part II. and the Staff Manual respectively. Title pages will be prepared in manuscript.

WAR DIARY
or
INTELLIGENCE SUMMARY.
(Erase heading not required.)

Army Form C. 2118.

Place	Date	Hour	Summary of Events and Information	Remarks and references to Appendices
HESDIGNEUL	7/5/18		to be perfected and then strengthening of walls outside to be pushed. ADS to be ready to hold a large number of lying casualties in these dugs [illegible]. Arranged for extra truck for casualties to go up to GREEN SPUR on return ste train nightly to bring sitting casualties to LA PIERRETTE. K2a 8.6.	
	8/5/18		Attended ADMS conference 10 am. Notified officers i/c ADSs of general arrangements in event of hostile enemy attack. Had satisfactory report from OC ADS GORRE re progress of improvements. At 11.55 pm had order from ADMS that enemy attack might take place about daybreak and that I should make necessary arrangements to start a walking wounded post at F13c 8.9. ~~[illegible]~~ Acted as requisite in the event of attack beginning	
	9/5/18		but the night passed quietly. Two members of the unit LCpl Connolly + Pte C Morris received cards of commendation from G.O.C. 46 Div. for their conduct at GORRE when bombarded with shell gas. One man who was gassed on that occasion Pte Batchelor died in 20 Gen. Hosp on 7th.	

D. D. & L., London, E.C.
(A8co4) Wt W1771/M2031 750,000 5/17 Sch. 52 Forms/C2118/14

Army Form C. 2118.

WAR DIARY
or
INTELLIGENCE SUMMARY.
(Erase heading not required.)

Instructions regarding War Diaries and Intelligence Summaries are contained in F. S. Regs., Part II. and the Staff Manual respectively. Title pages will be prepared in manuscript.

Place	Date	Hour	Summary of Events and Information	Remarks and references to Appendices
HESDIGNEUL	25/5/18		Fine day - camp drying rapidly. Inoculation carried out of men who have gone 10 months since last being done. QMr & Hon. Capt J. King proceeded a month special leave to G.B. Lt Richard struck off strength on posting to 1/5 S. Staffs Rgt as medical officer. Capt. (a/Major) S.S.B. Harrison MC joined unit from 1/5 S Staffs & posted to command of C. section. Paid unit amounts indented for by them.	
	26/5/18		Church Parade 10.15 am. Field Ambulance played Divisional Supply Column at cricket & got soundly whacked. 137 Brigade Band played during afternoon and evening for the two Field Ambulances. Usual desultory shelling round GORRE and ESSARS: the latter place is becoming distinctly less healthy than a few weeks ago.	
	27/5/18		Re-organisation of 'C' section proceeding: continued bomb protection of huts and horse standings. Received one officer re-inforcement Lt J. CHARNLEY RAMC (SR). After consultation with ADMS ~~[illegible]~~ wrote M.O. 231 Bde R.F.A. handing over to him RAMC post at F13C5.9 for RAMC purposes (RAP etc) and withdrew Field Ambulance holding party.	

D. D. & L., London, E.C.
(A8co4) Wt W1771/M2031 750,000 5/17 Sch. 52 Forms/C2118/14

Instructions regarding War Diaries and Intelligence Summaries are contained in F. S. Regs., Part II. and the Staff Manual respectively. Title pages will be prepared in manuscript.

WAR DIARY
or
INTELLIGENCE SUMMARY.
(Erase heading not required.)

Army Form C. 2118.

Place	Date	Hour	Summary of Events and Information	Remarks and references to Appendices
LABEUVRIERE	27/3/18		I saw O.C. 8 San Section there in afternoon and agreed that he should have two thirds of the barn at Ferme Du Lecoq for his workshops & that the CRS pack store should remain. That 1 Armstrong Hut should be handed over to him as an office & that I should find billets for his personnel, temporarily with the Field Ambce & later on their own: messing etc also arranged amicably.	
			Capt Douglas MC 92 Fd Amb, for a short time in 1916 a member of this unit spent night in village i/c of Fd Amb transport in lieu of march from Belgium over entertained at the mess.	
			Cold windy day & cloudy: no raiding aeroplane over. Concert party gave entertainment to patients in theatre	
	28/3/18		Capt A.W. Millar MC and Lieut Richard detailed for duty with 1/1 NMFA for ADS work on LENS front.	
			Lent 1 G.S.W. to 1/1 NMFA to assist him with move to AIX NOULETTE.	
			Cleared Barn ready for No 8 San Section to occupy, transferring Shoemaker etc temporarily to former scabies pack store.	
			Started on protection of huts against bomb splinters.	

A7092. Wt. W12839/M1293. 750,000. 1/17. D. D & L., Ltd. Forms/C2118/14.

Instructions regarding War Diaries and Intelligence Summaries are contained in F. S. Regs., Part II. and the Staff Manual respectively. Title Pages will be prepared in manuscript.

WAR DIARY
or
INTELLIGENCE SUMMARY
(Erase heading not required.)

Army Form C. 2118.

Place	Date	Hour	Summary of Events and Information	Remarks and references to Appendices
LABEUVRIERE	25		Attended conference ADMS office. Received instructions to evacuate as many patients as possible in view of impending operations.	
			Detailed Capt. SUTTIE to attend sick daily at 46th Div. Depot Bn.	
	26		D.D.M.S I Corps visited Hospital and expressed himself as greatly pleased with the arrangements and improvements.	
			Received urgent orders from ADMS to 46th DIV. to detail 20 convalescent patients to report to 1/1 N.M. F. Amb. to work on a sanitary construction under A.D.M.S. orders. Detailed 16 party.	
			Detailed Cpl. Ball for duty with 46th DIV. baths at BULLY GRENAY	
	27	4 p.m.	Despatched Capts. HERGA and SUTTIE, 6 additional bearers, 3 Motor Ambs. to report to O.C. 1/2 N.M. F. Amb. at AIX NOULETTE at 5 p.m.	
		7 p.m.	Capt. HERGA returned with the information that the operations were postponed. The motor ambulances had returned via BULLY GRENAY and brought back to Hospital the 20 convalescent patients mentioned above 25.6.17.	

Instructions regarding War Diaries and Intelligence Summaries are contained in F. S. Regs., Part II. and the Staff Manual respectively. Title pages will be prepared in manuscript.

WAR DIARY
or
INTELLIGENCE SUMMARY.
(Erase heading not required.)

Army Form C. 2118.

Place	Date	Hour	Summary of Events and Information	Remarks and references to Appendices
VENDELLES	23/9/18		Motor ambulances of 1/1st, 1/2nd & 1/3rd N. Mid. F. Ambs. pooled at VENDELLES. Twenty bearers arrived from 1/1st & eighteen from 1/2nd N. M. F. Ambs. & were sent up to ADS. Twenty more bearers of 1/2nd N. M. F. Amb held in readiness at VENDELLES ACY	
	24/9/18		At 5 AM 5th Leicesters attacked village of PONTRUET. About 120 casualties dealt with at Right ADS during day & about 40 at Left ADS. Evacuation proceeded smoothly. Visited Right ADS in morning.	
			Walking wounded on Right sector walked to VADENCOURT whence they were conveyed by lorries to POEUILLY; on left sector they were met at LE VERGUIER by horsed ambulances & conveyed to Walking Wounded Post at VENDELLES staffed by 1/2nd N. M. F. Amb ACY	
	25/9/18.		Visited Right ADS in morning; all quiet. Established walking wounded post at VADENCOURT. Bearers of 1/1st & 1/2nd N. M. F. Ambs. returned to their units. Motor ambulances pooled at HANCOURT, two remaining on duty at each ADS. ACY	
	26/9/18		Attended ADMS conference re impending operations. Visited Right ADS & Walking Wounded Post at VADENCOURT. ACY	

D. D. & L., London, E.C.
(A8co4) Wt W1771/M2031 750,000 5/17 Sch. 52 Forms/C2118/14

Army Form C. 2118.

Instructions regarding War Diaries and Intelligence Summaries are contained in F. S. Regs., Part II. and the Staff Manual respectively. Title pages will be prepared in manuscript.

WAR DIARY
or
INTELLIGENCE SUMMARY.
(Erase heading not required.)

Hour, Date, Place	Summary of Events and Information	Remarks and references to Appendices
March 4 15	INVENTOR sailed 5.30 pm -	
March 5 15.	CHYBASSA sailed 8 pm - INVENTOR disembarked HAVRE - 1/2 unit marched to No 1. REST CAMP HAVRE	
March 6, 15.	CHYBASSA disembarked HAVRE. Second half unit disembarked at 1 pm - bivouacked at Shed near DOCKS -	
March 7. 15.	Whole unit entrained at 7.30 am for Rail Head via St OMER.	
March 8 15	Arrived BAVINCHOVE at 8 am - detrained & marched to billets ARNEKE -	
March 9 15.	Marched with STAFFS Inf Brigade to BORRE - via WAEMARS CAPPEL - BAVINCHOVE - QUEUE de BAVINCHOVE - LES CISCAUX - Cross Roads South of first H in HONDEGHEM - L'HOFFAND - Billeted in BORRE. HQ unit at School ~~[illegible]~~	

Army Form C. 2118.

Instructions regarding War Diaries and Intelligence Summaries are contained in F. S. Regs., Part II. and the Staff Manual respectively. Title pages will be prepared in manuscript.

WAR DIARY
or
INTELLIGENCE SUMMARY.
(Erase heading not required.)

Place	Date	Hour	Summary of Events and Information	Remarks and references to Appendices
FRESNOY	22/12/18		G.O.C. & B.G.C. called & inspected hospital. ACT	
"	26.12.18		Attended ADMS conference. G.O.C. called. ACT	
"	27.12.18		Inspected cookhouses of 1/6th. S. Staff. R. ACT	
"	28.12.18		Inspected cookhouses of 1/6th. N. Staff. R. ACT	
"	29.12.18		Inspected cookhouses of 137th. Bgde. Hdqrs. & of 137th. T.M.B. ACT	
"	30.12.18		Inspected cookhouses of 1/5th. S. Staff. Regt. ADMS called & inspected hospital	

A. C. Turner
LIEUT.-COL. COMMDG.
1/3rd N. MID. FIELD AMB.
R.A.M.C.

D. D. & L., London, E.C.
(A8c04) Wt W1771/M2031 750,000 5/17 Sch. 52 Forms/C2118/14

Instructions regarding War Diaries and Intelligence Summaries are contained in F. S. Regs., Part II. and the Staff Manual respectively. Title Pages will be prepared in manuscript.

WAR DIARY
or
INTELLIGENCE SUMMARY
(Erase heading not required.)

Army Form C. 2118

Place	Date	Hour	Summary of Events and Information	Remarks and references to Appendices
ST AMAND	17/12/16		This scheme involves construction of shelter for bearers as requested & obtained permission for bearers to use shelter post to be built by 137 Bde & the same spot to be available to assist in running coffee stall etc of Bde when not otherwise employed. This scheme approved by ADMS & GOC 137 IB.	
	18/12/16		Attended weekly conference at ADMS office – Subject mainly SCABIES disposal: – visited bearer post in middle sector. Greater attention needs to be paid to gas trapping.	
	19/12/16		Inspected progress of construction work at BIENVILLERS. Trench tube in position and all communication cut between cellars & suitably revetted. Inspected Horse transport lines & quarters at GAUDIEMPRÉ.	
	20/12/16		Inspected ADS FONQUEVILLERS. – owing to subsidence work required a trench from house to dugouts.	
	21/12/16		Inspected bearer posts at Barrier on HANNESCAMP Road and in CROSS S^t – Gas trapping not satisfactory & to be remedied at once. Visited Bde drying room in CROSS S^t and arranged for relief of RAMC working there.	

1875 Wt. W593/826 1,000,000 4/15 J.B.C. & A. A.D.S.S./Forms/C. 2118.

Instructions regarding War Diaries and Intelligence Summaries are contained in F. S. Regs., Part II. and the Staff Manual respectively. Title Pages will be prepared in manuscript.

WAR DIARY
or
INTELLIGENCE SUMMARY
(Erase heading not required.)

Army Form C. 2118

Place	Date	Hour	Summary of Events and Information	Remarks and references to Appendices
GAUDIEMPRÉ	11/6/16		Patients in Field Ambulance inspected by DADMS under orders from G.O.C. on account of large number of cases being evacuated. Numbers in consequence reduced by transfer of cases of Fever N.Y.D. being sent for observation to 1/2 N. Mid. Field Amb. A large number of cases of pyodermia which had been choking the accommodation for some time having sufficiently recovered were returned to regiments. A small number of trivial cases which had been sent in by regimental medical officers were returned for regimental treatment.	
	12/6/16		Extra men (30) arrived from 1st + 2nd N.M.F. Ambs for getting huts for purpose of ~~—~~ making road in front of new hut hospital.	
	13/6/16		Huts will be in sufficiently advanced state for occupation by Field Ambulance on 19th.	
	15/6/16		Major CASTIDSTON returned to unit from Div. Sanitary School.	
	16/6/16		Attended conference of Field Amb commanders at ADMS office to consider medical arrangements in event of active operations.	

1875 Wt. W593/826 1,000,000 4/15 J.B.C. & A. A.D.S.S./Forms/C. 2118.

Confidential

1/3 N Midland Field Ambulance
RAMC TF

Army Form C. 2118.

WAR DIARY
or
INTELLIGENCE SUMMARY.
(Erase heading not required.)

Instructions regarding War Diaries and Intelligence Summaries are contained in F. S. Regs., Part II. and the Staff Manual respectively. Title pages will be prepared in manuscript.

Hour, Date, Place	Summary of Events and Information	Remarks and references to Appendices
Feb 19. 1915	The 1/3 N Mid Field Ambulance proceeded by train to GREAT HALLINGBURY PARK near BISHOP-STORTFORD & were inspected by H.M The KING returning by train the same afternoon -	
Feb. 28. 15	The unit departed from NEWPORT ESSEX 8.30 pm & entrained in two trains at	
March 1 15	ELSENHAM at 12.20 am & 2.20 am reaching SOUTHAMPTON 6 am & 8 am & detrained. Unit & horses proceeding to Rest Camp 2½ miles from SOUTHAMPTON.	
March 3. 15.	Embarked on H.M.T. INVENTOR & HMT CHYEBASSA.	

Instructions regarding War Diaries and Intelligence Summaries are contained in F.S. Regs., Part II. and the Staff Manual respectively. Title Pages will be prepared in manuscript.

WAR DIARY
or
INTELLIGENCE SUMMARY
(Erase heading not required.)

Army Form C. 2118

Place	Date	Hour	Summary of Events and Information	Remarks and references to Appendices
			before any comfort for the troops can be ensured.	
			Consulted with the R.M.O's as to provision of means for drying clothes and attending to "Foot trouble" and represented as the absolute minimum that should be done directly the men get to Rest billets from trenches, was to remove wet boots socks & puttees and dry the feet and legs thoroughly with firm friction with a towel and that the duty of seeing this carried out rested with the Company officers.	
	26/11/15		Took over from 138 Brigade chateau at R.21c.0.5 (Bethune combined sheet) and equipped it as Divisional Rest Hospital accommodating 6 officers and also moved Field Ambulance office and Headquarters to chateau.	
	29/11/15		Closed A.D.S. at ~~Kings Road~~ KINGS ROAD X.11.b handing it over to 138 Bde for rest billets.	
			Visited 137 Bde Hqrs and arranged with them to render assistance with RAMC personnel to work battalion wash houses and drying houses in their billeting area.	
			Work on improvement of quarters and transport lines proceeds steadily.	
			A.E. Hodder	
			COMM DG 3rd N. MID. FIELD AMB. R.A.M. CORPS	

1875 Wt. W593/826 1,000,000 4/15 J.B.C. & A. A.D.S.S./Forms/C. 2118.

[Instructions] regarding War Diaries and Intelligence Summaries are contained in F. S. Regs., Part II. and the Staff Manual respectively. Title pages will be prepared in manuscript.

WAR DIARY
or
INTELLIGENCE SUMMARY.
(Erase heading not required.)

Army Form C. 2118.

Place	Date	Hour	Summary of Events and Information	Remarks and references to Appendices
FOUQUIERES	20/1/18		Lieut G. R. Sharp returned from temporary duty with 1/5 N. Staffs Regt. Visited 33 Field Amb in connection with deferred moves.	
	21/1/18		Capt G. STODDART RAMC (TC) reported for duty & was taken on the strength.	
			Sent advanced party under Capt HERGA to near station at ANNEZIN.	
			Advanced party from 33 Field Amb arrived here.	
			After ~~the above~~ changes had taken place orders were received that completion of Field Amb moves was postponed till 24th.	
			Attended conference on "economy" at ADMS office in afternoon.	
	23/1/18		Capt G. D. Fairley struck off strength on re-posting.	
	24/1/18		Field Ambulance moved to ~~new~~ new quarters at ANNEZIN - school house as Hospital: billets in neighbourhood for personnel. Base 1 Corps Rest Stn handed over to 33 Field Amb. Move effected without incident.	

Army Form C. 2118

Instructions regarding War Diaries and Intelligence Summaries are contained in F. S. Regs., Part II. and the Staff Manual respectively. Title Pages will be prepared in manuscript.

WAR DIARY
or
INTELLIGENCE SUMMARY
(Erase heading not required.)

Place	Date	Hour	Summary of Events and Information	Remarks and references to Appendices
GAUDIEMPRÉ	21/3/17		Went over Hospital site at COUIN with a view to taking over at an early date: under orders from ADMS began clearing the Hospital of patients.	
	22/3/17		Completed clearing of Hospital – Moved Hdqrs of Field Amb. to BUS les ARTOIS leaving small holding party at GAUDIEMPRÉ. Notified B.R.C.S. to collect their property and handed other stores to appropriate authorities, R.E.; Town Major etc.	
~~23/3/17~~ BUS les ARTOIS	23/3/17		Withdrew holding party from GAUDIEMPRÉ, handing over site & fixtures to Town Major	
	24/3/17		Moved Hdqrs to CONTAY via BERTRANCOURT & ACHEUX.	
CONTAY	25/3/17		Moved Hdqrs to VILLERS BOCAGE via BEAUCOURT & MOLLIENS.	
VILLERS BOCAGE	26/3/17		Moved Hdqrs to SAVEUSE (5 km. S.W. of AMIENS). Personnel carried in Busses: transport ~~by~~ with brigaded transport via BERTANGLES and AILLY sur SOMME.	

1875 Wt. W593/826 1,000,000 4/15 J.B.C. & A. A.D.S.S./Forms/C. 2118.

Instructions regarding War Diaries and Intelligence Summaries are contained in F. S. Regs., Part II. and the Staff Manual respectively. Title pages will be prepared in manuscript.

WAR DIARY
or
INTELLIGENCE SUMMARY.
(*Erase heading not required.*)

Army Form C. 2118.

Place	Date	Hour	Summary of Events and Information	Remarks and references to Appendices
PREDEFIN	20/2/18		Attended ADMS conference 10 am. Out door training & lectures continued to O.R. Lt Sharp to 1/6 SSR & Lt Richard to 1/5 SSR for temporary duty. Sent 3 O.R. to HESDIGNEUL for trade test. Held practice run of 3 miles for Div. Cross Country race. A poor result only 18 out of 44 starters finishing within the time limit. Sent 1 NCO to I Army School for the 6th course. DDMS visited improvised hospital: no adverse comments. Assisted farmer Fauconnier with loan of wagon & team once for shifting manure on to fields. Charges of local civilians to men for washing clothes are extortionate 2-3 francs per set of underclothing. To counter this arranged purchase of 2 cu metres of cord wood from neighbouring village to enable clothing to be washed by unit. Fuel allowance at present 1/4 lb of coal per head per day only. The wood component of the ration viz 2 3/4 lb per head is generally lacking.	

A7092 Wt. W12839/M1293. 750,000. 1/17. D. D & L., Ltd. Forms/C2118/14.

Instructions regarding War Diaries and Intelligence Summaries are contained in F. S. Regs., Part II. and the Staff Manual respectively. Title pages will be prepared in manuscript.

WAR DIARY
or
INTELLIGENCE SUMMARY.
(Erase heading not required.)

Army Form C. 2118.

Place	Date	Hour	Summary of Events and Information	Remarks and references to Appendices
PRÉDEFIN	17/2/18		Went to Final of Divisional Football League at CRÉPY. A good turn out with massed bands but a poor match. 1/6 SSR defeated 1/5 NSR with ease contrary to expectations. Collected all P.H. Helmets for handing in, in accordance with recent G.R.O. Men at a certain billet have been acquiring eggs by unorthodox means so took steps to ensure a refund of the value of the eggs to the owner. Paid unit at normal rates.	
	18/2/18		Outdoor training continued: inspection of SBR & drill therein showed a falling off in quickness of adjustment and some inconvenience in wearing the respirator.	
	19/2/18		Route march for unit in light order. Left PRÉDEFIN 9.30 am marched via EQUIRRE doing deployment & company drill on fields as opportunity offered to CRÉPY. Thence through the woods, sweeping in extended order to TENEUR: resumed close order & marched to EPS which was reached 1.30. Halted 1 hour for meal which was served from wagon sent on in advance. Resumed march 2.30 passing over downs to HEUCHIN & so home. Reached quarters 4 pm. Hot water ready for foot washing on arrival & foot inspection carried out. All men comfortably tired.	

Instructions regarding War Diaries and Intelligence Summaries are contained in F. S. Regs., Part II. and the Staff Manual respectively. Title pages will be prepared in manuscript.

WAR DIARY
or
INTELLIGENCE SUMMARY.
(Erase heading not required.)

Army Form C. 2118.

Place	Date	Hour	Summary of Events and Information	Remarks and references to Appendices
MERICOURT		10/10/18	Hurried orders to move at night from near MAGNY to MERICOURT + attached to 139 Bde Group. Camped in fields outside MERICOURT in open - wet night + none too pleasant.	
			Since 4/10/18 3 officers } evacuated to C.C.S. - 3 O.R. wounded 32 O.R. } others gassed	
			During this move was notified to forward names of Scottish soldiers with the unit so that a flag emblem might be distributed to each on St Andrews day!! Bairnsfather might have gloried in this! GGH	
"		11/10/18	Evacuated sick &c of 139 Bde + established bivouacs &c notified of death of Pte CAPLE from gas shell (w) on 8th inst GGH	
		12/10/18	Orders from A.D.M.S. to detach from 139 Bde + establish HQrs at FRESNOY-LE-GRAND. This carried out on afternoon. Capt REID + 24 O.R. from 139 Bde reported back but to remain at short notice to return to Bde GGH	

D. D. & L., London, E.C. (A8co4) Wt W1771/M2031 750,000 5/17 Sch. 52 Forms/C2118/14

7

Instructions regarding War Diaries and Intelligence Summaries are contained in F. S. Regs., Part II. and the Staff Manual respectively. Title pages will be prepared in manuscript.

WAR DIARY
or
INTELLIGENCE SUMMARY.

(Erase heading not required.)

Army Form C. 2118.

Vol 41

Place	Date	Hour	Summary of Events and Information	Remarks and references to Appendices
	July 1918		C O N F I D E N T I A L.	140/3134
			W A R D I A R Y	
			O F	
			1/3. N O R T H M I D L A N D . F I E L D A M B U L A N C E .	
			F R O M 1/7/18. to 31/7/18.	

(A7092). Wt. W12839/M1293 75,0.0. 1/17. D. D. & L., Ltd. Forms/C.2118/14.

Instructions regarding War Diaries and Intelligence Summaries are contained in F. S. Regs., Part II. and the Staff Manual respectively. Title pages will be prepared in manuscript.

WAR DIARY
or
INTELLIGENCE SUMMARY.

(Erase heading not required.)

Army Form C. 2118.

Place	Date	Hour	Summary of Events and Information	Remarks and references to Appendices
LABEUVRIERE	25/3/18		Lieut Tabuteau & rear party of 1/3 E. Lancs Field Amb. departed to rejoin unit.	
			Major Bradley & Lieut Richard of this unit turned back from Boulogne on their way on leave reported having had an adventurous & highly uncomfortable journey up.	
	26/3/18		DDMS I Corps visited Rest Station & discussed contemplated improvements.	
			O.C. 8 San. Section visited C.R.S. in connection with new Bath installation & delousing chamber	
	27/3/18		Field Engineer I Corps inspected bath installation for replacement of which an indent had been submitted & also advised as to protection of hutments against bomb splinters with earth ramps.	
			Major Higgs & Capt Millar inspected 190 R.E. and graded into categories A & B.	
			DDMS again visited CRS and gave permission for me and O.C. 8 San. Section to arrange for the accommodation of the latter on CRS premises to our mutual satisfaction	

A5092. Wt. W12859/M1293. 750,000. 1/17. D. D & L., Ltd. Forms/C2118/14.

Army Form C. 2118

Instructions regarding War Diaries and Intelligence Summaries are contained in F. S. Regs., Part II. and the Staff Manual respectively. Title Pages will be prepared in manuscript.

WAR DIARY
or
~~INTELLIGENCE SUMMARY~~
(Erase heading not required.)

Place	Date	Hour	Summary of Events and Information	Remarks and references to Appendices
BAILLEUL aux CORNAILLES.	22/4/16		Started to clean all premises and put up necessary latrines and soak pits etc: fatigues put on to clean road channels & roads.	
Map sheet 36B. V 19 b.	24/4/16		Despatched one officer – Capt SSB Harrison – to take charge of divisional baths at ~~[illegible]~~ St Pol.	
	25/4/16		Dry weather enabled canvas to be put up to accommodate sick	
	27/4/16		Hospital inspected by D.M.S. 3rd Army: Fire ~~[illegible]~~ picquet started to patrol hospital & barn at night and fire orders remodelled to suit changed conditions.	
	28/4/16		Capt J C Harris & Lieut J N J Hartley received orders to report for temporary duty to ADMS – 25th Division	
	29/4/16		Capt F G Bennett sent from 1/1 N M F. Amb. to assist during absence of Capt Harris & Lt Hartley	
	30/4/16		Average number accommodated in Field Amb. Hospital since arrival at BAILLEUL aux CORNAILLES – 58 per diem.	

A E Hodder
Lt Col cdg

1875 Wt. W593/826 1,000,000 4/15 J.B.C. & A. A.D.S.S./Forms/C. 2118.

Army Form C. 2118.

WAR DIARY
or
INTELLIGENCE SUMMARY
(Erase heading not required.)

Instructions regarding War Diaries and Intelligence Summaries are contained in F. S. Regs., Part II. and the Staff Manual respectively. Title Pages will be prepared in manuscript.

Place	Date	Hour	Summary of Events and Information	Remarks and references to Appendices
	JUNE			
LABEUVRIERE	13		Detailed Capt. HERGA for temporary duty with 231 Bde. R.F.A. Entered 1 G.S. wagon and 1 horse ambulance and water cart for competition at 46th DIV Horse Show. Sent the Sanitary Sergeant and party of men to view the Sanitary Exhibits. D.D.M.S. I Corps visited Hospital and thought the place was much cleaner.	
	14.		Lieut. ATTENBOROUGH arrived for temporary duty from 1/1 N.M. F. Amb. By order ADMS despatched two motor ambulances to report to bearer post BULLY GRENAY	
	15.		Lieut PHIBBS returned from leave. Received congratulatory message from D.D.M.S. I Corps on the conduct of R.A.M.C. during the operations at LIEVIN on the night 8/9 June 1917.	

2449 Wt. W14957/M90 750,000 1/16 J.B.C. & A. Forms/C.2118/12.

Instructions regarding War Diaries and Intelligence Summaries are contained in F. S. Regs., Part II. and the Staff Manual respectively. Title pages will be prepared in manuscript.

Army Form C. 2118.

WAR DIARY
or
INTELLIGENCE SUMMARY.
(Erase heading not required.)

Hour, Date, Place	Summary of Events and Information	Remarks and references to Appendices
22-4-15	The DDMS also inspected a collapsible 2 wheeled Stretcher carriage invented by one of my Motor Ambulance Drivers, Sgt James by name - This appliance is very collapsible - 12 could be carried to the front by one Motor Ambulance - Their use there would greatly help the removal of wounded from near the firing line to an advanced dressing Station - Sgt James who is himself a manufacturer in WOLVERHAMPTON purchased the wheels & iron at BAILLEUL & had the machine made in the Motor Repair Shop attached to the Motor Ambulances of the Division - My opinion is that the machine is of considerable utility	
25-4-15.	Sgt Murray one of the Sergeants of the Unit - who is in private life an expert chemist & a PhD LEIPSIC detailed to assist Lt McRAE RAMC in his investigations of the "gases" & poisonous	

Instructions regarding War Diaries and Intelligence Summaries are contained in F. S. Regs., Part II. and the Staff Manual respectively. Title pages will be prepared in manuscript.

WAR DIARY
or
INTELLIGENCE SUMMARY.
(Erase heading not required.)

Army Form C. 2118.

Place	Date	Hour	Summary of Events and Information	Remarks and references to Appendices
BRUAY	21/4/18		Took steps as requisite to ensure hot baths and change of underclothing for all convalescents of first batch previous to discharge and as far as possible for all cases admitted on 22nd & subsequent days. & also arranged with Scabies centre ALLOUAGNE to disinfest blankets daily as needed.	
	22/4/18		Harassing fire occurred about 4 am. but no casualties brought here. Sent 350 blankets to ALLOUAGNE for disinfestation. Set up dressing room for wounded, to simplify working of admissions & keep them separate from sick. In evening as result of further shelling some civilian patients brought in and disposed of to S.P.O.	
	"		Epidemic of catarrhal fever extending in 138 I.B. All three battalions now affected in some degree & also 46 Batt. M. Gunners.	
	23/4/18		No fresh cases from 1/5 Leicesters but more cases from 4th Leics & 5 Lincolns & Machine gun batt. With A.D.M.S. & Major Haga visited No 8 F. Amb & then inspected Regimental aid posts & Field Amb posts on ESSARS section. And arranged details of relief with O.C. E F. Amb. 1 Officer 21 OR 2 motor Amb & motor cyclist required to staff posts.	

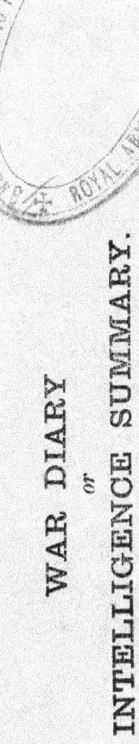

D. D. & L., London, E.C. (A8c04) Wt W1771/M2031 750,000 5/17 Sch. 52 Forms/C2118/14

Instructions regarding War Diaries and Intelligence Summaries are contained in F. S. Regs., Part II. and the Staff Manual respectively. Title pages will be prepared in manuscript.

WAR DIARY
or
INTELLIGENCE SUMMARY.
(*Erase heading not required.*)

Army Form C. 2118.

MEDICAL

Place	Date	Hour	Summary of Events and Information	Remarks and references to Appendices
BRUAY	1/9/18		1st. Lieut. E.M. MORRIS M.R.C USA reported for duty from 1/1st N.M.F. Amb. Car post established at LE TOURET X.16.d.4.8 RAP at X.17.d.4.6 ACY	
	2/9/18		Visited ADS's & RAP's together with ADMS. Capt. A.C. Reid with 13 extra bearers & 2 motor ambulances proceeded to ESSARS in anticipation of an attack. Lieut. MORRIS relieved Lieut. DOYLE at GORRE. Major HARRISON proceeded on leave Capt. BELANGER returned to 1/2nd. N.M.F. Amb. ACY	
	3/9/18		Visited ADS ESSARS. ACY.	
	4/9/18		At 5.15 AM 1/8th Sherwoods on left & 1/5th Leicesters on right advanced & occupied old British front line meeting little resistance. Eighteen extra bearers sent up to ESSARS in morning; they returned to Hdqrs. the same evening. Visited ADS ESSARS & attended ADMS conference. ACY.	
	5/9/18		Together with ADMS 46th Div. & ADMS 19th Div. visited ADS's & car posts. Two horsed ambulance waggons detailed to follow 137th Bgde. from FOUQUIERES to BURBURE in the evening. ESSARS ADS & bearer posts were handed over to 58th. F. Amb. & GORRE ADS to 57th. F. Amb. ACY	

D. D. & L., London, E.C. (A8co4) Wt W1771/M2031 750,000 5/17 Sch. 52 Forms/C2118/14

Instructions regarding War Diaries and Intelligence Summaries are contained in F. S. Regs., Part II. and the Staff Manual respectively. Title pages will be prepared in manuscript.

WAR DIARY
or
INTELLIGENCE SUMMARY.
(*Erase heading not required.*)

Army Form C. 2118.

Place	Date	Hour	Summary of Events and Information	Remarks and references to Appendices
PRÉDEFIN	20/2/18		Had practice run 3 miles. Only 44 started and only 18 of these finished within time limit.	
	21/2/18		Lectured to officers of 1/6 S. Staffs on Sick Wastage. Visited 452 & 453 Coys. A.S.C. at AUCHY au BOIS in reference to sick parade ~~taken~~ inspection. Instructed Lt Sharp temporarily doing duty at 1/6 S. Staffs to carry out this duty at 9.30 ~~pm~~ am daily.	
	22/2/18		Route march in morning 14 km. Very heavy going in places but good enough on the roads. In afternoon S.B.R. drill and exercises. Lectured to officers of 1/6 N.S.R. at 6.30 pm on Sick Wastage.	
	23/2/18		Lecture to own unit by QM on Food equivalents. Drills & physical exercises & tent pitching in morning. 3 miles run in afternoon. Number of men getting in within the time limit is very small. I regard these cross country runs for men relatively heavily clad and half trained as a great mistake from a health point of view and valueless as recreational training unless embarked on systematically as at Universities.	

Instructions regarding War Diaries and Intelligence Summaries are contained in F. S. Regs., Part II. and the Staff Manual respectively. Title Pages will be prepared in manuscript.

WAR DIARY

or

~~INTELLIGENCE SUMMARY~~

(Erase heading not required.)

Army Form C. 2118

Place	Date	Hour	Summary of Events and Information	Remarks and references to Appendices
ECOIVRES	13/4/16		Completed exchange of sections at advanced dressing posts in NEUVILLE ST VAAST and AUX RIETZ	
	16/4/16		Field Ambulance inspected by D.M.S 3rd Army.	
	18/4/16		Conducted O.C. 75 Field Amb. round Advanced Dressing Stations and regimental aid posts.	
	20/4/16		"C" section moved to BAILLEUL aux CORNAILLES to quarters about to be vacated by 75 Field Amb.	
			One section of 75 Field Amb. arrived at ECOIVRES and proceeded to AUX RIETZ and NEUVILLE ST VAAST taking over advanced dressing stations from "B" section of this unit:	
	21/4/16		Handed over Hospital and Headquarters at ECOIVRES to 75th Field Amb. and at 9 am marched to BAILLEUL aux CORNAILLES. Established Hospital in large farm – men billeted in barn in the village. Quarters good – village dirty.	

1875 Wt. W593/826 1,000,000 4/15 J.B.C. & A. A.D.S.S./Forms/C. 2118.

Instructions regarding War Diaries and Intelligence Summaries are contained in F. S. Regs., Part II. and the Staff Manual respectively. Title pages will be prepared in manuscript.

WAR DIARY
or
INTELLIGENCE SUMMARY.
(Erase heading not required.)

Army Form C. 2118.

Place	Date	Hour	Summary of Events and Information	Remarks and references to Appendices
FRESNOY-LE-GRAND	19/10/18		Capt REID + all bearers from A.D.S. returned - No casualties. Sjepts BILL + NUTTALL awarded M.M. for gallantry about 29th Sept. Several H.E. shells fell near Ambce HQrs - One man of H.T. being killed. (T/213517 Dvr. SMITH J.H.) SGH	
"	20.10.18		Uneventful day - Usual routine. 24 Bearers, tempy attached to 137 Bde battalions returned to unit. SGH	
"	21/10/18		Capt ELLENBOGEN J. RAMC } reported for duty. " GILLIES D. " } SGH	
			Usual routine.	
	22/10/18		Advised M M awarded to A/cpl White B.A } RAMC; Pte Walker B. }; Pte Kay J. B. M.T. A.S.C	

D. D. & L., London, E.C. (A8c04) Wt W1771/M2031 750,000 5/17 Sch. 52 Forms/C2118/14

WAR DIARY
or
INTELLIGENCE SUMMARY
(Erase heading not required.)

Army Form C. 2118

Place	Date	Hour	Summary of Events and Information	Remarks and references to Appendices
La Herlière.	17.10.16.		B. section relieved C. section at ~~Berles~~ BERLES C. section returned to LAHERLIERE for duty at Hospital	
	22.10.16		Dr Preston having reported here from 1st N.M.F. Amb. is taken on the strength of the Unit.	
	24	10.16.	Lt Phibbs left the Unit to day for temporary duty with 1st/8th Notts + Derbys Reg.	
	25	10.16.	Lieut Waterhouse reported here for duty to day + is taken on strength of the Unit. This officer has no previous military experience.	
	26 27		Extra Bearers + Cars sent to Berles on both nights in case of casualties while gas was carried in. During the last fortnight improvements have been made to Dressing Station + Dug out at Berles to make them stronger + gas proof	

Instructions regarding War Diaries and Intelligence Summaries are contained in F. S. Regs., Part II. and the Staff Manual respectively. Title Pages will be prepared in manuscript.

WAR DIARY
or
INTELLIGENCE SUMMARY
(Erase heading not required.)

Army Form C. 2118

1/3 NM Fd Amb
Vol 21

MEDICAL

Place	Date	Hour	Summary of Events and Information	Remarks and references to Appendices
	1/11/16		Field Ambulance moved from BREVILLERS to OUTREBOIS under orders of 137 Infy. Brigade. [Ref. sheet LENS 11 1/100 000] Routine collection of sick carried out - cases evacuated to 19 C.C.S. DOULLENS. Distance of march 8 miles.	
LINE OF MARCH	3/11/16		Moved from OUTREBOIS to GAPENNES (17 miles). No men fell out. A long march well borne - all transport kept well closed up notwithstanding some severe hills.	
	4/11/16		Found quarters for reception of limited number of patients at QUESNOY FARM [Ref. sheet ABBEVILLE - 1/100 000] 1.5 Km. N.W. of G. in GAPENNES. - Set about erecting vapour baths for use of 137 I.B.	
	5/11/16		Lt PHIBBS rejoined from temporary duty with 8th Sherwood Foresters.	
	6/11/16		Training begun in accordance with scheme set out by ADMS. Riding school instituted for newly joined officers.	
	7/11/16		Lieut E. T. WILLANS reported for duty. - This officer has had 14 mos experience in Egypt with a Field Amb. on SALONIKA front.	

1875 Wt. W593/826 1,000,000 4/15 J.B.C. & A. A.D.S.S./Forms/C. 2118.

Army Form C. 2118

Instructions regarding War Diaries and Intelligence Summaries are contained in F. S. Regs., Part II. and the Staff Manual respectively. Title Pages will be prepared in manuscript.

WAR DIARY
or
INTELLIGENCE SUMMARY

(Erase heading not required.)

3RD NORTH MIDLAND FIELD AMBULANCE ROYAL ARMY MEDICAL CORPS.

Place	Date	Hour	Summary of Events and Information	Remarks and references to Appendices
LA HERLIÈRE	13/7/16		Sent an officer & 80 OR up to A.D.S. 10pm as last night with same result.	
	14/7/16		Made preparations again for a show opposite our own sector — nothing unusual occurred in way of casualties. Inspected F. Amb. Transport	
	15/7/16		Visited HQrs 230 Bde RFA and completed arrangements for evacuation and evacuation of sick & wounded from batteries of centre group RA.	
	17/7/16		Lieut C. L. HAWKINS (T.C.) reported for duty with F. Amb. " C. ROBERTSON (T.C.) "	
			Inspected Personnel of Bearer & Transport sections	
	18/7/16		Visited N. Staff aid post and HQrs 137 I.B. and fixed up arrangements for supply of medical stores to 137 Bde units.	
			Inspected Bearer section again 3.30pm	
	19/7/16		Inspected bearers again 3.30pm.	
	20/7/16		Inspected Transport dismounted 9 am	
			" " vehicles & harness 3.30pm	
	22.7.16		G.O.C. 46 Div inspected F. Amb. today.	

1875 Wt. W593/826 1,000,000 4/15 J.B.C. & A. A.D.S.S./Forms/C. 2118.

Army Form C. 2118

Instructions regarding War Diaries and Intelligence Summaries are contained in F. S. Regs., Part II. and the Staff Manual respectively. Title Pages will be prepared in manuscript.

WAR DIARY
or
INTELLIGENCE SUMMARY
(Erase heading not required.)

Place	Date	Hour	Summary of Events and Information	Remarks and references to Appendices
LA HERLIÈRE	8/9/16		Capt H GREY detached for temporary duty with VIIth Reserve Park.	
		10pm	Reinforced A.D.S. BERLES with extra bearers & transport in view of small operation on this sector of front. Their services were not needed.	
			Took over Sanitary supervision of N.M. Mobile Vety section.	
	9/9/16		Divisional Disinfecting Station at LA CAUCHIE opened today staffed by personnel of this unit; provision made for dealing with 100 contacts per day. If not needed for this purpose at any time the Russian Bath is available & will bath a Battalion per day	

Confidential

Instructions regarding War Diaries and Intelligence Summaries are contained in F. S. Regs., Part II. and the Staff Manual respectively. Title pages will be prepared in manuscript.

WAR DIARY
or
INTELLIGENCE SUMMARY.
(*Erase heading not required.*)

Army Form C. 2118.

1/3rd North Midland Field Ambulance R.A.M.C.T.F.

Hour, Date, Place	Summary of Events and Information	Remarks and references to Appendices
3 - 4 - 15	Marched to farm on the left of the road which runs from the BAILLEUL - ARMENTIERS Road to NEUVE EGLISE + 1 mile from the latter place - Took over the advanced Dressing Station there from the 17th FIELD AMBULANCE. A section of the Field Ambulance (3rd N. Midland) opened there + at night collected wounded from Regimental Aid posts at The DRESSING FARM + St QUENTINS CABARET - Billeted rest of unit here -	/
5 - 4 - 15	Sent one officer + 10 NCO's + men of B section to take over the Infectious Hospital in BAILLEUL - One officer + 5 men of the same section took over Divisional Baths at PLAS PLICHON BAILLEUL	
11 - 4 - 15.	Handed over the Baths in BAILLEUL - One officer + 12 men took over the STAFFS BRIGADE baths in NEUVE EGLISE =	
12 - 4 - 15	TOOK over from the 15th Field Ambulance Divisional Convalescent Hospital - capable of accomodating 100 cases - at 32 RUE DE MUSEE DE PUYDT BAILLEUL	

Instructions regarding War Diaries and Intelligence Summaries are contained in F. S. Regs., Part II. and the Staff Manual respectively. Title pages will be prepared in manuscript.

WAR DIARY
or
INTELLIGENCE SUMMARY.
(Erase heading not required.)

Army Form C. 2118.

Place	Date	Hour	Summary of Events and Information	Remarks and references to Appendices
			to assist Major LANE M.C. Hdqrs together with Major Harrison MC & Capt Bradley returned to VENDELLES The captures made by the 46th Division included the villages of BELLENGLISE, MAGNY LA FOSSE & LEHAUCOURT, 4,200 prisoners, 40 field guns, two batteries of heavy guns, 300 machine guns & numerous trench mortars. The prisoners did good work in bringing down wounded & greatly relieved the strain on the stretcher bearers. Touch was lost with nearly all the RMO's very early in the attack; this was owing to the dense fog which made it impossible to see more than a few yards. Most excellent work was done by the bearer officers later in the day in finding the RMO's & re-establishing contact A C Turner LIEUT.-COLONEL COMM'DG. 3rd N. MID FIELD AMB R. A. M. CORPS.	

D. D & L., London, E.C.
(A8c04) Wt W1771/M2031 750,000 5/17 Sch. 52 Forms/C2118/14

Instructions regarding War Diaries and Intelligence Summaries are contained in F. S. Regs., Part II. and the Staff Manual respectively. Title pages will be prepared in manuscript.

WAR DIARY
or
INTELLIGENCE SUMMARY.
(Erase heading not required.)

Army Form C. 2118.

Hour, Date, Place	Summary of Events and Information	Remarks and references to Appendices
28 – 4 – 15.	Summary for 24 hours up to 6 pm – Admissions 106 Remained from 27.4.15 – 12 – Transfers 84 Deaths 6 – Prisoner 1. (transferred) Remaining 30.	
29 – 4 – 15.	Patients in:- Admissions 51 Remained 30 Transfers 16 Deaths 3 Remaining 62	
30 – 4 – 15	Sgt James A.S.C. Motor Driver attached proceeded to G.H.Q with ~~a~~ a Wheeled Collapsible Stretcher Carrier – This carrier was suggested by Captn J. Miller of the unit + worked out by Sgt James – Sgt James is a manufacturer in WOLVERHAMPTON + was instrumental in raising one Gift Motor Ambulance for the unit from the town of WOLVERHAMPTON + enlisted specially to drive the Car –	

Instructions regarding War Diaries and Intelligence Summaries are contained in F. S. Regs., Part II. and the Staff Manual respectively. Title Pages will be prepared in manuscript.

WAR DIARY
or
INTELLIGENCE SUMMARY
(Erase heading not required.)

Army Form C. 2118

Place	Date	Hour	Summary of Events and Information	Remarks and references to Appendices
MAISON ROLAND	24/7/16		Move of Field Ambulance postponed. Received 8 reinforcements.	
	25/7/16		Moved Field Ambulance Headquarters to MESNIL-DOMQUEUR. Average number of patients in hospital at LONGVILLERS - 65. Received 1 reinforcement.	
MESNIL-DOMQUEUR	26/7/16		Provided 2 men for water & RAMC duties with 137 Bde Machine Gun Coy	
	27/7/16		Measles revealed in one of the drivers who arrived as reinforcement on 24th. According to his statement measles is prevalent among the details at Base at ROUEN. - Issued instructions as regards segregation of contacts - see App 2. - and evacuated patient to Highland C.C.S. - Notified 137 Brigade of the occurrence as reinforcements were received by them at same time who travelled up in close contact with the driver who developed the disease.	
	29/7/16		A and C sections of Field Amb. moved under orders of G.O.C 137 Bde to billets at MONPLAISIR - near HEM. (ref map sheet - LENS 11 1/100000). The move was accomplished without casualty of any kind. Motor Ambulances employed fully in transporting lightly sick of 137 Bde to their new billets. B section by order of ADMS immobilised for 3 days to dispose of sick in hospital at LONGVILLERS and close the Hospital.	

A E Hodder Lt Col

LIEUT.-COLONEL. COMM'DG. 3RD N. MID FIELD AMB R. A. M. CORPS.

1875 Wt. W593/826 1,000,000 4/15 J.B.C. & A. A.D.S.S./Forms/C. 2118.

Instructions regarding War Diaries and Intelligence Summaries are contained in F. S. Regs., Part II. and the Staff Manual respectively. Title pages will be prepared in manuscript.

WAR DIARY
or
INTELLIGENCE SUMMARY.
(Erase heading not required.)

Army Form C. 2118.

Place	Date	Hour	Summary of Events and Information	Remarks and references to Appendices
HESDIGNEUL	18/6/18		Continuation of bivouac building for men + bomb proof walls to horse lines	ACH
	19/6/18		For raid by 1/5 Notts + Derby Regt. despatched a further 16 men + 1 N.C.O. to Essars sector – 8 of these bearers at disposal of Battn M.O. – Evacuation of casualties rapidly carried out – Pte Cutler L.C. slightly wounded, also Pte King of 1/2 NMFA Sergt. Holyland + Pte McCUSKER ~~evacuated~~ to C.C.S. "Sick"	ACH
–	20/6/18		LT McCREA returned to duty from 1/1 N.M.F.A. Six men lent to No 6 C.C.S. ~~there~~ to be trained in nursing duties.	ACH
	21/6/18		Unit paid. The usual popular parade	ACH
	22/6/18		"C" Section relieved "A" section at GORRE – uneventful. Lt CHARNLEY returned from 1st Army RAMC School Sergt. MILLARD + 25 O.R began building new R.A.P. ESSARS.	ACH
	23/6/18		LT CHARNLEY to 1/5 NOTTS + DERBY Regt for temporary duty. Notified CAPT REID's leave extended to 3/7/18 Usual night working party for ESSARS R.A.P. Normal ESSARS relief.	ACH

D. D. & L., London, E.C.
(A8c04) Wt W1771/M2031 750,000 5/17 Sch. 52 Forms/C2118/14

Army Form C. 2118

WAR DIARY
or
INTELLIGENCE SUMMARY
(Erase heading not required.)

Instructions regarding War Diaries and Intelligence Summaries are contained in F. S. Regs., Part II. and the Staff Manual respectively. Title Pages will be prepared in manuscript.

3RD NORTH MIDLAND FIELD AMBULANCE ROYAL ARMY MEDICAL CORPS.

Place	Date	Hour	Summary of Events and Information	Remarks and references to Appendices
LA HERLIÈRE	25.7.16		Capt. J C Harris of the unit injured by being thrown from his horse & evacuated to no 20 C.C.S.	
	26.7.16		Inspected Transport in marching order.	
	29.7.16		Visited Hqrs 137 IB and 230 Bde R.F.A to enquire into working of medical arrangements.	
			A section relieved B section in charge of A.D.S. at BERLES au BOIS.	

A E Hodder
Lt Col.
LIEUT.-COLONEL,
COMM'DG. 3rd N. MID FIELD AMB
R. A. M. CORPS.

Instructions regarding War Diaries and Intelligence Summaries are contained in F. S. Regs., Part II. and the Staff Manual respectively. Title Pages will be prepared in manuscript.

WAR DIARY
or
INTELLIGENCE SUMMARY
(Erase heading not required.)

Army Form C. 2118

Place	Date	Hour	Summary of Events and Information	Remarks and references to Appendices
LA HERLIÈRE	14/10/16		Village of BERLES au BOIS was shelled ~~for~~ by enemy from 7am to 1.45pm. – 23 wounded were treated at A.D.S. there – one motor ambulance loaded with wounded was slightly injured by a shell exploding close by & one of the patients got a further slight wound – No material damage done to Field Ambulance quarters & no RAMC injured. This is the third day in four that this village has been shelled – as it appears to be developing into a habit, the A.D.S. party will cease to use the upper parts of buildings for a time and retire to cellars.	
			L/Cpl. Hawkins is struck off strength – permanently appointed to 1/5 S. Staffs.	

Instructions regarding War Diaries and Intelligence Summaries are contained in F. S. Regs., Part II. and the Staff Manual respectively. Title Pages will be prepared in manuscript.

WAR DIARY
or
INTELLIGENCE SUMMARY
(Erase heading not required.)

Army Form C. 2118

Place	Date	Hour	Summary of Events and Information	Remarks and references to Appendices
LA HERLIÈRE	14/8/16		Cases to the north of No 3 post will be evacuated if possible down NEWARK St straight to RAVINE. Cases in the neighbourhood of No 3 post [Trench 93 bay 4 to Trench 92 bay 6] will be evacuated down sap (NITRATE St) to support line & thence to NEVERENDING LANE - Cases on southern side of Bearer post 8 will be evacuated along 91 street into NEVERENDING LANE. Each bearer will carry 1 shell dressing & one tin box of ammonia capsules, and each N.C.O. a shell dressing haversack. Transport — On receipt of warning - 2 horsed ambulances and 2 G.S. wagons will proceed to rendezvous at W 14 central whence they will proceed to ADS BERLES as called for. Each wagon orderly will be responsible for 1 G.S. wagon in addition to 1 horsed ambulance. Six motor ambulances will proceed at 10 minute intervals to BERLES where they will remain under cover close to ADS till required. References. Trench map RANSART 1/10000 and France 51c 1/40000	

1875 Wt. W593/826 1,000,000 4/15 J.B.C. & A. A.D.S.S./Forms/C. 2118.

Instructions regarding War Diaries and Intelligence Summaries are contained in F. S. Regs., Part II. and the Staff Manual respectively. Title Pages will be prepared in manuscript.

WAR DIARY
or
INTELLIGENCE SUMMARY
(Erase heading not required.)

Army Form C. 2118

Place	Date	Hour	Summary of Events and Information	Remarks and references to Appendices
LABOURSE	25/7/17		DDMS I Corps visited Main dressing Station LABOURSE and A.D.S. PHILOSOPHE. I visited advanced bearer posts and regimental aid posts at St George, Halfway House, Wings Way and Port Street. Requested Regimental MOs in sector concerned to submit suggestions for improvements in the system of evacuation, if any occur to them. Found bearer posts fairly satisfactory as regards protection and the new post on right sector near Port Street well advanced towards completion. This will be a Field Ambulance Post and not an R.A.P. The main communication trenches such as 10th avenue, Wings way & Port Street are in bad order and contain a good deal of water though there has been little rain. The carrying is therefore difficult & slow. By night it is	

2449 Wt. W14957/M90 750,000 1/16 J.B.C. & A. Forms/C.2118/12.

(Ref: Bethune Combined Sheet 1/40000 and Trench Maps LOOS 1/10000)

Army Form C. 2118.

Instructions regarding War Diaries and Intelligence Summaries are contained in F. S. Regs., Part II. and the Staff Manual respectively. Title pages will be prepared in manuscript.

WAR DIARY
or
INTELLIGENCE SUMMARY.
(Erase heading not required.)

Place	Date	Hour	Summary of Events and Information	Remarks and references to Appendices
BRUAY	31/8/18		Together with ADMS visited ADS ESSARS & RAP's. Arranged for a Ford motor ambulance to be stationed at bearer post at LES FACONS (X.15.a.7.5) to assist in evacuating casualties. RAP of 1/6th Sherwoods advanced from LOISNE to LE TOURET X.17.d.40.60; casualties evacuated to ADS ESSARS instead of GORRE. B section relieved A section at ESSARS.	

A. C. Turner
LIEUT.-COLONEL
COMM'DG. 1/3rd N. MID FIELD AMB.
R. A. M. CORPS.

D. D. & L., London, E.C.
(A8c04) Wt W1771/M2031 750,000 5/17 Sch. 52 Forms/C2118/14

Appendix I to War Diary Aug. 1917.

I CORPS MAIN DRESSING STATION.

On notification being received that large casualties may be expected the following measures will be put into force:-

A. GENERAL- (1) All patients remaining, including officers, will be disposed of to C.C.S. or C.R.S., or their wagon lines for light duty.

(2) All beds on ground floor will be removed and stacked outside, matting, etc: rolled up and rooms cleared entirely.

(3) Ward No:1 will be equipped as a Dressing Room in which 3 Medical Officers may work simultaneously.

(4) Wards No:2 and 4 will be sued to accommodate patients before they are dressed: the more serious cases being put in the former, the less so in the latter.

(5) The present Dressing Room will be sued as a Reception Room and for making the preliminary records, which will later be passed to the A & D Book clerks working in the Orderly Room.

Permission having previously been obtained for their use, the forms and desks will be removed from school rooms on the ground floor at the west end of the building and these rooms used to accommodate cases that have been passed for evacuation.

M.A.C. cars will come into School yard and clear from the doors of these rooms.

(7) Wounded officers will be received into No:2.

(8) The Bath House will be used as a temporary Mortuary and a reliable private put in charge.

(9) As far as possible all personnel will be disposed so that each individual gets 8 hours complete rest out of 24.

B. CLERICAL- Sergt: Fellows will directail recording and clerical work.

(1) A.F.W.3210 will be used for all cases.

(2) All Field Medical Cards must be made out exactly so that in the case of every patient, full information is available at a glance to Receiving Officer at C.C.Stn.

(3) Clerks must be able at any moment to give information to A.D.M.S., or D.D.M.S., regarding numbers received, evacuated, and remaining. Cases will be shewn as evacuated to No: M.A.C.

C. 'Q' Department- (1) Lt: and Q.Master J.King will make all the usual arrangements for supplying drinks and suitable food to patients, and will dispose of cooking staff suitably.

(2) Under his direction the Corporal i/c Packstore will prepare to deal with large quantities of rifles and equipment: and a N.C.O., will be detailed to deal with belongings of patients dying in hospital.

(3) Drinks to be available in Evacuation wards as well as 2 and 4.

(4) An urgent indent for dressings will be put in by Pte: Jukes who will maintain them and keep them up to requirements.

D. RECEIVING- An officer will see all cases on admission and will direct them to the appropriate wards.

He will be in charge of all bearers on his sid e and see that no delay occurs in unloading cars, and that the proper exchanges of blankets, etc: are effected.

EVACUATING- A senior N.C.O., will be in charge of evacuations and will direct the bearers on his side.

He will remove the serial number from each patient before he goes into the M.A.C. car and hand in the checks to A & D Book clerks.

Also he will see that hot water bottles etc: are available as required for collapsed cases and that blankets are received in exchange for outgoing ones.

Blankets will be folded round patients in the manner set out in directions posted in hospital.

E. NURSING- Sergt: Major will carefully inform all men of their duties as detailed in the operation schedule of duties whcih will be published, and ensure that each man clearly understands his part, and that there is no overlapping.

He will exercise general supervision of all nursing arrangements and see that bed pans, urinals, feeding cups are available in all wards.

He will maintainan adequate supply of stretchers and blankets on receiving side of hospital, and will see that all soiled clothing and

Instructions regarding War Diaries and Intelligence Summaries are contained in F. S. Regs., Part II. and the Staff Manual respectively. Title pages will be prepared in manuscript.

WAR DIARY
or
INTELLIGENCE SUMMARY.
(Erase heading not required.)

Army Form C. 2118.

Place	Date	Hour	Summary of Events and Information	Remarks and references to Appendices
HESDIGNEUL	10/5/18		Notified 1pm by ADMS that medical arrangements for night of 9/10 will be repeated for night 10/11.	
			Got rid of a vicious draught horse that we have been unable to work for 6 months - a bad kicker in harness.	
			At 7pm an advanced party of an American Engineer Regt arrived near the camp so invited the two officers in charge to dinner & established friendly relations with our allies.	
			At 10pm all RAMC parties in position ~~of~~ for stand to, as last night. Our own heavies pretty active but enemy artillery reply negligeable.	
	11/5/18		5.30am. situation normal so RAMC stood down and dispersed to their normal stations.	
			Decided to collar for RAMC as emergency dressing station the farm buildings cellar at F13c.5.9 occupied by a holding party of 1 NCO & 4 men to hold it and put it in order: strengthening it as necessary & possible with material at hand and. This party would also be ~~at hand~~ on the spot rather to carry in with walking wounded if necessary.	
			Posted 1 NCO at Speedwell Spur E22 d 1.8 on light Railway to ~~[illegible]~~ accompany outgoing freight train to Green Spur & return with patients from La Pierrette.	

D. D. & L., London, E.C.
(A8004) Wt W1771/M2031 750,000 5/17 Sch. 52 Forms/C2118/14

Instructions regarding War Diaries and Intelligence Summaries are contained in F. S. Regs., Part II. and the Staff Manual respectively. Title Pages will be prepared in manuscript.

WAR DIARY
or
INTELLIGENCE SUMMARY
(Erase heading not required.)

Army Form C. 2118

Place	Date	Hour	Summary of Events and Information	Remarks and references to Appendices
AIX-NOULETTE	19/4/17		Field Amb moved to AIX-NOULETTE: quarters in Brewery at R22a.7.2. (sheet 36B.) Accommodation in cellars good.	
	20/4/17		Inspected ADS & bearer post in LIEVIN. ~~Iam~~ neither satisfactory as protection from shell fire practically nil: work of improvement put in hand at once.	
			Reconnoitred routes of evacuation & submitted report to ADMS.	
	21/4/17		Capt G D FAIRLIE rejoined from leave.	
	22/4/17		Visited LIEVIN and found affairs at ADS & bearer post much improved. Reinforced ADS with 16 additional men.	
			Situation of bearer post M27b4.3 CITE de ROLLENCOURT.	
			ADS M28b7.2. White House LIEVIN	
			also bearer post at R29b3.0. BETHUNE-ARRAS road.	
			this last to deal with casualties among artillery & Road construction parties in neighbourhood.	
			Lt QMr J King reported from leave.	
			Capt J. MILLER departed on leave	
	23/4/17		Main dressing station fairly busy in morning owing to casualties incurred by 139 Bde. in attack on enemy. Visited A.D.S. in afternoon to inquire into working of evacuation	

Instructions regarding War Diaries and Intelligence Summaries are contained in F. S. Regs., Part II. and the Staff Manual respectively. Title pages will be prepared in manuscript.

WAR DIARY
or
INTELLIGENCE SUMMARY.
(Erase heading not required.)

Army Form C. 2118.

Place	Date	Hour	Summary of Events and Information	Remarks and references to Appendices
FRESNOY LE GRAND	3.2.19		Capt. D. GILLIES returned from leave. ACY	
"	5.2.19		Major E.J. BRADLEY M.C. proceeded on leave. ACY	
"	7.2.19		Capt. D. GILLIES evacuated to no. 12 CCS sick. ACY	
"	16.2.19		Proceeded to MAUROIS to reconnoitre new billeting area. Village occupied by artillery of 18th Division. No accommodation. ACY	
"	21.2.19		Lieut. CHAPELL, dentist, arrived for temporary duty with this unit. ACY	
"	26.2.19		Called on ADMS. Inspected sanitary arrangements of 216 POW Camp BOHAIN & of 302 POW Camp FRESNOY. ACY	
	27.2.19		Inspected cookhouses, water carts, & latrines of 1/5th. S. Staff. Regt. Called on ADMS re demobilisation. ACY	
	28.2.19		Inspected cookhouses, water-carts, & latrines of 1/6th. S. Staff. Regt. ACY	

A C Turner
LIEUT.-COL. COMMDG.
1/3rd N. MID. FIELD AMB.
R. A. M. C.

D. D. & L., London, E.C.
(A8c04) Wt W1771/M2031 750,000 5/17 Sch. 52 Forms/C2118/14

Army Form C. 2118

Instructions regarding War Diaries and Intelligence Summaries are contained in F. S. Regs., Part II and the Staff Manual respectively. Title Pages will be prepared in manuscript.

WAR DIARY
or
INTELLIGENCE SUMMARY
(Erase heading not required.)

1/3 N M Fd Amb

Vol 22

MEDICAL

Place	Date	Hour	Summary of Events and Information	Remarks and references to Appendices
BREVILLERS	1/12/16		Remaining in quarters, taking in Scabies cases from 137 Bde units in neighbourhood – accommodation quite unfit for patients. Vapour bath got going for them but no means available for disinfecting clothing. Arranged for carriage to Oculist No 6 Stationary Hosp by M.A.C. cars of short sighted men of 137 Bde.	
	4/12/16		Inspected quarters at ST AMAND proposed for occupation by Field Amb. – this is not good – two decent iron huts holding 30 each and 5 canvas roofed huts which let in wet freely – No possibility at all of accommodating patients and accommodation in the canvas covered huts is not good enough for the season of the year. No billets as yet available for officers – No accommodation for Transport. Capt Miller with one section (A) departed to take over advanced dressing stations at FONQUEVILLERS and BIENVILLERS. 1 Section of 1/2 West Riding Field Amb came into BREVILLERS.	
	5/12/16		Sent Capt Strange to ST AMAND in connection with Transport accommodation & billets for officers. Former to be fixed up at GAUDIEMPRÉ – billets for officers found.	

1875 Wt. W593/826 1,000,000 4/15 J.B.C. & A. A.D.S.S./Forms/C. 2118.

WAR DIARY
or
INTELLIGENCE SUMMARY.
(Erase heading not required.)

Army Form C. 2118.

Instructions regarding War Diaries and Intelligence Summaries are contained in F. S. Regs., Part II. and the Staff Manual respectively. Title pages will be prepared in manuscript.

Place	Date	Hour	Summary of Events and Information	Remarks and references to Appendices
ANNEZIN (P de C)	7/2/18		Had 1 riding horse cast for remount reasons & received fresh animal in exchange. 2 Sunbeam motor ambulances met with mishap yesterday on road & have had to go into workshop for repair. Capt E.C. BRADLEY returned from temporary duty with 1/6 N.S.R. and resumed command of "C" section.	
	8/2/18		Holding party of 1 Sergt & 2 men from 2/1 Wessex Field Amb. arrived and took over stores pertaining to Field Amb. site.	
	9/2/18		Field Ambulance marched with 137 Brigade group to quarters for night at NÉDON via LAPUGNOY - LOZINGHEM - AUCHEL. G.O.C. 46 Div. inspected column en route & expressed his satisfaction with the turn-out & march discipline.	
NÉDON (P de C.)	10/2/18		Field Ambulance resumed line of march 10 a.m. the starting point NÉDONCHELLE. arrived at quarters PRÉDEFIN. 3 p.m. Column again inspected by G.O.C. & again satisfactory. Billets scattered - one building taken into use as a hospital with accommodation for about 50 cases on stretchers.	
PRÉDEFIN (P de C)	11/2/18		Field Ambulance acting as detention hospital for divisional receiving house for all special cases. No resting & cleaning equipment: C section detailed for all the hospital duties.	

A7092 Wt. W12839/M1293. 750,000. 1/17. D. D & L., Ltd. Forms/C2118/14.

Instructions regarding War Diaries and Intelligence Summaries are contained in F. S. Regs., Part II. and the Staff Manual respectively. Title Pages will be prepared in manuscript.

WAR DIARY
or
INTELLIGENCE SUMMARY
(Erase heading not required.)

Army Form C. 2118

Place	Date	Hour	Summary of Events and Information	Remarks and references to Appendices
	12/12/15		Completed exchange of horses H.D. for horses LD & mules. Completed total — Mules — 43 Horses (LD) — 14 " Riding — 14 " LD — 1 } attached. " Riding — 4 }	
	14/12/15		Received reinforcements from Guards and XIXth divisions for RAMC and Transport sections.	
	18/12/15		Received 6 drivers ASC as muleteers.	
	19/12/15		Field Ambulance moved quarters to billets along BUSNES — S[t] VENANT Road P20b 2.8 — P14b 7.2 (BETHUNE combined sheet). March effected without mishap or incident — Billets occupied are satisfactory generally, but the Field Ambulance is a good deal scattered as no one billet will accommodate a whole section.	
BUSNES - S[t] VENANT Road	20/12/15		All sections occupied with internal economy, chiefly in preparing wagons [illegible] [illegible] for long journey & completing equipment.	

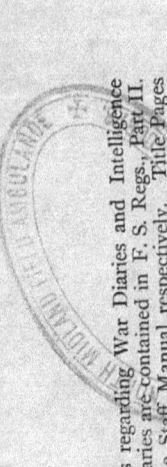

Instructions regarding War Diaries and Intelligence Summaries are contained in F. S. Regs., Part II. and the Staff Manual respectively. Title pages will be prepared in manuscript.

WAR DIARY
or
INTELLIGENCE SUMMARY.
(Erase heading not required.)

Army Form C. 2118.

Place	Date	Hour	Summary of Events and Information	Remarks and references to Appendices

MEDICAL. CONFIDENTIAL.

WAR DIARY

OF

1/3rd N.M.Field Ambulance.

1st December 1918 to 31st December 1918.

(A7092). Wt. W12839/M1293. 750,000. 1/17. D. D. & L., Ltd. Forms/C.2118/14.

Instructions regarding War Diaries and Intelligence Summaries are contained in F. S. Regs., Part II. and the Staff Manual respectively. Title Pages will be prepared in manuscript.

WAR DIARY
or
~~INTELLIGENCE~~ SUMMARY
(Erase heading not required.)

Army Form C. 2118

Place	Date	Hour	Summary of Events and Information	Remarks and references to Appendices
IVERGNY	6/3/16		Arrived 1pm after leaving BAILLEUL aux CORNAILLES at 8am. No mishaps on road - no men fell out - distance 12 miles. Capt Starrs and 'A' section move to Advanced Dressing Station at FONQUEVILLERS. E27a 7.4 [Sheet 57D]	
	7/3/16		Moved to GAUDIEMPRÉ in wake of 139 I.B. Motor cars hard worked carrying non marchers of 139 I.B. number carried including those of 1st Monmouth Rgt 118 - Mileage run by cars 692. This was effected without mishap. Quarters in GUADIEMPRÉ D16 8.3 poor: insufficient accommodation for personnel & none for patients	
	8/3/16		Erected all available canvas for patients in orchard of farm: inspected Advanced Dressing Station at FONQUEVILLERS: Surroundings as a whole distinctly theatrical more picturesque than safe.	

Instructions regarding War Diaries and Intelligence Summaries are contained in F. S. Regs., Part II. and the Staff Manual respectively. Title pages will be prepared in manuscript.

WAR DIARY
or
INTELLIGENCE SUMMARY.
(Erase heading not required.)

Army Form C. 2118.

Place	Date	Hour	Summary of Events and Information	Remarks and references to Appendices
PREDEFIN	24/7/18		Rest day for all ranks:- hair cutting & cleaning of kit the order of the day. Football team played Tank Corps Workshops at ERIN	
	25/7/18		A very wet morning: outdoor work hardly possible. Weather improved in afternoon & we were able to put in some physical training.	
	26/7/18		Parade of RAMC in marching order for inspection. On the whole satisfactory. Tent pitching followed & occupied the remainder of the morning. In the afternoon squad drill & physical jerks. ~~Lect~~ CO & Capt Herga (?) attended lecture at noon at I Army School on the Rôle of the Rest Station. At 4 pm CO lectured on Sick Wastage to officers of M.G.C. Lt Richard returned from temporary duty with 1/5 S.S.R.	
	27/7/18		Attended ADMS weekly conference at 10 am. Subjects discussed - inspecting rooms (?), recent GRO affecting acting ranks & small matter of economy. Men all bathed at LISBOURG. CO lectured to 1/5 S. Staffs Rgt 5.30 pm	

Instructions regarding War Diaries and Intelligence Summaries are contained in F. S. Regs., Part II. and the Staff Manual respectively. Title pages will be prepared in manuscript.

WAR DIARY
or
INTELLIGENCE SUMMARY.
(Erase heading not required.)

Army Form C. 2118.

Place	Date	Hour	Summary of Events and Information	Remarks and references to Appendices
ANNEZIN	29/1/18		Personnel other than those employed in Hospital duty route marched with all available wagons in morning. Carried out Recreational training (football) in afternoon.	
	30/1/18		Last night about 12.15 am hostile bombing attack by aeroplanes in immediate neighbourhood followed by bursts of machine gun fire from the attacking planes.	
			Attended ADMS conference at 10 am: subjects discussed 1) Protection of hutments & stables from bombing attacks 2) Reduction of RAMC divisional establishments 3) Sphere of duties of Field Ambulance Commanders as SMOs of Brigades.	
			In afternoon made sanitary visitation to 1/5 and 1/6 S. Staffs Rgts. Personnel employed all day in making protection to Horse standings.	
	31/1/18		Small party did some sanitary work in the village which was badly needed. Further work in horse standings carried out. Turned out ceremonial funeral party to attend burials of Railway operators killed in enemy air raid on 28/1/18	

16

Instructions regarding War Diaries and Intelligence Summaries are contained in F. S. Regs., Part II. and the Staff Manual respectively. Title pages will be prepared in manuscript.

WAR DIARY
or
INTELLIGENCE SUMMARY.
(Erase heading not required.)

Army Form C. 2118.

1/3 N M Fd Amb

Vol 36

MEDICAL

Place	Date	Hour	Summary of Events and Information	Remarks and references to Appendices
ANNEZIN	1/2/18		Personnel other than Hospital section employed in morning on extending protection to Horse standings. In afternoon squad drill and physical exercises carried out. Inspection of fire appliances made & steps taken to increase the number of fire buckets by 10. Garden plot for the Field Ambulance occupying these premises started at E9a.7.6 ANNEZIN. Working party of 12 O.R. sent to 22 C.C.S.	
	2/2/18		Some bombing by E.A. in evening but none near by.	
	3/2/18		More bombing by E.A. about 6.30 am.	
	4/2/18		Visited HEUCHIN with the prospect of relieving Field Ambulance at present occupying that site. Accommodation fair for 50-60 patients. Billets for personnel not good; fixed sanitary appliances nil. Civilian stables mostly infected with mange. Country around hilly & looks suitable for training.	
	5/2/18		Visited 137 Bde Hdqrs & conferred with S.C. as to quarters in new area: Capt. BEARD RAMC(SR) to 1/1 CCS - Scabies.	
	6/2/18		Attended ADMS conference 10 am. Capt AU MILLAR and Lt GR SHARP + 2 NCOs left for 5th course at I Corps RAMC School.	

A5092. Wt. W12839/M1293. 750,000. 1/17. D. D & L. Ltd. Forms/C2118/14.

Instructions regarding War Diaries and Intelligence Summaries are contained in F. S. Regs., Part II. and the Staff Manual respectively. Title pages will be prepared in manuscript.

WAR DIARY
or
INTELLIGENCE SUMMARY.
(*Erase heading not required.*)

Army Form C. 2118.

Place	Date	Hour	Summary of Events and Information	Remarks and references to Appendices
FOUQUIÈRES	15/12/17		Capt J. S. Ullman US MORC left for duty at 33 C.C.S & was struck off strength of Field Ambulance	
	17/12/17		G.O.C. 46 Dn. visited CRS and conversed with patients in the wards.	
	18/12/17		4 Officer reinforcements arrived from Base making the Field Ambulance up to strength. Rendered Report on I.C.T. to A.D.M.S. Sent Miller-James wheeled stretcher carrier to 33 C.C.S. for the inspection by American medical officers there.	
	19/12/17		Newly joined officers taken round main dressing station LABOURSE and A.D.S.s PHILOSOPHE & FORT GLATZ by Capt Herga. for instruction. 1 Party of American medical officers visited CRS and were given all information possible in regard to those institutions.	

A7092 Wt. W12859/M1293 750,000. 1/17. D. D & L., Ltd. Forms/C2118/14.

Instructions regarding War Diaries and Intelligence Summaries are contained in F. S. Regs., Part II. and the Staff Manual respectively. Title pages will be prepared in manuscript.

WAR DIARY
or
INTELLIGENCE SUMMARY.
(Erase heading not required.)

Army Form C. 2118.

Place	Date	Hour	Summary of Events and Information	Remarks and references to Appendices
HESDIGNEUL	11/8/18		General routine. during last few days Enemy air craft v. active at night bombs being dropped in in locality numerous forward areas. Casualties from these insignificant. SSH	
	12/8/18		Visited ADS. GORRE ref to 6" How. guns placed awkwardly for us. Arranged satisfactorily. SSH	
	13/8/18		Enemy 'planes busy over district of HESDIGNEUL generally during the day – apparently observing. SSH	
	14/8/18		At 1.30 a.m. + again at 3.30 a.m. camp shelled by enemy. In all 20 5.9" H.V. shells. Two MOs + 5 O.R. recd injuries – one man of 1/3 NMFA attached dying of wounds later at midday two more shells fired just over camp. Evacuated camp, men sleeping out in the open + officers with 1/1 NMFA for the night. SSH	
BRUAY	15/8/18		HQrs. of Unit – transport &c moved to BRUAY. HQrs 31 Rue de la GARE. Troops satisfactorily housed. SSH	

D. D. & L., London, E.C.
(A8c04) Wt W1771/M2031 750,000 5/17 Sch. 52 Forms/C2118/14

Instructions regarding War Diaries and Intelligence Summaries are contained in F. S. Regs., Part II. and the Staff Manual respectively. Title Pages will be prepared in manuscript.

WAR DIARY
or
INTELLIGENCE SUMMARY
(Erase heading not required.)

Army Form C. 2118.

Place	Date	Hour	Summary of Events and Information	Remarks and references to Appendices
LABEUVRIERE	6/6/17		Detailed Lieut. R.H.G. OULTON to attend a one day course at 41 Sanitary Section. A.D.M.S. 46 Division visited hospital. Received report that Capt. MILLER at A.D.S. MAROC had been somewhat heavily shelled and had to vacate the upper portion of the dressing station to occupy the cellars.	
	7/6/17		Detailed 3 horse ambulances to report to O.C. 1/1 N.M. F. Amb. to assist in the ensuing operations.	
	8/6/17		Detailed Capt. HERGA to report at AIX NOULETTE to O.C. 1/2 N.Mid. F. Amb. and all available motor ambulances to attend to report at 8.0 p.m. at same place. Transport inspected by Capt. BEST 453 Coy. A.S.C.	
	9/6/17		All motor ambulances returned from AIX NOULETTE at 7-30. a.m. D.D.M.S. I Corps visited hospital and interviewed all Scabies patients. Visited B. Section	

Instructions regarding War Diaries and Intelligence Summaries are contained in F. S. Regs., Part II. and the Staff Manual respectively. Title Pages will be prepared in manuscript.

WAR DIARY
or
INTELLIGENCE SUMMARY
(Erase heading not required.)

Army Form C. 2118

Place	Date	Hour	Summary of Events and Information	Remarks and references to Appendices
MAISON ROLLAND	30/1/16		Opened A section for reception of patients from 1/6 Sherwood Frs.	

LIEUT.-COLONEL.
COMM'DG 3RD N. MID. FIELD AMB. R.A.M. CORPS

1875 Wt. W593/826 1,000,000 4/15 J.B.C. & A. A.D.S.S./Forms/C. 2118.

Instructions regarding War Diaries and Intelligence Summaries are contained in F. S. Regs., Part II. and the Staff Manual respectively. Title Pages will be prepared in manuscript.

WAR DIARY
or
INTELLIGENCE SUMMARY
(Erase heading not required.)

Army Form C. 2118

Place	Date	Hour	Summary of Events and Information	Remarks and references to Appendices
AIX-NOULETTE	9/5/17		Reported on S. Sgt Green sent up from Base Depot as a reinforcement as unfit for the post of S. Sgt in a Field Ambulance & recommended his return to Base duties.	
	10/5/17		Inspection of Field Amb. Transport by O.C. 46 Div. Train. Animals & vehicles good - harness on the whole not good. Necessary disciplinary action taken.	
			Capt GAVIN RAMC (T.C.) reported for duty.	
	11/5/17		Visited ADS and all posts in LIÉVIN. Enemy using gas shells freely each night necessitating wearing of S.B.R. frequently. Improvements in ADS & posts mentioned above (9th) making good progress.	
			Military medals awarded to Sgt Collins and privates Barlow and Conolly.	
			ADMS inspected main dressing station AIX-NOULETTE	

Army Form C. 2118.

Instructions regarding War Diaries and Intelligence Summaries are contained in F. S. Regs., Part II. and the Staff Manual respectively. Title Pages will be prepared in manuscript.

WAR DIARY
or
INTELLIGENCE SUMMARY
(Erase heading not required.)

Place	Date	Hour	Summary of Events and Information	Remarks and references to Appendices
LABOURSE	25/7/17		feasible to carry on top and preferable to do so. Have increased the number of wheeled carriers at St George's: Submitted proposal to ADMS for equipping A.D.S. with electric light from Pit head near by. Applied to C.R.E. for material (red shale) for extending horse standings. Lieut HOMAN RAMC(TC) attached for instruction prior to posting to 46 Div. Train.	
	26/7/17		Commenced instruction of Lieut Homan. Ordinary routine duties – applied for extension of accommodation for personnel in loft over school.	
	27/7/17		Obtained use of loft over school & started re-assortment of billets: put H.T. men into billets – struck tents.	

2449 Wt. W14957/M90 750,000 1/16 J.B.C. & A. Forms/C.2118/12.

Army Form C. 2118.

WAR DIARY
or
INTELLIGENCE SUMMARY.
(*Erase heading not required.*)

Instructions regarding War Diaries and Intelligence Summaries are contained in F. S. Regs., Part II. and the Staff Manual respectively. Title pages will be prepared in manuscript.

3RD NORTH MIDLAND FIELD AMBULANCE ROYAL ARMY MEDICAL CORPS

Place	Date	Hour	Summary of Events and Information	Remarks and references to Appendices
LABEUVRIÈRE	10/4/18		Fixed up bathing & disinfestation of clothing for personnel of N.F.A. Brigade here.	
	11/4/18		Agreement of shelling of CHOCQUES and the railway between ~~[illegible]~~ it & here. A troop train hit. 12 wounded & 5 dead brought in here.	
			CRS section at FOUQUIÈRES cleared & set up a Main dressing station: 51 patients received here from them.	
			~~Party of No 2 [illegible]~~	
			Men on detached duty returned to unit.	
			ADMS I Division visited CRS.	
	12/4/18		No 2 Field Amb. took over CRS.	
			Avery busy day in LABEUVRIÈRE: quantities of transport & refugees passing through.	
			EA dropped 4 bombs near mess in evening: 3 civilians wounded – all sent to 23 C.C.S.	
DIVION	13/4/18		Field Amb. left LABEUVRIÈRE 8am arr. DIVION 10.30am. Found quarters in Chau LEGAY J 23 d 95 45 sheet 36B. Visited ADMS for orders: own to be ready to move at 2 hours notice: Officer returned from 1/1 NMFA	

A7092 Wt. W12859/M1293 750,000. 1/17. D. D. & L., Ltd. Forms/C2118/14.

Army Form C. 2118.

Instructions regarding War Diaries and Intelligence Summaries are contained in F. S. Regs., Part II. and the Staff Manual respectively. Title pages will be prepared in manuscript.

WAR DIARY
or
INTELLIGENCE SUMMARY.
(Erase heading not required.)

140/3401 45

Place	Date	Hour	Summary of Events and Information	Remarks and references to Appendices
Nov. 1918			**MEDICAL.**	
			From November 1st. 1918 to November 31st. 1918.	
			O.C. 1/3rd.N.M. Field Ambulance.	

(A7092). Wt W12839/M1293 75,000. 1/17. D. D. & L., Ltd. Forms/C.2118/14.

Instructions regarding War Diaries and Intelligence Summaries are contained in F. S. Regs., Part II. and the Staff Manual respectively. Title Pages will be prepared in manuscript.

WAR DIARY
or
INTELLIGENCE SUMMARY
(Erase heading not required.)

Army Form

Place	Date	Hour	Summary of Events and Information	Remarks and references to Appendices
St AMAND	4/1/17		In company of Bde Major 137 I.B. and Officer i/c detachment Special Bde RE reconnoitred all trenches on 137 Bde sector with a view to medical arrangements in the event of gas operations. Communication trench from left to right not being possible owing to waterlogged state of trenches it was necessary to provide for medical service being conducted from both flanks. Submitted detailed recommendations thereon to ADMS.	
	5/1/17		Inspected Advanced Dressing Station FONQUEVILLERS – owing to incursion of water and to dilapidation due to weather and occasional enemy shells incessant work is necessary here, repairing rebuilding and draining.	
	6/1/17		Brigade Rest Billet transferred from POMMIER to St AMAND and established in large I.P. marquee under control of this Field Ambulance – conditions not good for the purpose but on the whole better than at POMMIER.	
	7/1/17		Reconnoitred trenches on 139 Bde sector to investigate means of evacuation of wounded. Conditions on right half are fair but on left half only one C.T. is in order, on extreme left and from most of that front evacuation must be done over the top.	
	8/1/17		Attended weekly conference at ADMS office and presentation of ribbons of decorations by Army Commander at Div. Hqrs. – Inspected Transport lines – great improvement is being effected on these by making a [illegible] on fascine bases up to then [illegible]	

Appendix III.

April 12th 15
to
May

1. Divisional Baths.
2. Infectious Hospital
3. Divisional Rest Hospital
+ later Casualty Clearing
Hospital

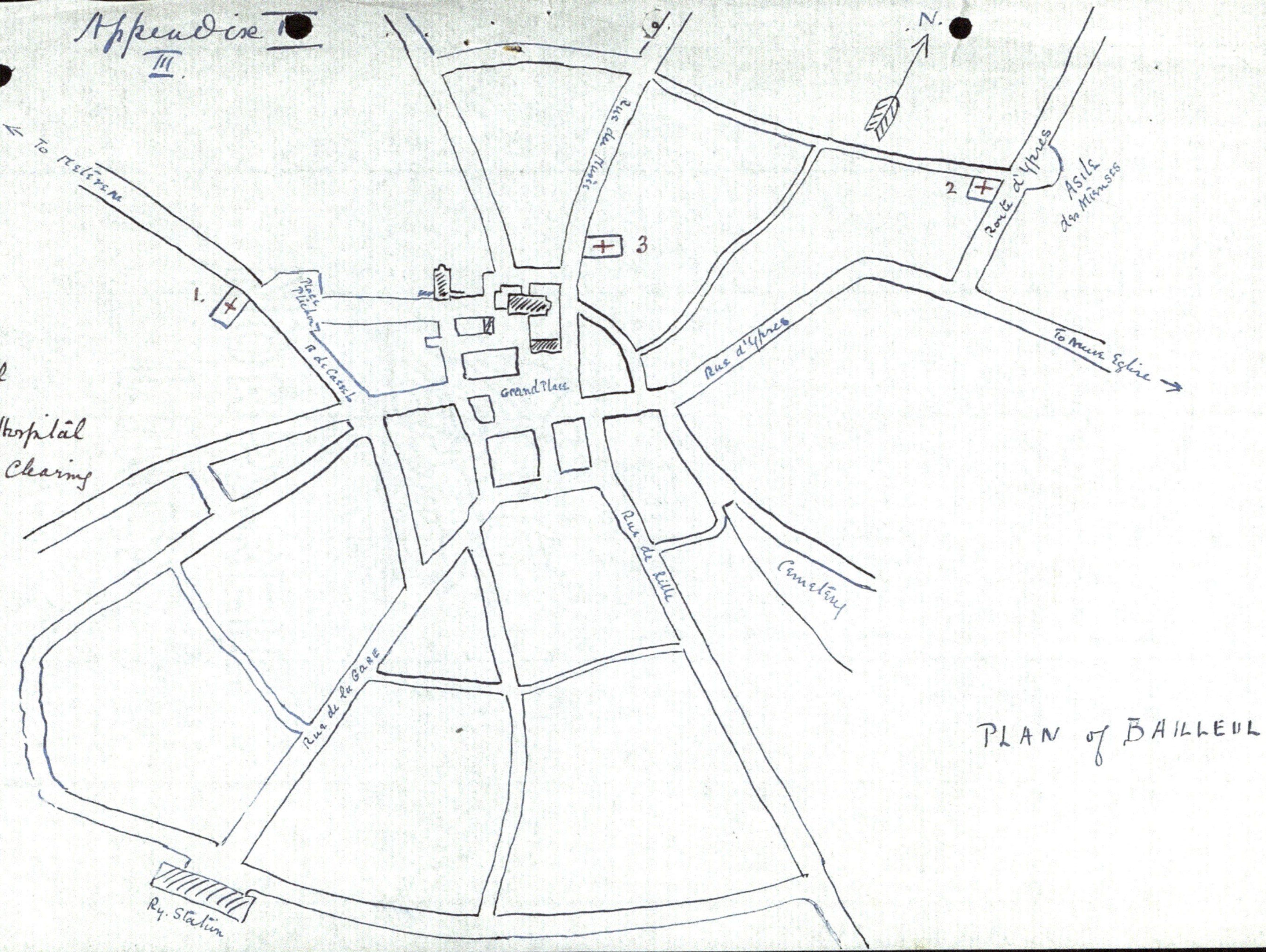

PLAN of BAILLEUL

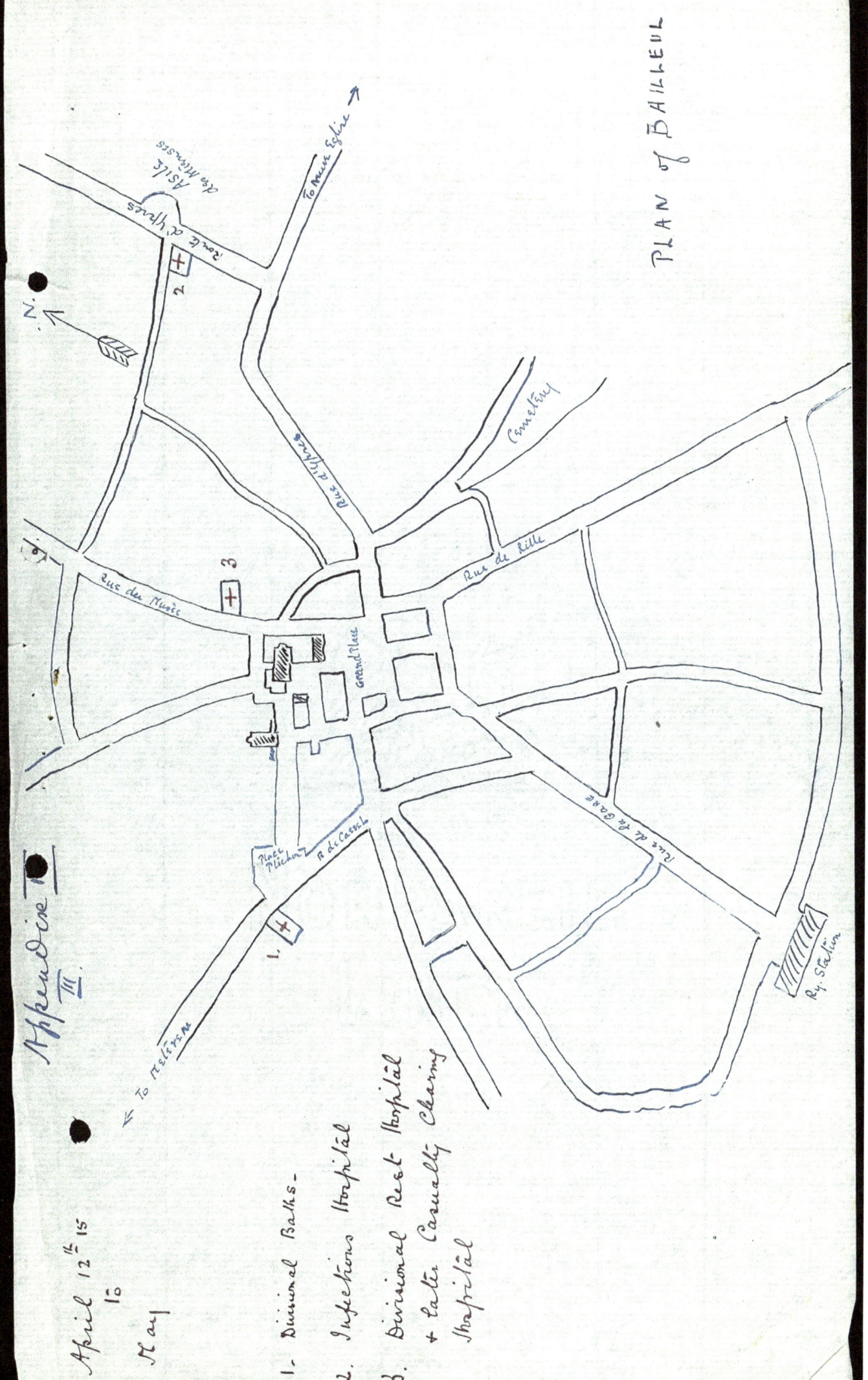

Instructions regarding War Diaries and Intelligence Summaries are contained in F. S. Regs., Part II. and the Staff Manual respectively. Title Pages will be prepared in manuscript.

WAR DIARY
or
INTELLIGENCE SUMMARY
(Erase heading not required.)

Army Form C. 2118

3RD NORTH MIDLAND FIELD AMBULANCE ROYAL ARMY MEDICAL CORPS.

Place	Date	Hour	Summary of Events and Information	Remarks and references to Appendices
ST AMAND	30/12/16		Visited ADS BIENVILLERS and went up to L sector along Raving to see what progress was being made with Brigade rest post - excavation is going on but will take another 10 days at least.	
			Work of Field Ambulance during past three weeks much handicapped by artisan members having called away to do tests in various Army & Corps workshops. - there are 79 such artisans in the unit and they are summoned at short notice without any regard to the efficiency of the Field Amb: This is felt particularly in transport section - at present there are not sufficient drivers to get the whole transport on the move in the event of orders to do so.	
	31/12/16		Visited men of unit employed at Divl Baths.	
			Visited men ~~[illegible]~~ ill - sent into 1/1 N M F Amb. Capt St. William	
			Lt ~~Capt~~ PHIBBS returns to ADS - FONQUEVILLERS.	
			A E Hodder. LIEUT.-COLONEL, COMM'DG 3RD N. MID. FIELD AMB. R.A.M. CORPS	

1875 Wt. W593/826 1,000,000 4/15 J.B.C. & A. A.D.S.S./Forms/C. 2118.

Instructions regarding War Diaries and Intelligence Summaries are contained in F. S. Regs., Part II. and the Staff Manual respectively. Title Pages will be prepared in manuscript.

WAR DIARY
or
INTELLIGENCE SUMMARY
(Erase heading not required.)

Army Form ..

Place	Date	Hour	Summary of Events and Information	Remarks and references to Appendices
ECQUEDECQUES	5/4/17		Capt. E.E. HERGA RAMC (TC) reported from Base for duty & was taken on the strength.	
	6/4/17		Inspected hospital at MAZANOY Fm.	
	7/4/17		Attended conference at ADMS office 10 am.	
			Reconnoitred ESTREE-BLANCHE district in afternoon with a view to medical arrangements in connection with divisional tactical exercise.	
			Lt A.M. CRAWFORD to No. 58 (2/1 W.R.) C.C.S. for duty (temp)	
	8/4/17		Attended conference ADMS office 11 am.	
			Inspected Hospital	
	9/4/17		Field Amb less personnel employed in Hospital took part in Divisional route march & inspection by Corps Commander. Left quarters 9.15 am returned at 10 pm.	

Army Form C. 2118

WAR DIARY
or
INTELLIGENCE SUMMARY
(Erase heading not required.)

Instructions regarding War Diaries and Intelligence Summaries are contained in F. S. Regs., Part II. and the Staff Manual respectively. Title Pages will be prepared in manuscript.

Place	Date	Hour	Summary of Events and Information	Remarks and references to Appendices
AIX-NOULETTE	28/4/1[illegible]		continued - Arranged for evacuation to be carried out by this route instead of via CITE CALONNE direct to main dressing station at this place - withdrew motor Amb off from CALONNE & posted it at RAMC post at CITÉ de ROLLENCOURT M27b 4.2. Prospective new site for ADS. jumped by an artillery battery.	
			Settled scheme of evacuation as follows. Right Brigade line approx from M18c central to M30d 2.3 RAPs at:- M28a.70.65 and M28b 25.01. ADS at White Chateau M28b 7.2. Thence ~~to RAMC post~~ by wheeled carrier to RAMC post at CITÉ de ROLLENCOURT M27b.4.2 whence by motor ambulance via ANGRES, road through M26 c+d, M25 d, (sheet 36c) R30b and point COLONELS HOUSE R29 d 6.6 (sheet 36b) on ARRAS-BETHUNE Road to AIX-NOULETTE.	

Instructions regarding War Diaries and Intelligence Summaries are contained in F. S. Regs., Part II. and the Staff Manual respectively. Title pages will be prepared in manuscript.

WAR DIARY
or
INTELLIGENCE SUMMARY.
(Erase heading not required.)

Army Form C. 2118.

Place	Date	Hour	Summary of Events and Information	Remarks and references to Appendices
BÉTHUNE	6/3/18		Attended ADMS conference 10am. Put reinforcement draft under Lt Sharp as a whole, to be trained into shape ab initio. Lt F.L. Richard sent to I Corps Scabies station for duty. Sent S Sgt POWIS DCM. to I Army RAMC school. Arranged bathing for 310 men of 1/5 Kings Liverpools beginning 7am on 7th. Capacity of baths 24 per hour.	
"	7/3/18		Lt Col A.E. Hodder departing for 14 days leave in U.K. Capt S.G. Herga assumed temp. command of unit. Usual drills & exercises for men not employed on hospital duties. —	
	8/3/18		Reinforcements showing better form. Lt Sharp having hopes of turning out a few good men after a week or two of training. Subject to notification in L. Gazette later promotion approved by G.O.C to rank of Major of Capt Herga & Capt Bradley.	

Instructions regarding War Diaries and Intelligence Summaries are contained in F. S. Regs., Part II. and the Staff Manual respectively. Title Pages will be prepared in manuscript.

WAR DIARY
or
INTELLIGENCE SUMMARY
(Erase heading not required.)

Army Form C. 2118

Place	Date	Hour	Summary of Events and Information	Remarks and references to Appendices
GAUDIEMPRE	24/7/17		Capt WLA HARRISON departed for temporary duty with 1/5 N. Staffs vice Capt A.V MILLAR sick	
	25/7/17		3am. received wire notifying retirement of enemy opposite 5th Corps and ordering stand by ready to move.	
			11am. standby cancelled.	
			Inspected ADS BERLES in afternoon.	
	26/7/17		Capt Walsh RAMC arrived from 1/1 N Mid Fd Amb for duty (temporary).	
			Capt J MILLER left for temp^y duty at ADMS office.	
	27/7/17		Lt AM CRAWFORD from 41st Div. reported for duty replacing Capt WLA HARRISON.	
	28/7/17		Capt WL. HARRISON left to report for duty with 41st Div.	
			A E Hodder Lieut Col cdg.	

1875 Wt. W593/826 1,000,000 4/15 J.B.C. & A. A.D.S.S./Forms/C. 2118.

Instructions regarding War Diaries and Intelligence Summaries are contained in F. S. Regs., Part II. and the Staff Manual respectively. Title Pages will be prepared in manuscript.

WAR DIARY
or
INTELLIGENCE SUMMARY
(Erase heading not required.)

Army Form C. 2118

Place	Date	Hour	Summary of Events and Information	Remarks and references to Appendices
GAUDIEMPRÉ	5/6/16		Capt J.C. Harris departed on short leave. Major C.H. Stidston took over charge of A.D.S. Started to build Russian vapour bath house for patients and personnel and built new type of incinerator for burning manure & faeces - built of corrugated iron sheets.	
	7/6/16		Lt J.R. Rutter reported to be attached temporarily for duty.	
	8/6/16		DMS 3rd Army inspected A.D.S. at 11 am and Headquarters dressing station at 12.45 pm. Major Stidston appointed to command Divisional Sanitary School at LUCHEUX. Capt E.W. Strange succeeds Major Stidston i/c A.D.S. Vapour bath erected works satisfactorily but defects are revealed which may be easily set right.	
	9/6/16		Withdrew all men of 1/1 N.M.F.A. attached from work on A.D.S trenches and handed them over to work under R.E. i/c construction of Hut hospital on GAUDIEMPRÉ - S AMAND road.	

Instructions regarding War Diaries and Intelligence Summaries are contained in F. S. Regs., Part II. and the Staff Manual respectively. Title Pages will be prepared in manuscript.

WAR DIARY
or
INTELLIGENCE SUMMARY
(Erase heading not required.)

Army Form C. 2118.

Vol 23

MEDICAL

Place	Date	Hour	Summary of Events and Information	Remarks and references to Appendices
ST AMAND	1/1/17		Attended ADMS conference at 10 am. Visited 137 Bde and inspected "Rest billet" in POMMIER and Brigade drying rooms: the former not satisfactory and not adequate for its purpose. Discussed an alternative arrangement with Staff Captain by which the "Rest Billet" should be moved to ST AMAND and put under the control of the Field Ambulance. Capt E.W. STRANGE returned from leave.	
	2/1/17		Inspected Sanitary conditions of one half of ST AMAND with Town Major. – visited advanced dressing stations at BIENVILLERS and FONQUEVILLERS. – daily working party required at latter to repair ravages of weather & occasional shells in trenches leading to Tube Dressing station: drainage of flood water presents great difficulties.	
	3/1/17		Completed sanitary inspection of ST AMAND. attended lecture by ADVS – inspected Transport lines at GAUDIEMPRE – Capt E T WILLIAMS returned to duty from 1/1 N M F Amb.	

Instructions regarding War Diaries and Intelligence Summaries are contained in F. S. Regs., Part II. and the Staff Manual respectively. Title pages will be prepared in manuscript.

WAR DIARY
or
INTELLIGENCE SUMMARY.
(*Erase heading not required.*)

Army Form C. 2118.

Place	Date	Hour	Summary of Events and Information	Remarks and references to Appendices
PREDEFIN	27/2/18		Submitted application for advancement to acting rank of Major of Capts Bradley & Herga. under G.R.O. 3448.	
			Returned statement of amounts of amounts invested in War Loan to I Corps during the period of campaign.	
			Total purchase £999.	
	28/2/18		Field Amb. concert party "The Rufflers" gave a performance at FONTAINE LES BOULANS for 1/6 S. Staff which gave great satisfaction.	
			Football team drew with 1/6 S. Staff in afternoon.	
			Made preparations for moving quarters tomorrow.	
			Summary of changes in personnel for month of February.	
			Increase { Officers – 0; O.R. – 8 Net increase 2. O.R.	
			Decrease { Officers – 1; O.R. – 6	
			A E Stoudse [?] Lt Col cdg 1/3 NMFA.	

A5092 Wt. W12859/M1293 750,000. 1/17. D. D & L., Ltd. Forms/C2118/14.

Army Form C. 2118

Instructions regarding War Diaries and Intelligence Summaries are contained in F. S. Regs., Part II. and the Staff Manual respectively. Title Pages will be prepared in manuscript.

WAR DIARY
or
INTELLIGENCE SUMMARY
(Erase heading not required.)

Place	Date	Hour	Summary of Events and Information	Remarks and references to Appendices
BREVILLERS	26/11/16		Billets at BREVILLERS crowded & bad – submitted report to ADMS on the filthy condition in which billets had been left by outgoing unit. – Made arrangements for sick of 137 I.B. [?] and various divisional units in neighbourhood. – Only accommodation available devoted to Scabies cases & that bad. Bathing of these cases carried on. Fitting of Box Respirators begun under Capt Stranger's [?] supervision.	
	29/11/16		All members of unit fitted with Box respirators & tested in gas with exception of men on leave.	

A E Hodder [?]
LIEUT.-COLONEL
COMMDG.

Instructions regarding War Diaries and Intelligence Summaries are contained in F. S. Regs., Part II. and the Staff Manual respectively. Title Pages will be prepared in manuscript.

Army Form C. 2118

WAR DIARY
or
INTELLIGENCE SUMMARY
(Erase heading not required.)

Place	Date	Hour	Summary of Events and Information	Remarks and references to Appendices
	18/9/16		Lt C. Robertson departed for G.B. on expiry of contract.	
			Stand to for Gas operations ordered 8pm - wash out.	
	19/9/16		Fire parade. Inspection of horses & transport	
	21/9/16		Capt A H Grey returned from temporary duty with VII Reserve Park	
	23/9/16		Capt A H Grey left to rejoin 16 M.A.C. Inspected Adv. dressing stations and Divisional Disinfecting Station.	
	28/9/16		Capt J.S.B Harrison went for temporary duty to 1/6 S. Staffs	

A E Houlder
Lieut Col

Instructions regarding War Diaries and Intelligence Summaries are contained in F. S. Regs., Part II. and the Staff Manual respectively. Title pages will be prepared in manuscript.

WAR DIARY
or
INTELLIGENCE SUMMARY.
(Erase heading not required.)

Army Form C. 2118.

Place	Date	Hour	Summary of Events and Information	Remarks and references to Appendices
FOUQUIÈRES	15/1/18		Sent one private to permanent duty at I Corps Schools. With Capt Hedges attended lecture on the P.U.O. group of cases given by Col Soltau RAMC at 22 C.C.S. A heavy gale with rain which is damaging roads.	
	16/1/18		Pumping station out of order owing to floods. All water supplied by carts from Village Hesdigneul temporarily. Attended at ADMS office for weekly conference. 10 am. Move of division to new area postponed owing to condition of roads.	
	17/1/18		Party of French civilian workmen arrived under orders from C.E. I Corps to demolish Hut no 4 condemned as unsafe. All transport on roads reduced to minimum on account of damage caused by past floods.	
	19/1/18		Lt F.L. Richard ~~and~~ & 1 NCO returned from course at I Army RAMC School.	
	18/1/18		Capt & QMr J. King returned from ordinary leave.	

Instructions regarding War Diaries and Intelligence Summaries are contained in F. S. Regs., Part II. and the Staff Manual respectively. Title Pages will be prepared in manuscript.

WAR DIARY
or
INTELLIGENCE SUMMARY
(Erase heading not required.)

Army Form C. 2118

Place	Date	Hour	Summary of Events and Information	Remarks and references to Appendices
Aix Noulette	25.5.17		About 40 casualties, sitting & walking cases & mostly of a slight nature arrived during the night. Received instructions to despatch all available motor amb & 2	
		2pm	H. ambulances to Bully Grenay. These were not required & were returned	
			Despatched 7 additional bearers to A.D.S. Maroc	
			Capt Harris with 1 Tent subdivision proceeded as advance party to Labeuvrière	
		8pm	Detailed transport guide with all necessary equipment for A.D.S. Maroc.	
			All equipment belonging to 1/3 N. Mid Field Amb returned to Aix Noulette in the empty waggons	
	26.5.17		Was much delayed by non-arrival of 2nd Field Amb equipment from Bully Grenay.	
			This arrived about 10 a.m. & later 2 officers & 30 men of the 2nd came to take over	
		1pm	All personnel & transport remaining at Aix Noulette set out for Labeuvrière	
			As active operations were pending I remained personally at Aix Noulette	
			until the arrival of O.C. 1/2 N. Mid Fd Amb at 2 pm.	

Instructions regarding War Diaries and Intelligence Summaries are contained in F. S. Regs., Part II. and the Staff Manual respectively. Title Pages will be prepared in manuscript.

WAR DIARY
or
INTELLIGENCE SUMMARY
(Erase heading not required.)

Army Form C. 2118

NORTH MIDLAND FIELD AMBULANCE
ROYAL ARMY MEDICAL CORPS

Place	Date	Hour	Summary of Events and Information	Remarks and references to Appendices
GAUDIEMPRÉ	20/2/17		Officers and O.R. of 2/3 N.C. Fd. Amb. rejoined their unit. ADMS 58th Div assumed medical administration of part of 46th Div. remaining in situ.	
	21/2/17		Visited A.D.S. BERLES & found all in good order. Nissen hut erected by XVIII Corps RE increases accommodation by 22 beds. New Kitchen fitment for boiling 12 dixies at once completed. Incinerator pulled down preliminary to reconstruction. Lt T Waterhouse of this unit evacuated to 43 CCS.	
	22/2/17		Hut for extension of Pack Store begun: when finished there will be good accommodation for 400 packs & kits.	
	23/2/17		Between 8 pm & 9.30 pm the enemy made a small attack with gas shells on our line east of BERLES: summary of report on cases dealt with by O/c ADS BERLES herewith	

1875 Wt. W593/826 1,000,000 4/15 J.B.C. & A. A.D.S.S./Forms/C. 2118.

Instructions regarding War Diaries and Intelligence Summaries are contained in F. S. Regs., Part II. and the Staff Manual respectively. Title Pages will be prepared in manuscript.

WAR DIARY
or
INTELLIGENCE SUMMARY
(Erase heading not required.)

Army Form C. 2118

1/3 N M Fd Amb

Vol 20

MEDICAL

Place	Date	Hour	Summary of Events and Information	Remarks and references to Appendices
LAHERLIÈRE	2/10/16		Lieut. J.L. PHIBBS - RAMC (TC) " H. ANGEL - " reported for duty (reinforcement) and were taken on the strength of the unit. Both these officers are entirely without previous training and experience in military duties.	
	4/10/16		5 Reinforcements (O.R) reported from Base and were taken on the strength.	
	9/10/16		1 Reinforcement arrived for duty on discharge from C.C.S. was restored to strength of unit.	
	11/10/16		2 Reinforcements (O.R) reported from Base depot & were taken on the strength. Two huts for patients which were previously covered only with sailcloths which let rain through have been made water tight by roofing with tarred felt laid on wire netting, the sailcloth being laid over all. & they are now fit for use again. The washerman's bench has been roofed & covered in so that they can work in any weather.	

1875 Wt. W593/826 1,000,000 4/15 J.B.C. & A. A.D.S.S./Forms/C. 2118.

75

Instructions regarding War Diaries and Intelligence Summaries are contained in F. S. Regs., Part II. and the Staff Manual respectively. Title Pages will be prepared in manuscript.

WAR DIARY
or
INTELLIGENCE SUMMARY
(Erase heading not required.)

Army 1/3 NM Fd Amb Vol 27

MEDICAL

Place	Date	Hour	Summary of Events and Information	Remarks and references to Appendices
AIX-NOULETTE	1/5/17		Relief of ADS parties LIÉVIN completed 5 pm.	
	2/5/17		Visited ADS and bearer post: Battn. Hdqrs having moved from "White House" the whole of the accommodation is now available for RAMC purposes. This greatly increases the accommodation and renders the quarters suitable for a main dressing station in the event of a retirement by the enemy. Interviewed G.O.C 137 I.B. on subject of lice & scabies and the establishment of Brigade Rest Camp at AIX-NOULETTE under supervision of Field Ambulance Commander.	
	4/5/17		DDMS I Corps inspected Hospital and Baths at AIX NOULETTE G.O.C. 46 Div. presented Cx de GUERRE with gold star to 7368 Pte W.P. PHELAN RAMC at the F. Amb. Hqrs 5 pm.	
	5/5/17		Capt E.E. HERGA lent to 2nd N.M.F. Amb for temporary duty at ADS. BULLY GRENAY	

Army Form C. 2118.

WAR DIARY
or
INTELLIGENCE SUMMARY.
(Erase heading not required.)

Instructions regarding War Diaries and Intelligence Summaries are contained in F. S. Regs., Part II. and the Staff Manual respectively. Title pages will be prepared in manuscript.

Place	Date	Hour	Summary of Events and Information	Remarks and references to Appendices
HESDIGNEUL	30/6/18		Rev. R. Street C.F. reported for duty. Apparently the Chaplain's Dept recognise our crying need!	
			Night working party for Essars discontinued + one N.C.O. + 8 men detailed as a day working party to remain at Essars. AEH	
			For the month 2 officers joined one left for duty elsewhere 6 O.R. " 10 left " " "	
"	1			
	1/7		Toured the A.D. Stations - bearer posts + RAPs both brigades in line with D.D.M.S. XIII Corps + A.D.M.S. 46 Div.	

A.E. Howell
Lt Col RAMC

D. D. & L., London, E.C.
(A8co4) Wt W1771/M2031 750,000 5/17 Sch. 52 Forms/C2118/14

Instructions regarding War Diaries and Intelligence Summaries are contained in F. S. Regs., Part II. and the Staff Manual respectively. Title Pages will be prepared in manuscript.

WAR DIARY
or
INTELLIGENCE SUMMARY
(Erase heading not required.)

Army Form C. 2118

Place	Date	Hour	Summary of Events and Information	Remarks and references to Appendices
GAUDIEMPRE	17/2/17		One officer and 29 OR. from 2/3 N.C Field Amb arrived to be att'd for instruction – 10 OR of these despatched to BERLES to learn ADS routine	
	18/2/17		Inspected ADS BERLES and caves no I in village with a view to rendering them better protected against gas. Following recommendations & suggestions of Gas officer 137 IB are concurred in though it is felt that a more radical treatment of the whole A.D.S. site would be better.	
			(1) Large cellar at present used as sleeping quarters by personnel to be used as Dressing station in event of gas attack – gas locks to be fitted in passage between the entrance	
			(2) Large room under shrine to be rendered gas tight the girders of roof to be strengthened with a double row of 9" pit props and a "cracker" layer to be added on top if possible	
			(3) Cave no I this to be used as emergency shelter for walking cases only – a short gas lock to be fitted in upper entrance & lower entrance to be blocked up with gas blanket & not used: a sentry being posted if necessary.	
			Lieut MAILE 2/3 N.C F. Amb. reported for instruction.	

1875 Wt. W593/826 1,000,000 4/15 J.B.C. & A. A.D.S.S./Forms/C. 2118.

5

Instructions regarding War Diaries and Intelligence Summaries are contained in F. S. Regs., Part II. and the Staff Manual respectively. Title pages will be prepared in manuscript.

WAR DIARY
or
INTELLIGENCE SUMMARY.
(Erase heading not required.)

Army Form C. 2118.

Hour, Date, Place	Summary of Events and Information	Remarks and references to Appendices
NEUVE EGLISE	Deep trench latrines answer best - Urine pits have been constructed & work well - These pits take the fluid drainage from the deep trench latrines - No nuisance comes from either, even in hot weather.	
	Stable shelters have been provided for horses - The men are bivouacing in shelters in the farm field -	
16 - 6 - 15 BAILLEUL	Remained 65 - Admitted 6 Duty 5 Transferred 1. Remaining 65.	
	Sgt JAMES ASC Motor Driver attached sent to D.G.M.S. G.H.Q re the MILLER-JAMES stretcher carrier - He proceeded to ENGLAND to have made an improved pattern for inspection -	

22

Instructions regarding War Diaries and Intelligence Summaries are contained in F. S. Regs., Part II. and the Staff Manual respectively. Title pages will be prepared in manuscript.

WAR DIARY
or
INTELLIGENCE SUMMARY.
(Erase heading not required.)

Army Form C. 2118.

3RD NORTH MIDLAND FIELD AMBULANCE ROYAL ARMY MEDICAL CORPS — 1/3 N M Fd Amb

Vol 3

Place	Date	Hour	Summary of Events and Information MEDICAL	Remarks and references to Appendices
BÉTHUNE	1/1/18		Extensive air raid by enemy on BÉTHUNE: on evening of 31.12.17. much damage done to 1/1 N.M. Fd Amb. quarters & as a result all transport vehicles of that unit sent up here & parked with those of this unit. Whist drive in evening for patients & personnel.	
	2/1/18		Attended conference at ADMS office. Principal objects discussed were War Economy Campaign and system of relief of RMOs going on leave. Capt. & QM J. King proceeded on ordinary leave.	
LEZ	4/1/18		In response to appeal from Corps Commander sent 130 francs subscribed by officers to collection for St Dunstans Hostel for the blind.	
FOUQUIÈRES	5/1/18		Captain Beard to 1/5 Leicesters temporarily.	
	9/1/18		DDMS I Corps inspected CRS in detail.	
			Lieut Sharp to 1/5 Sherwood Foresters temporarily	
			Lieut Richard & 1 NCO to I Army RAMC school.	
			G.O.C. 46 Div. visited C.R.S: sent 29 O.R. to 18 C.C.S. for duty.	
	10/1/18			
	11/1/18		D.M.S. I Army inspected C.R.S. and expressed his approval of all he saw.	

A7092. Wt. W12839/M1293. 750,000. 1/17. J. B. C. & A. Forms/C2118/14.

14

Instructions regarding War Diaries and Intelligence Summaries are contained in F. S. Regs., Part II. and the Staff Manual respectively. Title pages will be prepared in manuscript.

WAR DIARY
or
INTELLIGENCE SUMMARY.
(Erase heading not required.)

Army Form C. 2118.

1/3 NM Fd Amb

Vol 34

MEDICAL

Place	Date	Hour	Summary of Events and Information	Remarks and references to Appendices
FOUQUIÈRES LEZ BÉTHUNE	1/12/17		Routine day. – Capt John Miller appointed a/Lieut Col. to command 1/2 N. Midland Field Amb.	
	2/12/17		Capt a/Lt Col J Miller took over command of 1/2 NM F Amb & was struck off strength. Instituted careful inquiry into duration of stay in the CRS of patients.	
	3/12/17		As result of the above sent a large number back to duty. Principal causes of admissions are P.U.O and I.C.T. of body & limbs. – Addressed W.Os & Sgts on "War savings"	
	5/12/17		Still only have 1 medical officer. Attended lecture at HOUDAIN by DMS I Army on Medical organisation. This was mainly for benefit of combatant officers & for A & Q staff.	

A5092. Wt. W12839/M1293. 750,000. 1/17. D. D & L., Ltd. Forms/C2118/14.

Instructions regarding War Diaries and Intelligence Summaries are contained in F. S. Regs., Part II. and the Staff Manual respectively. Title Pages will be prepared in manuscript.

NORTH MIDLAND FIELD AMBULANCE ROYAL ARMY MEDICAL CORPS

WAR DIARY
or
INTELLIGENCE SUMMARY
(Erase heading not required.)

Army Form C. 2118

Place	Date	Hour	Summary of Events and Information	Remarks and references to Appendices
	15/11/15		Represented to ADMS that present Headquarters are quite unsuitable as a place in which to detain sick; it is fit for use as a rest billet or as a place in which cases of scabies may be accommodated, but facilities for adequate treatment of "itch" are entirely lacking.	
	18/11/15		Capt E. W. Strange rejoined for duty after sick leave. Sent 1 Corporal and 1 private for duty with Divisional Supply Column who have no medical establishment or equipment.	
	19/11/15		Visited Div. Supply Col. at E 16 c (BÉTHUNE Combined Sheet) and arranged with O.C. 36 Field Amb to see any sick of the D.S.C. during remainder of their stay near BÉTHUNE.	
	[illegible]		Transport employed in drawing brushwood from FORÊT DE NIEPPE and other personnel in making fascines to serve as basis for paths & horse lines.	
	20/11/15		Haulage of shale from ESTAIRES begun. Visited Rest billets of Regts of 137 Inf Bde:- found those at CROIX BARBÉE (M 26 c. sheet as above) in very bad state of repair and needing a great deal of work put into them	

1875 Wt. W593/826 1,000,000 4/15 J.B.C. & A. A.D.S.S./Forms/C. 2118.

Instructions regarding War Diaries and Intelligence Summaries are contained in F. S. Regs., Part II. and the Staff Manual respectively. Title pages will be prepared in manuscript.

WAR DIARY
or
INTELLIGENCE SUMMARY.
(Erase heading not required.)

Army Form C. 2118.

Place	Date	Hour	Summary of Events and Information	Remarks and references to Appendices
PREUX.	1.12.18		DDMS XIII Corps called & inspected sanitary arrangements of 137th Bgde. Capt. D. GILLIES RAMC detailed for temporary duty with 230 Bgde. RFA. ACY	
	4.12.18		Capt. J. ELLENBOGEN RAMC reported for duty from 1/6th. S. Staff. Regt. ACY	
	5.12.18		Capt. J. ELLENBOGEN RAMC departed for duty in England. ACY	
	9.12.18		Major HERGA M.C. with 18 O.R's ~~departed~~ proceeded to new Billets at FRESNOY LE GRAND as advance party. ACY	
BUSIGNY	11.12.18		Unit left PREUX at 9.30 AM & proceeded by route march to BUSIGNY arriving 3.30 PM. Very wet day. ACY	
FRESNOY LE GRAND	12.12.18		Unit left BUSIGNY at 10 AM & proceeded by route march to FRESNOY LE GRAND arriving at 1 PM. Very wet day. Billets fairly good. ACY	
"	13.12.18		Hospital established in convent. Accommodation 50. ACY	
"	14.12.18		Capt. & 2 M. KING returned from leave. ACY	
"	17.12.18		1st. Lieut. E.M. MORRIS USMC returned from leave. ACY	
"	20.12.18		Croix de Guerre awarded to Major E.E. HERGA M.C. ACY	

D. D. & L., London, E.C.
(A8004) Wt W1771/M2031 750,000 5/17 Sch. 52 Forms/C2118/14

Instructions regarding War Diaries and Intelligence Summaries are contained in F. S. Regs., Part II. and the Staff Manual respectively. Title Pages will be prepared in manuscript.

WAR DIARY
or
INTELLIGENCE SUMMARY
(Erase heading not required.)

Army Form C. 2118

Place	Date	Hour	Summary of Events and Information	Remarks and references to Appendices
Aix Noulette	18.5.17		Lieut Z. B. Sacks joined from base. Completed relief of personnel at A.D.S. & Bearer post.	
	19.5.17		Inspected baths at Aix Noulette & reported to A.D.M.S. who obtained permission for the personnel of 46th Div to continue to run the baths.	
	20.5.17		With ~~Lieut Sacks~~ Capt Gavin visited A.D.S. & all the bearer posts in Liévin. Found the arrangements at Rollencourt quite satisfactory. Gave instructions for a trench to be dug to accommodate a new latrine at this post, the present one being in a very dangerous position. Left Capt Gavin for duty at A.D.S.	
	21.5.17		Attended conference at A.D.M.S. Main dressing station was shelled at 8.15 p.m with two salvoes of 4 shells each, three of which struck the building. They were shells of a great type, detonating on striking the tiles of the roof, sending forward a shower of splintered shell case, but spreading quite horizontally. Seven of the personnel were wounded (3 gravely)	

1875 Wt. W593/826 1,000,000 4/15 J.B.C. & A. A.D.S.S./Forms/C. 2118.

MEDICAL

Instructions regarding War Diaries and Intelligence Summaries are contained in F. S. Regs., Part II. and the Staff Manual respectively. Title Pages will be prepared in manuscript.

WAR DIARY
or
INTELLIGENCE SUMMARY
(Erase heading not required.)

1/3 NM 3d Amb

Army Form C. 2118

Vol 19

Place	Date	Hour	Summary of Events and Information	Remarks and references to Appendices
LA HERLIÈRE	1/9/16		Further report received to day from O/c ADS BERLES on Gas operation of night 30/31 August points out that between 9am + 6pm on 31st 15 cases were sent to ADS exhibiting ~~delayed~~ symptoms of gas poisoning whose onset was delayed till the men got back to billets – in most of these the gas had been inhaled while uncoupling the pipes from the cylinders after the gas attack. All these cases were sent to Field Amb. of 51st Division at GAUDIEMPRÉ. These bring up the total of own men more or less gassed in course of this operation to 22.	
		9.30 pm	Under instruction from ADMS – took over A.D.S. at BIENVILLERS [E2c9.8] from 1/2 N.M. F. Amb. supplying personnel of 1 off. 8 men and necessary equipment – this to be regarded as annexe to A.D.S. BERLES & to be visited daily by one of the officers stationed there –	

Instructions regarding War Diaries and Intelligence Summaries are contained in F. S. Regs., Part II. and the Staff Manual respectively. Title Pages will be prepared in manuscript.

WAR DIARY
or
INTELLIGENCE SUMMARY
(Erase heading not required.)

Army Form C. 2118

Place	Date	Hour	Summary of Events and Information	Remarks and references to Appendices
[illegible]	30/6/16		All excreta carefully covered & guarded against flies. Mud road along west side of Hospital has been covered with metal as far as possible to render it fit for use in wet weather. All Buildings are suitably connected with paths of Duck boards. Capacity of Hospital :- 250 lying cases in E huts + 100 in Adrian Huts + Accommodation under canvas as needed. A.L. Woodson [illegible] Lieut Col. Cdg 1/3 N M F Amb [illegible]	

1875 Wt. W593/826 1,000,000 4/15 J.B.C. & A. A.D.S.S./Forms/C. 2118.

App. I

106 MEN OF 1/5th. LEICESTERSHIRE REGT. UNDER OBSERVATION IN 1/3RD. N.M. FIELD AMBULANCE.

****

Dates of exposure to gas (shell).	Number of men exposed of 64 interrogated.
8th. April.	53.
9th. "	60.
10th. "	53.
11th. "	56.
12th. "	46.

ONSET OF SYMPTOMS.

DATE.	NUMBERS.
11th. April.	1.
12th. "	5.
13th. "	11.
14th. "	35.
15th. "	30.
16th. "	20.
17th. "	2.
18th. "	1.

Febrile symptoms preceded sore throat in 100 cases.

FREQUENCY OF SYMPTOMS.

SYMPTOM.	PRESENT IN CASES.	
Vomiting.	57.	
" without reference to coughing.	19.	(In a few cases after food, in most un-provoked
Sore mouth.	16.	
Soreness of throat, described as "raw" or "burning"	102.	
Soreness in upper part of chest.	103.	
Cough.	106.	
Hoarseness.	97.	
" amounting to loss of voise	25.	
Pain in epigastrium on coughing.	65.	
Headache.	106.	
Pains in back.	83.	
Pains in legs.	94.	

NATURE OF GASES TO WHICH EXPOSED.

96 men state that gas irritated their noses at the time. Most of the men profess to have experience of "Mustard" (Yellow Cross) gas. 19 say they detected it. Shells exploding like ordinary H.E. (? Blue Cross) and quietly exploding shells were used. Yellow stained shell-holes noticed. Some men describe smell of rotten onions, and one Sergt. says this is attempt to describe a quite new smell.

6 men had sores on Ears and Face.

ANALYSIS OF TEMPERATURE AND PULSE RATES SINCE ADMISSION.

Evening of 18th. April.		Morning of 19th. April.	
Temperatures of 99° and over.	20.	Temperatures of 99° and over.	8.
" " 100° " "	13.	" " 100° " "	3.
" " 101° " "	7.	" " 101° " "	1.
" " 102° " "	5.	" " 102° " "	0.
" under 98°	17.	" under 98°	41.
" " 97°	2.	" " 97°	24.
" " 96°	1.	" " 96°	15.

Instructions regarding War Diaries and Intelligence Summaries are contained in F. S. Regs., Part II. and the Staff Manual respectively. Title Pages will be prepared in manuscript.

WAR DIARY
or
INTELLIGENCE SUMMARY
(Erase heading not required.)

Army Form C. 2118

Place	Date	Hour	Summary of Events and Information	Remarks and references to Appendices
AIX-NOULETTE	29/4/17		Notified that 7368 Pte W. R. PHELAN of this unit had been awarded CROIX de GUERRE for an act of gallantry in rescuing two French civilians whose house at BERLES au BOIS had been blown in by large gas shell on 6.3.17.	
	30/4/17		Attended ADMS conference at 10 am. afterwards visited LIEVIN and arranged for relief of ADS and bearer post parties. Relief to be completed by 5 pm 1/5/17	
			Summary of changes in personnel Month of March 1917	
			Struck off strength Officers – 1 (Capt E.W. Strange to 1st Army School)	
			OR – RAMC 9 (one killed in action)	
			~~ASC~~ – ASC 3	
			Taken on strength Officers – 2 Capt L.E. HERGA & Lt WATERHOUSE	
			OR – RAMC 13	
			ASC 2	
			Required to complete to estab. 5. OR. RAMC: 2 OR ASC.	

A.E. Stoudler[?]
Lt Col.

Instructions regarding War Diaries and Intelligence Summaries are contained in F. S. Regs., Part II. and the Staff Manual respectively. Title Pages will be prepared in manuscript.

WAR DIARY
or
INTELLIGENCE SUMMARY
(Erase heading not required.)

Army Form C. 2118

Place	Date	Hour	Summary of Events and Information	Remarks and references to Appendices
MARSEILLE	24/1/16	4.30pm	Received notice to entrain whole unit at midnight. Capt Harris + Transport section less vehicles from LA VALENTINE and Capt Jameson c B section from SANTI Camp rendezvoused with remainder of F. Amb. at GARE ARENC at 11.45 pm: Lt H W Greig detached for duty on train c 4th N.M. Bde RFA. Amm Col.	
	27/1/16		Entrainment begun 0.15 am: considerable delay in entraining owing 1/ to train being too long for platform: so that animals and vehicles could not be entrained simultaneously, 2 most inconvenient types of trucks provided 3 Difficulties in loading motor ambulances on the trucks in question. Train moved out 5.15 am — Picked up Dr Bendall of 1st N M Bde RFA Amm. Col at LYON.	
PONTREMY MAISON ROLLAND	29/1/16		Arrived PONT-REMY 5 am. detrained at once, and moved to billeting area at MAISON ROLLAND. Officers + men on detached duty all rejoined except Lt ARMITAGE + 1 man.	

1875 Wt. W593/826 1,000,000 4/15 J.B.C. & A. A.D.S.S./Forms/C. 2118.

Instructions regarding War Diaries and Intelligence Summaries are contained in F. S. Regs., Part II. and the Staff Manual respectively. Title Pages will be prepared in manuscript.

WAR DIARY
or
INTELLIGENCE SUMMARY
(Erase heading not required.)

Army Form C. 2118

Place	Date	Hour	Summary of Events and Information	Remarks and references to Appendices
Aix Noulette	15/5/17		By orders I Army Major J. A. Barron 1/1 North Mid Field Ambulance was appointed to temporary command of the unit.	
	16/5/17		With Capt J. Miller visited the A.D.S. & all bearer posts at Lievin. Found good progress had been made at No 1 post Rollencourt. The 3 cellars being well connected. At A.D.S. the shoot for lowering stretchers into the cellar had been completed & was very satisfactory. Arranged with Capt Harris for the relief of all bearers with men from main dressing station.	
			Sergt Holyland R.D 1/2 N Mid Fd Amb joined from base	
	17/5/17		Lieut R. H. G. Dalton RAMC (T.C.) joined from the base	
			Capt Best 453 Coy. A.S.C. inspected horses & transport. He considered the horses to be in excellent condition & the waggons quite satisfactory. He thought that there was still too much oil & grease on the harness.	

Army Form C. 2118

Instructions regarding War Diaries and Intelligence Summaries are contained in F. S. Regs., Part II. and the Staff Manual respectively. Title Pages will be prepared in manuscript.

WAR DIARY
or
INTELLIGENCE SUMMARY
(Erase heading not required.)

Place	Date	Hour	Summary of Events and Information	Remarks and references to Appendices
AIX - NOULETTE	23/4/17		continued - Visited Hqrs 139 I.B. and arranged for notification direct to O i/c A.D.S. of impending operations to allow him to make adequate preparations and a saving of time.	
	24/4/17		Shell of large calibre fell in courtyard of A.D.S. killing S. Sgt. Stevens RAMC T of this unit: two other N.C.Os injured also & temporarily incapacitated.	
	25/4/17		Visited A.D.S. at LIEVIN and inspected proposed new site for A.D.S. which seemed [illegible] satisfactory. Put gang of men in to clean out and prop cellars.	
	27/4/17		Capt G D Fairlie replaced Lt J L Phibb in medical charge of Div. Depot Battalion.	
	28/4/17		Visited LIEVIN & A.D.S. in morning: road direct via ANGRES and main BETHUNE - ARRAS Road at R29 d 6.6 now open for traffic.	

Instructions regarding War Diaries and Intelligence Summaries are contained in F. S. Regs., Part II. and the Staff Manual respectively. Title Pages will be prepared in manuscript.

WAR DIARY
or
INTELLIGENCE SUMMARY
(Erase heading not required.)

Army Form C. 2118

Place	Date	Hour	Summary of Events and Information	Remarks and references to Appendices
St AMAND	8/12/16		Inspected stations at FONQUEVILLERS – Both in good order and well adapted to their purpose. – practically no new work needed on them but repairs will constantly be called for.	
			Capt E W Strange with (B) section took over control of Divisional Laundry at PAS.	
			Capt S C Harris took over command at BIENVILLERS	
	9/12/16		Again inspected ADS at BIEVILLERS: am of opinion that station at E 8 a 4.4. affords bad accommodation & is in part of village that receives most attention from enemy, also off main route of evacuation. – that it should be given up or at ~~least and~~ most used as an over flow station and that quarters at E 2 d 2.5. should be further protected & adapted to take all cases.	
	11/12/16		Attended weekly conference at ADMS office and afterwards inspected advanced dressing stations at BIENVILLERS and FONQUEVILLERS.	
	14/11/16		Capt E T Williams returned from temporary duty with 231 Bde RFA	

1875 Wt. W593/826 1,000,000 4/15 J.B.C. & A. A.D.S.S./Forms/C. 2118.

Army Form C. 2118

Instructions regarding War Diaries and Intelligence Summaries are contained in F. S. Regs., Part II. and the Staff Manual respectively. Title Pages will be prepared in manuscript.

WAR DIARY
or
INTELLIGENCE SUMMARY
(Erase heading not required.)

Place	Date	Hour	Summary of Events and Information	Remarks and references to Appendices
St AMAND	13/11/16		Visited BIENVILLERS ADS – discussed plans for increasing accommodation for patients at ADS in POMMIER Rd and settled on course to be pursued. When completed this will provide accommodation well protected for at least 18 stretcher cases and up to 30 sitting as well as a French tube dressing room & quarters for two officers and 16 O.R. Work to be put in hand at once.	
	16/11/16		Inspected ADS FONQUEVILLERS. – Capt M H BARTON. MC reported for duty ovous taken on strength – Lt PHIBBS left for duty 1/5th Leicesters	
	17/11/16		Reconnoitred evacuation routes from L sector of division between BERLES - MONCHY and BIENVILLERS - MONCHY Road and made recommendations to ADMS (1) That casualties should be evacuated via NEVERENDING STREET to RAVINE & thence through BERLES and 30th Division. (2) If this is not desirable, that bearer post be established in RAVINE along NABOTH St and that cases be brought from there to BIENVILLERS by trolley railway.	

11

Instructions regarding War Diaries and Intelligence Summaries are contained in F. S. Regs., Part II. and the Staff Manual respectively. Title pages will be prepared in manuscript.

WAR DIARY
or
INTELLIGENCE SUMMARY.
(Erase heading not required.)

Army Form C. 2118.

Vol 40

Place	Date	Hour	Summary of Events and Information	Remarks and references to Appendices
June 1918.			MEDICAL.	140/3076.
			CONFIDENTIAL.	
			WAR DIARY OF THE	
			1/3. NORTH MIDLAND. FIELD AMBULANCE.	
			FOR JUNE. 1918.	

A5834 Wt. W4973/M687 750,000 8/16 D. D. & L. Ltd. Forms/C.2118/13.

App I

Subject:-Improvement to Billets.see D.R.O.1130 of 8/2/16.

From:-
O.C.
3rd:North.Midland.Field.Ambulance.

3RD NORTH MIDLAND FIELD AMBULANCE ROYAL ARMY MEDICAL CORPS 18/5/16

To:-
The A.D.M.S.
46th:Division.

Taken over from No:10 Field Ambulance 29/1/16.	To be left by 3rd:North.Midland. Field.Ambulance.
At Mme:B.Tellier.	1.All structures taken over,as per schedule herewith,
Bath room,brick floor locally made, containing-	
Fire place " "	2.Officers' latrine,tin roof,locally made.
2 seats " "	
6 foot gratings " "	3.Grease pit and trap/with trough, tinned and soldered.
6 bath tubs Ordnance.	
In drying room. 10	4.New floor to wash-house,can pavement
1 brick fire place for camp kettles.	and cinders.
***************	5.Tin surface to scrubbing table for clothes in wash-house.
At M.Lardi.	
48 stretcher trestles.	6.New 4 chambered field oven of brick, clay and oil drums,with flue.
1 fire stove Ordnance.	
1 brick made kitchen.	7.Additional patients' latrine.
1 wash-house. locally built.	
1 latrine " " under existing roof.	In general drainage,improvements and extensions have been effected, paths made and existing structures kept in repair.
1 brick incinerator.	
***************	Roads have been swept,and water channels cleaned daily,and drain opened to clear M.Lardi's farmyard.
At M.Leroux.	
1 brick incinerator.	
1 brick fireplace.	
1 covered latrine locally made.	
***************	

(At M. Lardi — items 2 to 7)

11/2/16.

A E Hodder
LIEUT.-COLONEL,
COMM'DG 3RD N. MID. FIELD AMB. R.A.M. CORPS

Instructions regarding War Diaries and Intelligence Summaries are contained in F. S. Regs., Part II. and the Staff Manual respectively. Title pages will be prepared in manuscript.

WAR DIARY
or
INTELLIGENCE SUMMARY.
(Erase heading not required.)

Army Form C. 2118.

Place	Date	Hour	Summary of Events and Information	Remarks and references to Appendices
LABOORSE	30/9/17		Attached Appendix I summarising medical arrangements on front ~~for~~ from which this Field Ambulance is responsible for evacuating casualties.	
			A E Hodder Lt Col cdg 1/3 N. Mid. Fd Amb.	

A7092. Wt. W12839/M1293. 750,000. 1/17. D. D & L., Ltd. Forms/C2118/14.

Instructions regarding War Diaries and Intelligence Summaries are contained in F. S. Regs., Part II. and the Staff Manual respectively. Title pages will be prepared in manuscript.

WAR DIARY
or
INTELLIGENCE SUMMARY.
(Erase heading not required.)

Army Form C. 2118.

Place	Date	Hour	Summary of Events and Information	Remarks and references to Appendices
LABOURSE	10.11.17		and men returned to LABOURSE. CAPT. HERGA remained at FORT GLATZ. attached for temp. duty with 1/2 N. M. F. Amb.	
			CAPT. STEEL. and 42 OR marched to B. Section 1st CORPS. REST STATION at FOURQUIERES. as an advanced party.	
FOUQUIERES.	12.11.17		B. Sect. 1st CORPS. REST STATION. taken over. and relief completed by 6 pm. CAPT. ULLMAN remaining at LABOURSE with 1/2nd NMFA. until return of Major TURNER.	
			CAPT. STEEL to 1/5 NOTTS + DERBY Regt. to relieve CAPT. G.S. BROWN. RAMC. proceeding on 14 days. leave.	
	14.11.17		CAPT + QM. KING. + fatigue party. by order of ADMS. 46 Div. cleaned out the Battalion Rest billets. at FOUQUIERES. They removed 9 Tip Cart loads of refuse. + 7 Sand bags full of Saw and lime-washed the billets.	
	15.11.17		CAPT. ULLMAN attached to 1/4 LINCOLN REGT. in place of CAPT. LUDOLF proceeding on 14 days leave.	
	16.12.17.		Cleaning of Battalion rest billets finished. Inspected by ADMS. Concert to Patients by 46. Amm. Sub Park.	
	17.12.17.		Concert by Band 137. Bde.	
	19.12.17		Floors of Cooks room and cutting up room. cemented. and drained. Visit from ADMS. 46 Div	

A7092 Wt. W12839/M1293. 750,000. 1/17. D. D & L., Ltd. Forms/C2118/14.

Instructions regarding War Diaries and Intelligence Summaries are contained in F. S. Regs., Part II. and the Staff Manual respectively. Title Pages will be prepared in manuscript.

WAR DIARY
or
INTELLIGENCE SUMMARY
(Erase heading not required.)

Army Form C. 2118.

Place	Date	Hour	Summary of Events and Information	Remarks and references to Appendices
LABEUVRIERE	June 3		Church Parade C of E. Nonconformists for the Patients. Attended Conference at Y.M.C.A. BRAQUEMONT convened by D.D.M.S. I Corps where it was decided that all Sanitary appliances should be standardised & made in Sanitary workshops or by R.E. under direction of Sanitary Officer	
	4		Attended conference at A.D.M.S. 46th DIV. Visited bearer post at BULLY GRENAY and found everything greatly improved. D.D.M.S. I Corps visited Hospital and inspected water carts.	
	5		General routine. By orders DDMS I Corps drew 46 pairs of stretcher trestles for use in Scabies Hut. Detailed 1 Sergt. and 1 man to act as guard at Civil & Military Hospital, BETHUNE	

2449 Wt. W14957/M90 750,000 1/16 J.B.C. & A. Forms/C.2118/12.

Instructions regarding War Diaries and Intelligence Summaries are contained in F. S. Regs., Part II. and the Staff Manual respectively. Title Pages will be prepared in manuscript.

WAR DIARY
or
INTELLIGENCE SUMMARY

(Erase heading not required.)

Army Form C. 2118.

Place	Date	Hour	Summary of Events and Information	Remarks and references to Appendices
LABEUVRIERE	June 1		Together with O.C. 1/1 N. Mid. F. Amb. visited the bearer post at BULLY GRENAY, expressed great dissatisfaction both with the condition of the post and also with the transport. Issued orders for many things to be done. Proceeded to A.D.S. MAROC under the command of Capt. T. MILLER who did not consider the Dressing Room above ground to be at all shell proof and was tunnelling and joining up a series of cellars below the Dressing station.	
	2		General Routine. The well at Quartermaster's stores from which the reservoirs of the hospital are filled pumped dry. Made arrangements for bathing large numbers of 1st Cavalry Division. Visited No. 1 Sanitary Section to make arrangements for sending Lieut. OULTON for a 3 days course	

2449 Wt. W14957/M90 750,000 1/16 J.B.C. & A. Forms/C.2118/12.

Instructions regarding War Diaries and Intelligence Summaries are contained in F. S. Regs., Part II. and the Staff Manual respectively. Title Pages will be prepared in manuscript.

WAR DIARY
or
INTELLIGENCE SUMMARY

(Erase heading not required.)

Army Form C. 2118.

Place	Date	Hour	Summary of Events and Information	Remarks and references to Appendices
LABOURSE	30/7/17		Attended ADMS meeting 10 am. Drew materials for rebuilding & extending horse standings & extra timber & wire netting for beds for personnel.	
	31/7/17		Accommodation of all personnel at M.D.S. completed and billets clearly defined. No overcrowding now exists. Work begun on horse standings. ~~Captain~~ ~~[illegible]~~ Lieut Stoman returned from period of instruction under M.O. 1/5th Staffs. Submitted details of evacuation from HULLUCH sector to A.D.M.S. Visited A.D.S. in afternoon & made arrangements conformably to wishes of RMO R. Battalion for evacuation of casualties during operations. This involves establishment temporarily of two more relay posts between front line & RAP & a reinforcement of Field Amb. bearers at RAP. Submitted to ADMS the arrangements I propose to adopt in event of active operations on HULLUCH sector	

2449 Wt. W14957/M90 750,000 1/16 J.B.C. & A. Forms/C.2118/12.

Instructions regarding War Diaries and Intelligence Summaries are contained in F. S. Regs., Part II. and the Staff Manual respectively. Title Pages will be prepared in manuscript.

WAR DIARY
or
INTELLIGENCE SUMMARY
(Erase heading not required.)

Army Form C. 2118

1/3 N M Fd Amb.

1/3 NORTH MIDLAND FIELD AMB. ROYAL ARMY MEDICAL CORPS

Vol 2

MEDICAL

Place	Date	Hour	Summary of Events and Information	Remarks and references to Appendices
St AMAND	2/3/17		Took over A.D.S. BERLES from 49th Div. F. Amb. and handed over A.D.S. at BIENVILLERS and FONCQUEVILLERS to 1/2 N. Mid. Fd. Amb.	
	3/3/17		Completed change with 1/2 N M F Amb & took over Main D.S. GAUDIEMPRÉ D2 c.0.8. Sheet 57D.	
GAUDIEMPRÉ			2 officers & 30 O.R. from 2/2 W.C. Fd Amb. 58th Div arrived for weeks instruction.	
	4/3/17		Sent one officer & 8 OR of attached to ADS BERLES for instruction in front line duties; remainder being employed in work at main D.S.	
	6/3/17		Inspected A.D.S.	
	7/3/17		Changed over party of attached at A.D.S.	
	10/3/17		Fresh party of 2 officers and 30 OR from 2/3 W.C. Field Amb arrived for instruction replacing former party returned to unit	

1875 Wt. W593/826 1,000,000 4/15 J.B.C. & A. A.D.S.S./Forms/C. 2118.

Instructions regarding War Diaries and Intelligence Summaries are contained in F. S. Regs., Part II. and the Staff Manual respectively. Title Pages will be prepared in manuscript.

WAR DIARY
or
INTELLIGENCE SUMMARY
(Erase heading not required.)

Army Form C. 2118

Place	Date	Hour	Summary of Events and Information	Remarks and references to Appendices
ECQUE-DECQUES.	10/4/17		Took part in Tactical Exercise for commanding officers of the Division at ESTRÉE-BLANCHE and neighbourhood. Lt & QM J. King departed on short leave 11th – 21st in U.K.	
	11/4/17		Lt T. Waterhouse RAMC (TC) reported for duty from Base after sick leave in Mickelham Home. Inspected Hospital MALANOY FARM.	
	13/4/17		Field Ambulance moved to BÉTHUNE being quartered in HOSPICE CIVILE – RUE ST PRY. Visited 137 Bde & made usual arrangements for collection etc of sick: Issued instruction to RMOs of Bde re measures prevention of venereal disease	
BÉTHUNE	16/4/17		Visited 139 Bde NOEUX-LES-MINES and made arrangements for collection of sick from units of that brigade.	
	17/4/17		Re-inoculation of unit with TAB completed.	
	18/4/17		Sent Capt J.C. Harris with advanced party to take over A.D.S. in LIÉVIN – AIX-NOULETTE from 7 Amb. 24th Div.	

1875 Wt. W593/826 1,000,000 4/15 J.B.C. & A. A.D.S.S./Forms/C. 2118.

Instructions regarding War Diaries and Intelligence Summaries are contained in F. S. Regs., Part II. and the Staff Manual respectively. Title Pages will be prepared in manuscript.

WAR DIARY
or
INTELLIGENCE SUMMARY
(Erase heading not required.)

Army Form C. 2118.

Place	Date	Hour	Summary of Events and Information	Remarks and references to Appendices
LABOURSE	31/7/17		Summary of personnel changes for July 1917	
			Officers On 5 Off. 4 - net increase 1	
			O.R. " 15 " 12 - net increase 3.	
			A E Hodder Lieut Col RAMCT Cdg 1/3 N Mid Field Amb	

Instructions regarding War Diaries and Intelligence Summaries are contained in F. S. Regs., Part II. and the Staff Manual respectively. Title Pages will be prepared in manuscript.

WAR DIARY
or
INTELLIGENCE SUMMARY
(Erase heading not required.)

Army Form C. 2118

Place	Date	Hour	Summary of Events and Information	Remarks and references to Appendices
SAUDIEMONT	23/2/17		Time of attack 8pm – 9.30 pm 23.2.17 Area affected – support lines & C.T. from NEWARK St to NEVERENDING St and from there over RAVINE. Number of cases dealt with – 10 Characteristics of gas – sweetish taste like pineapple. No effect on metal buttons (not chlorine). Gave rise in most cases to frontal headache, sickness or eructation and some soreness of throat. Pulse & respiration not affected. None of the cases showed any serious symptoms before reaching there or ... Treatment at ADS and ... was (1) Rest (2) Inhalation of Ammonia and in one case that showed slight cyanosis (3) oxygen and by mouth hot soup. All cases evacuated direct to 43 C.C.S. in view of the possibility of delayed serious symptoms. The S.B.R. seem to have been put on quickly in most cases but in one or two instances they did not seem to fit well. The gas shells were mixed with H.E. shells & T.M. bombs.	

Instructions regarding War Diaries and Intelligence Summaries are contained in F. S. Regs., Part II. and the Staff Manual respectively. Title Pages will be prepared in manuscript.

WAR DIARY
or
INTELLIGENCE SUMMARY
(Erase heading not required.)

Army Form C. 2118.

Place	Date	Hour	Summary of Events and Information	Remarks and references to Appendices
LABEUVRIERE	9/6/17		I Corps rest station FOUQUIERES.	
	10/6/17		Capt. Hogg returned from LIEVIN, from temp'y duty with 1/2 N. Mid. F. Amb. The three horse amb. also detailed with this unit returned. Detailed Lieut. R. H. G. OULTON for duty with 1/6 N. Staffs.	
	11/6/17		Attended conference ADMS 46th DIV. Found that Lieut. R. H. G. OULTON had not arrived at 1/6 N. Staffs.: proceeded to Hqrs. 137 Bde. and discovered by telephone that Lieut. OULTON had gone by mistake to Transport Lines but was proceeding forthwith to Hqrs. of Battalion. Visited A.D.S. at MAROC and bearer post at BULLY GRENAY	
	12/6/17		General routine. With Capt. Harris proceeded to Exhibition of Sanitary appliances by Sanitary Sections of I Corps.	

2449 Wt. W14957/M90 750,000 1/16 J.B.C. & A. Forms/C.2118/12.

Instructions regarding War Diaries and Intelligence Summaries are contained in F. S. Regs., Part II. and the Staff Manual respectively. Title pages will be prepared in manuscript.

WAR DIARY
or
INTELLIGENCE SUMMARY.
(Erase heading not required.)

Army Form C. 2118.

Place	Date	Hour	Summary of Events and Information	Remarks and references to Appendices
LABEUVRIERE	29/8		called on for fatigues, that this block is the only one on which Nursing personnel are needed i.e. that by the above means it will be possible to run the rest station of 500 beds with 1 section of a F. Amb. if necessary without loss of efficiency.	
			In afternoon visited Corps Scabies station in order to get an insight into its working.	
			Arranged a detail of daily collection sick from Fosse 10. Horsed Amb leaves here daily 2 pm. puts up for the night at Fosse 10 returns with patients in morning	
			Detailed 1 Motor Ambulance for duty at Corps Scabies Station.	
			Horsed Transport now fully occupied: as 8 G.S.W. will till further notice draw 2 loads of shale daily from BRUAY in addition to the transport necessary to draw [illegible] rations, forage etc.	
	30/8		Sent two men, who have been trained in cement work to Corps Scabies Station to make concrete baths	
			Very wet in latter part of day: 8 G.S.W. loads shale drawn and roadmaking pushed	

A7092. Wt. W12839/M1293. 750,000. 1/17. D. D & L., Ltd. Forms/C2118/14.

Instructions regarding War Diaries and Intelligence Summaries are contained in F. S. Regs., Part II. and the Staff Manual respectively. Title Pages will be prepared in manuscript.

WAR DIARY
or
INTELLIGENCE SUMMARY
(Erase heading not required.)

Army Form C. 2118

Place	Date	Hour	Summary of Events and Information	Remarks and references to Appendices
S^T AMAND	19/1/17		Inspected posts at BIENVILLERS and progress of new bearer post on NAKED S^t	
	21/1/17		Inspected posts at FONCQUEVILLERS with ADMS 138 Bde drying room in the village. – Capt WLA HARRISON RAMC reported for duty.	
	22/1/17		ADMS's conference 10 am – inspected with him the post in NAKED S^t which is now in operation and evacuations from extreme left of Divisional front will now be conducted via NAKED S^t & trolley line to ADS BIENVILLERS instead of via NOBODYS BOTTOM & BERLES through adjoining division. Received 1 reinforcement MT ASC & 1 H.T.	
	24/1/17		Capt WLA HARRISON left for course at 3rd Army Sanitary School. Inspected advanced dressing station on both sectors.	
	25/1/17		Received 2 reinforcements RAMCT.	
	26/1/17		ADMS XVIII Corps inspected ADS BIENVILLERS and medical arrangements generally of L half of Div: front	

17

Instructions regarding War Diaries and Intelligence Summaries are contained in F. S. Regs., Part II. and the Staff Manual respectively. Title pages will be prepared in manuscript.

WAR DIARY
or
INTELLIGENCE SUMMARY.
(Erase heading not required.)

Army Form C. 2118.

1/3 NM Fd Amb

Vol 37

Place	Date	Hour	Summary of Events and Information — MEDICAL	Remarks and references to Appendices
WESTREHEM	1/3/18		Field Ambulance moved this morning to WESTREHEM with 137 Infy Bde group. – inspected by G.O.C 137 Bde en route.	
			Uneventful march 8km. Billets at WESTREHEM good.	
	2/3/18		Standing fast. – usual inspections and exercise for men	
	3/3/18		Standing fast. very cold with snow.	
			Paid unit: prepared for move tomorrow.	
	4/3/18		Field Ambulance moved to INSTITUT ST VAAST BÉTHUNE – 25 km. at 9.30 am. arriving 3 pm.	
			Midday halt had to curtailed to 40 minutes owing to the bitterly cold wind. A very satisfactory march, but easy as I was able to carry the packs in an empty Horsed Ambulance.	
			Quarters very good at Institute.	
			Detailed 'A' section to run the Hospital for local sick.	
			1/2 N.M. F.A also in same Institute but doing no Hospital work there. No wounded taken in.	
			This unit will also collect & dispose of all special cases eyes, ears etc. & will accommodate the dentist on his visit	

A5092—Wt. W12839/M1293 750,000. 1/17. D. D & L., Ltd. Forms/C2118/14.

B.E.F.

13rd N. Mid. F.A. 46th Divn. 2nd Corps. WESTERN FRONT.

O.C. Lt. Col. A.E. Hodder D.S.O. April. '17.

1st Army. 1.

1st Corps from 19/4/17.

Phase "B" Battle of Arras. April- May- 1917.

1st Period Attack on Vimy Ridge April.

1917.	Headquarters.	at Ecque-Docques.
April 1st.	Medical Arrangements:	Temp. Hospital was opened at Malancy from Map 36a O.31.a.5.5.
15th.	Moves.	To Bethune.
18th.	Moves Detachment:	A.D.S. in Liévin and Aix-Moulette taken over from Field Ambulance 24th Divn.
19th.	Moves:	To Aix-Noulette R.22.a.7.2.
	Transfer.	To 1st Corps.

WAR DIARY
or
INTELLIGENCE SUMMARY
(Erase heading not required.)

Army Form C. 2

Place	Date	Hour	Summary of Events and Information	Remarks and references to Appendices
GAUDIEMPRE	6/3/17		rescue of two old civilians whose cottage was perforated by a large gas shell: sent recommendation for reward to French Mission in duplicate through ordinary channel.	
			At 4pm ADS party was relieved by 1/3 N.C.F. Amb and rejoined at HdQrs.	
	7/3/17		Received notification Capt L T WILLIAMS to be struck off the strength of the unit as from 16/2/17	
	8/3/17		Capt FAIRLEY. RAMC (TC) from 51st Div. reported for duty.	
	9/3/17		Capt FAIRLEY to 1/5th Leicester Rgt for duty (temporary)	
	10/3/17		Supplied Horsed Amb to follow A & B. Batts 137 Bde from HALLOY area to SOUASTRE area.	
	11/3/17		Supplied Horsed Amb to follow remainder of 137 Bde from HALLOY area to BAYENCOURT & SOUASTRE.	
			Visited HQrs 137 Bde & made routine arrangements for collection of sick.	
			Visited 95. F. Amb. COIGNEUX in view of possibility of relieving them. Capt S.Y. WALSH left for temporary duty 4th Lincs.	

1875 Wt. W593/826 1,000,000 4/15 J.B.C. & A. A.D.S.S./Forms/C. 2118.

WAR DIARY
or
INTELLIGENCE SUMMARY
(Erase heading not required.)

Army Form C. 2118

Instructions regarding War Diaries and Intelligence Summaries are contained in F. S. Regs., Part II. and the Staff Manual respectively. Title Pages will be prepared in manuscript.

3RD NORTH MIDLAND FIELD AMBULANCE ROYAL ARMY MEDICAL CORPS

Place	Date	Hour	Summary of Events and Information	Remarks and references to Appendices
LA HERLIERE	10/7/16		Accompanied ADMS the Sanitary Officer on inspection of advanced dressing stations & R.A.P.s	
	11/7/16		A.D.S. at BERLES moved from site on POMMIER ROAD W15c73 to Billet no 47. at W21b0.2. [Map sheet 57C 1/40000] Cellar accommodation in new quarters good, buildings well sheltered and rather nearer the evacuation trenches. Ample accommodation & well protection for transport; The billet in POMMIER Rd retained as overflow. Visited advanced bearer post at W10d central and directed some necessary alterations to entrance and enlargement of Gas lock to 8 feet so as to accommodate a stretcher. Handed over advanced dressing station at BAILLEULVAL to 1/1 N. Mid. Fd Amb. closing its personnel in on ADS at BERLES.	
	12/7/16		Sent 1 Officer and 20 OR with necessary equipment to ADS 10pm in expectation of a show – nothing happened as the wind changed so they returned 1am	

1875 Wt. W593/826 1,000,000 4/15 J.B.C. & A. A.D.S.S./Forms/C. 2118.

Instructions regarding War Diaries and Intelligence Summaries are contained in F. S. Regs., Part II. and the Staff Manual respectively. Title pages will be prepared in manuscript.

WAR DIARY
or
INTELLIGENCE SUMMARY.
(*Erase heading not required.*)

Army Form C. 2118.

Place	Date	Hour	Summary of Events and Information	Remarks and references to Appendices
BETHUNE 22/3/18			A quiet morning. A few small calibre shells being hopped into the town about 1.15.	
			Majr Bradley & Lt Richard departed 14 days leave to U.K.	
			During the last 4 or 5 days work continued at horse-lines — now showing result.	
			Men generally occupied fatigues & exercises.	
			Fire picquet exercise	
[illegible]	23/3/18		Had sudden orders to ~~turn~~ take over charge of Asst. CRS at LABEUVRIÈRE from 1/3 E. Lancs. Fd. Amb. to hand over whole of Institute St Vaast to 1/2 N.M. Fd Amb and duties as regards local sick to 1/1 N.M. Fd Amb which was taking over premises at ANNEZIN.	
LABEUVRIÈRE			Carried on as requisite to effect this & assumed charge of C.R.S. midday.	
			Lt Col A.H. Hodder returned to duty from ordinary leave.	
			A number of enemy bombing machines passed over in the evening between 7pm and midnight on their way to & from distant objectives. No bombs dropped near here. Our own scouts active also "Archies"	

Instructions regarding War Diaries and Intelligence Summaries are contained in F. S. Regs., Part II. and the Staff Manual respectively. Title pages will be prepared in manuscript.

WAR DIARY
or
INTELLIGENCE SUMMARY.
(Erase heading not required.)

Army Form C. 2118.

Place	Date	Hour	Summary of Events and Information	Remarks and references to Appendices
HESDIGNEUL	24 6/18		Five further men sent for nursing instruction &c at No 6 C.C.S. Usual night working party for ESSARS & RAP AHH	
	25 6/18		Uneventful AHH	
	26 6/18		Lt McCREA left for duty with 50th Divn & accordingly struck off strength. Usual ESSARS working party. CAPT KING returned from leave today AHH	
	27 6/18		Uneventful.	
	28 6/18		Divn transferred to XIII Corps. Capt Florian MRC USA reported for duty night of 27 6/18 & left today to replace Lt Charnley (sick) with 1/5 Sherwoods AHH. M2/134554 Pte Williams A awarded D.C.M.	
	29 6/18		Twenty eight O.R. with "A" Sect Equipment be sent to run XIII Corps Scabies Stn Allouagne. Up to date working party of Sgt Millard + 25 men sent nightly to work at RAP Essars. AHH	

D. D. & L., London, E.C. (A8co4) Wt W1771/M2031 750,000 5/17 Sch. 52 Forms/C2118/14

Instructions regarding War Diaries and Intelligence Summaries are contained in F. S. Regs., Part II. and the Staff Manual respectively. Title Pages will be prepared in manuscript.

WAR DIARY
or
INTELLIGENCE SUMMARY
(Erase heading not required.)

Army Form C. 2118

Place	Date	Hour	Summary of Events and Information	Remarks and references to Appendices
SAVEUSE	27/3/17		Reconnoitred roads in neighbourhood and entraining facilities at SALEUX.	
	28/3/17		Reconnoitred entraining station BACOUEL pursuant to change of orders	
	29/3/17		Closed Hdqrs SAVEUSE 9.30 am. marched to BACOUEL entrained & left station 4 pm	
	30/3/17		Detrained at BERGUETTE 4.30 am in pouring rain marched to quarters at ECQUEDECQUES. via LILLERS.	
ECQUE-DECQUES	31/3/17		Headquarters established V 8 d. 9.1 (sheet 36 A 1/40000) Inspected MELANOY FARM (O31a central) with a view to occupying it as a hospital for sick. Saw all medical officers of 137 Bde and acquainted them with provisional arrangements for sick	

A E Hodder
Lieut Col.

1875 Wt. W593/826 1,000,000 4/15 J.B.C. & A. A.D.S.S./Forms/C. 2118.

Instructions regarding War Diaries and Intelligence Summaries are contained in F. S. Regs., Part II. and the Staff Manual respectively. Title Pages will be prepared in manuscript.

WAR DIARY
or
INTELLIGENCE SUMMARY
(Erase heading not required.)

3RD NORTH MIDLAND FIELD AMBULANCE — ROYAL ARMY MEDICAL CORPS

Army Form C. 2118

Place	Date	Hour	Summary of Events and Information	Remarks and references to Appendices
ST AMAND	12/1/17		Floor of room at ADS BIENVILLERS which was wrecked by shell yesterday has been covered with 2 feet of sand bags. Struts as fire to protect cellar beneath which is sleeping quarters of personnel.	
	13/1/17		Inspected A.D.S. Fonquevillers – further constructional work at a standstill owing to lack of material.	
			Quarters of transport section and wagon lines again altered at GAUDIEMPRÉ owing to incoming troops.	
	14/1/17		Visited A.D.S. BIENVILLERS in morning – in aft. GAUDIEMPRÉ to get satisfactory arrangements for transport section quarters	
	15/1/17		A.D.M.S. conference 9.30 am. – Inspected transport lines and quarters	
	16/1/17		Escorted ADMS 69th Division round BIENVILLERS ADS and bearer post HANNESCAMPS	
			Capt E.T WILLANS departed for Officers Convalescent Hosp CAP MARTIN	
	17/1/17		Showed Lt Col ~~[illegible]~~ DAWSON cdg 2/1 N. Mid Field Amb 69th Div round all dressing stations, bearer posts and gave all information in my power regarding collection & evacuation	

Army Form C. 2118.

WAR DIARY
or
INTELLIGENCE SUMMARY.
(Erase heading not required.)

Instructions regarding War Diaries and Intelligence Summaries are contained in F. S. Regs., Part II. and the Staff Manual respectively. Title pages will be prepared in manuscript.

Place	Date	Hour	Summary of Events and Information	Remarks and references to Appendices
LABOURSE	31/8/17		Summary of changes of personnel for month of August 1917.	
			Struck off strength – Officers 2 { Capt D.C. Sutton to No1 CCS for duty; Capt J.C. Harris killed in action }	
			O.R. 6 – one killed in action	
			Taken on strength – Officers – nil	
			O.R. – 15.	
			A.C. Haddow Lt Col cmdg 1/3 NMFA.	

A7092. Wt. W12839/M1293. 750,000. 1/17. D. D & L., Ltd. Forms/C2118/14.

Instructions regarding War Diaries and Intelligence Summaries are contained in F. S. Regs., Part II. and the Staff Manual respectively. Title Pages will be prepared in manuscript.

WAR DIARY
or
INTELLIGENCE SUMMARY

(Erase heading not required.)

1/3 NM Fd Amb

Vol 25

MEDICAL

Place	Date	Hour	Summary of Events and Information	Remarks and references to Appendices
GAUDIEMPRÉ	1/3/17		Enemy used gas shells extensively in BERLES and 22 sect. 16 shell gassed cases sent down, 7 of whom were detained in F. Amb. as likely to be able to return to duty in a few days.	
	2/3/17		Inspected ADS BERLES. - Gas trapping in ADS cellar now completed. - 2 reinforcements received	
	3/3/17		Inspection of all ranks RAMC in marching order.	
	4/3/17		Inspection of Transport Section in order for the road.	
	5/3/17		Conference at ADMS office 10 am	
	6/3/17		BERLES heavily gas shelled night of 5th–6th. Advanced dressing station invaded by French civilians who in their panic rushed through & destroyed the gas traps protecting cellar dressing station which filled with gas & became untenable. All casualties therefore were dealt with in the courtyard. Sent memo. to French Mission re subject of the civilians & their behaviour which would have been the cause of many casualties if the enemy had mixed shrapnel with his gas shells. Pte PHELAN effected a gallant	

Instructions regarding War Diaries and Intelligence Summaries are contained in F. S. Regs., Part II. and the Staff Manual respectively. Title Pages will be prepared in manuscript.

WAR DIARY
or
INTELLIGENCE SUMMARY
(Erase heading not required.)

Army Form C. 2118

Place	Date	Hour	Summary of Events and Information	Remarks and references to Appendices
St AMAND	24/12/16		Visited ADS Bienvillers in morning – attended lecture by ADMS on Trench foot in afternoon.	
	25/12/16		Visited all posts at which members of the Field Amb. were on duty – forward line in morning; transport and Divl. Baths in afternoon – All men in good spirits. Xmas Dinner, Roast pork, vegetables, plum pudding, beer, canned cherries & smokes: these supplemented by mens own purchases in many cases.	
	28/12/16		Inspected Transport lines – sent loaded wagons to be unloaded into store hut so as to relieve wear on limited number of wagons & also preserve equipment. Also inspected ADS BIENVILLERS which in all essentials is now completed – some more timber etc is needed to make racks for stretchers so as further to economise space.	
	29/12/16		Inspected ADS FONQUEVILLERS in morning: enemy shelling orchard on hand at back of ADS – more damage to trenches & drainage channels being choked up.	

1875 Wt. W593/826 1,000,000 4/15 J.B.C. & A. A.D.S.S./Forms/C. 2118.

Instructions regarding War Diaries and Intelligence Summaries are contained in F. S. Regs., Part II. and the Staff Manual respectively. Title Pages will be prepared in manuscript.

WAR DIARY
or
INTELLIGENCE SUMMARY
(Erase heading not required.)

Army Form C. 2118

Place	Date	Hour	Summary of Events and Information	Remarks and references to Appendices
LA HERLIÈRE	14/8/16		D.D.V.S. 3rd Army inspected Horses of Transport section.	
	15/8/16		Sent Capt Harrison and 40 Bearers to BERLES in readiness for "Gas operations"	
	17/8/16		2 RAMC reinforcements received	
	18/8/16		Bearers returned from BERLES to stand to on receipt of warning from Div Hqrs or direct from OC Special Bde RE. i/c of Gas Operations.	
	19/8/16		Stand to for "Gas" ordered 8 30 pm: Bearers & transport moved up to BERLES at once in accordance with orders issued as above – Stand down ordered 2 am.	
	20/8/16		Another Stand to at 10 pm – washed out / 1 ASC reinforcement received.	
	21/8/16		Another stand to at 10 pm – washed out	
	22/8/16		Between 9 pm & 11 pm 16 men were brought in to ADS suffering from gas poisoning owing to an enemy shell	

Instructions regarding War Diaries and Intelligence Summaries are contained in F. S. Regs., Part II. and the Staff Manual respectively. Title Pages will be prepared in manuscript.

WAR DIARY
or
INTELLIGENCE SUMMARY

(Erase heading not required.)

Army Form C. 2118

Place	Date	Hour	Summary of Events and Information	Remarks and references to Appendices
ZELOBES	1/12/15		Occupied quarters at LOCON vacated by 57th Field Amb: with C section who established a hospital for lightly sick.	
			Personnel of 6 NCOs and 15 men sent to assist in working of washing and drying house of 137 I.B. and Capt MILLER put in charge.	
	4/12/15		The Division having received orders to move back, closed Officers Rest Hospital;	
	5/12/15		In pursuance of the orders withdrew section from LOCON.	
	6/12/15		Personnel attached to 137 I.B. washing house withdrawn	
	7/12/15		Under orders from "Q" office exchanged 16 horses H.D. for 32 mules	
	8/12/15		All animals in charge tested with Mallein – no suspicious symptoms evoked: exchanged further 2 horses H.D. for 8 mules or light draught horse	
	9/12/15		Moved to billets at BOIS DE PACAUT – Q 33 b. (BETHUNE combined sheet) Impossible to park transport on fields owing to flood water. Owing to increase of draught animals without any increase of transport personnel great difficulties were experienced in making the move	

Instructions regarding War Diaries and Intelligence Summaries are contained in F. S. Regs., Part II. and the Staff Manual respectively. Title pages will be prepared in manuscript.

WAR DIARY
or
INTELLIGENCE SUMMARY.
(Erase heading not required.)

Army Form C. 2118.

Place	Date	Hour	Summary of Events and Information	Remarks and references to Appendices
BETHUNE	9/3/18		Usual drills, exercises &c. Football match v. 1/2 N.M.F.A. easily won. Unit marched to FOUQUIERES to attend match.	
	10/3/18		A most uninteresting day.	
	11/3/18		A.D.C. made rapid tour of grounds, as a result of his observations, work of building up ramps around horse standings to height of 6 feet pushed along. Sent Sgt Collins + 2 corporals to HARLEY ST (A.D.S. of 1/1 N.M.F.A.) for a 2 days tour of line. 14 local wounded admitted + evacuated.	
	12/3/18		Capt A.W. Mallor + Sgt Bore sent up to [illegible] front to learn routes of evacuation of wounded. Unit mainly employed on horse line work.	
	13/3/18		Attended A.D.M.S. Conference, plans discussed for front line evacuation of wounded. Sgt Collins + 2 corporals returned from Cambrin. Investigated sites for signboards (→ Ambulance)	

Instructions regarding War Diaries and Intelligence Summaries are contained in F. S. Regs., Part II. and the Staff Manual respectively. Title Pages will be prepared in manuscript.

WAR DIARY
or
INTELLIGENCE SUMMARY
(Erase heading not required.)

Army Form C. 2118

3 N M Fd Amb

46 D

Vol 26

Place	Date	Hour	MEDICAL. Summary of Events and Information	Remarks and references to Appendices
ECQUE-DECQUES	1/4/17		Opened temporary hospital at MALANOY FARM - (O 31 a. 5.5 sheet 36a) with 2 officers + one tent subdivision.	
			Visited 230 and 231 Bdes R.F.A. to inform them of arrangements for sick collection.	
			Capt E.W. STRANGE left for instruction in administrative duties under D.D.M.S. II Corps.	
	2/4/17		Attended ADMS conference 10 am.	
			Inspected Hospital 11 am.	
			Took sick parade A.S.C. companies 2 pm.	
	4/4/17		Capt J. MILLER returned from duty as a/DADMS.	
			Inspected Hospital in morning.	
			Submitted scheme to ADMS for light mobile detachment of officers + O.R. plus transport - including 2 pack mules - for following in close touch with Infantry in event of advance.	
			Inoculation of whole unit practically completed.	
			Inspection of SBR and PH helmets completed.	
			1 Horse Amb or Water cart to 1.O.M. II Corps Workshops for repair	

Instructions regarding War Diaries and Intelligence Summaries are contained in F. S. Regs., Part II. and the Staff Manual respectively. Title pages will be prepared in manuscript.

WAR DIARY
or
INTELLIGENCE SUMMARY.
(Erase heading not required.)

Army Form C. 2118.

Place	Date	Hour	Summary of Events and Information	Remarks and references to Appendices
BETHUNE	18/3/18		During afternoon enemy fired on observation balloon nr Bethune several shells exploding on ground contact. One casualty – old woman slightly wounded.	
	19/3/18		Near midday enemy shelled town with supposed 7" Naval shells – Some 40 Casualties amongst civilians & troops 35 more serious cases evacuated to Lapugnoy 18 C.C.S.	
	20/3/18		Further shelling of Bethune with few casualties ADMS. Conference attended. Useful results Nil.	
	21/3/18		Enemy began to shell town at 5 a.m for an hour, no one injured. Intermittent fire during day a nuisance as all civilians refused to be dragged from cellars into their shops, estaminets &c. Ambulance Troupe gave concert from 6 pm – 8 pm. – At 8.10 pm the Boche planes began a demonstration which lasted until 10 pm. – They left their mark in the town. At midnight further shelling, – including supposed Gas shells in the vicinity. During afternoon Lt Reid & nursing subsection of "B" section left for tempy duty at 58 C.C.S. LILLERS.	

A.7092 Wt. W12839/M1293. 750,000. 1/17. D. D & L., Ltd. Forms/C2118/14.

Confidential

Instructions regarding War Diaries and Intelligence Summaries are contained in F. S. Regs., Part II. and the Staff Manual respectively. Title pages will be prepared in manuscript.

WAR DIARY
or
INTELLIGENCE SUMMARY.
(Erase heading not required.)

3rd FIELD AMBULANCE
46th DIVISION

Army Form C. 2118.

Hour, Date, Place	Summary of Events and Information	Remarks and references to Appendices
Near TOPERINGHE July 1. 1915	In the rear of our billetting field a well has been dug by the men of the unit capable of supplying 350 gallons a day. A spring has been dammed & a wooden bath let into the same for bathing the men. This work has been carried out by carpenters in the unit, the material being obtained from the Divisional Engineers.	
July 2. 15.	Went with ADMS 46 Division to KRUISSTAAT & inspected a field there at ROAD JUNCTION H 18 d 10.5 (1/40,000 No 28) Dug outs capable of holding 20 men to be made here. One MO & 20 Bearers will be here & collection of wounded go on through the day. A pump obtained from Engineers for drawing	

Instructions regarding War Diaries and Intelligence Summaries are contained in F. S. Regs., Part II. and the Staff Manual respectively. Title Pages will be prepared in manuscript.

WAR DIARY
or
INTELLIGENCE SUMMARY
(Erase heading not required.)

Army Form C.

1/3rd NORTH MIDLAND FIELD AMBULANCE ROYAL ARMY MEDICAL CORPS

Place	Date	Hour	Summary of Events and Information	Remarks and references to Appendices
GAUDIEMPRE	11/2/17		Received 8 O.R. reinforcements from Base Depot.	
	14/2/17		D.D.M.S. XVIII Corps inspected ADS BERLES. Positions of ADS & bearer posts as follows. Mapsheet 51C 1/10000 — ADS — W.21.b.0.9. Bearer post } W 16 d 4.7 in Farnborough Road Trench. 1 RAP } 1 Bearer post } W 22.a.7.5 in Nobody's Bottom 1 R.A.P. } where BERLES-MONCHY Road crosses Ravine.	
	16/2/17		Main dressing station visited by DMS 3rd Army & two officers of [illegible] Army Medical Service. DDMS corps outlined changes contemplated at site to enable it to accommodate Corps Rest Station as well as main dressing station. Erection of huts to begin at once. Capt J. C. Harris returned from short leave.	

1875 Wt. W593/826 1,000,000 4/15 J.B.C. & A. A.D.S.S./Forms/C. 2118.

Instructions regarding War Diaries and Intelligence Summaries are contained in F. S. Regs., Part II. and the Staff Manual respectively. Title pages will be prepared in manuscript.

WAR DIARY
or
INTELLIGENCE SUMMARY.
(Erase heading not required.)

Army Form C. 2118.

Hour, Date, Place	Summary of Events and Information	Remarks and references to Appendices
25 – 4 – 15	liquids used by the Germans against our troops N of YPRES – He proceeded with Lt McNee to HAZEBROUCK – At noon orders received from Col Geddes DDMS to evacuate all sick + prepare for the reception of wounded – All evacuated either to Regiments, another Divisional Rest Station or to No 8 Casualty Clearing Hospital by 3.30 pm – The Rest Hospital to be an overflow from No 8 Casualty Clearing Hospital + to be part of this unit – The personnel to be officers NCOs + men of "A" Section of the 1/3 North Midland Field Ambulance – Lt McNee came in and asked for the help of Lt Boyd to assist him in examining the blood of soldiers poisoned by "Gas" used by the Germans – Lt Boyd sent to him –	

(9 29 6) W4141—463 100,000 9/14 H W V Forms/C. 2118/10

Phase "B" cont.

2nd Period cont.

1917. May.25th.	Casualties. About 40 wounded dealt with during the night.
26th.	Moves: To La Beuvriere.
27th.31st.	General routine and organisation.

Instructions regarding War Diaries and Intelligence Summaries are contained in F. S. Regs., Part II. and the Staff Manual respectively. Title Pages will be prepared in manuscript.

WAR DIARY
or
INTELLIGENCE SUMMARY
(Erase heading not required.)

Army Form C. 2118

Place	Date	Hour	Summary of Events and Information	Remarks and references to Appendices
ST AMAND	22/11/16		Capt BARTON. MC. of this unit wounded in foot ~~while~~ while walking from N dressing station to South ADS FONQUEVILLERS – Major P A Lloyd Jones DSO DADMS 46 Div who was wounded at same time ~~was~~ died of wounds a couple of hours later. Capt Barton evacuated to 20 CCS. – likely to be incapacitated three months.	
	23/11/16		Visited advanced dressing station FONQUEVILLERS. Enemy are putting a good many shell – whizzbangs and 105 mm apparently about the latter dressing station & damaging the shelter trenches: this necessitates constant work repairing damage done by shell & wet. Dube dressing station has to be pumped out daily. Represented Field Amb at funeral of Major P. A. Lloyd Jones. DSO.	

1875 Wt. W593/826 1,000,000 4/15 J.B.C. & A. A.D.S.S./Forms/C. 2118.

Instructions regarding War Diaries and Intelligence Summaries are contained in F. S. Regs., Part II. and the Staff Manual respectively. Title pages will be prepared in manuscript.

WAR DIARY
or
INTELLIGENCE SUMMARY.
(Erase heading not required.)

Army Form C. 2118.

Place	Date	Hour	Summary of Events and Information	Remarks and references to Appendices
ANNEZIN	31/1/18		Changes of personnel in month of January Officers – on 3 off 2 O.R. – on nil off 8. 2. O.R. attended to receive medal ribbons at hands of Army Commander at Divl HdQrs.	

A E Hodder
Lt Col RAMC OC 1/3 N.M. Fd Amb.

A7092. Wt. W12839/M1293. 750,000. 1/17. D. D & L., Ltd. Forms/C2118/14.

Instructions regarding War Diaries and Intelligence Summaries are contained in F. S. Regs., Part II. and the Staff Manual respectively. Title Pages will be prepared in manuscript.

WAR DIARY
or
INTELLIGENCE SUMMARY
(Erase heading not required.)

Army Form C. 2118

Place	Date	Hour	Summary of Events and Information	Remarks and references to Appendices
Aix Noulette	23.5.17		at Labourse. Visit OC 1/2 N. Mid Fd Amb inspected the hospital when doing so received wire from ADMS postponing the relief until May 26th. Notified Capt Butler that in consequence of operations I should not further relief men of 1/2 N Mid Field Amb on May 24th. Capt Sproson 2 NCOs & 15 men arrived from Maroc & proceeded to Lievin requested Major Farrer to return to Main Dressing Station an equal number of NCOs & men. Interpreter Mr le Blanc returned from leave	
"	24.5.17		Despatched to Capt Mellor ADS Maroc 2 NCO & 38 men. Sent 2 acting NCOs to report to OC 1/2 N Mid Field Amb to be instructed in duties of billet warden & scabies inspector. Detailed 1 horse amb to report at Dressing Station Bully Grenay 8 pm. Warned remaining horse ambulances & all motor ambulances to stand to.	

1875 Wt. W593/826 1,000,000 4/15 J.B.C. & A. A.D.S.S./Forms/C. 2118.

Army Form C. 2118.

Instructions regarding War Diaries and Intelligence Summaries are contained in F. S. Regs., Part II. and the Staff Manual respectively. Title pages will be prepared in manuscript.

WAR DIARY
or
INTELLIGENCE SUMMARY.

(Erase heading not required.)

Place	Date	Hour	Summary of Events and Information	Remarks and references to Appendices
LABEUVRIERE	31/3/18		Summary of changes of personnel for month	
			Officers — on 1 — off 2 (chaplains attd)	
			OR — 28 — 9	
			A. E. Hodder Lt Col cdg 1/3 N. Mid. Fd. Amb	
			In the field 31/3/18	

A7092. Wt. W12839/M1293. 750,000. 1/17. D. D & L., Ltd. Forms/C2118/14.

To Officer Commanding,
1/3 N. Midland Field Ambulance

Sir

Herewith as you requested I send some notes on the roads in the area through which we might have to evacuate wounded, together with a rough tracing from Map 13.28.SW 1/20000 on which I have graded the roads with particular reference to their suitability for Ambulance transport. The grading of these roads is based on my own knowledge: all those graded I have been over myself either on foot or on horseback under varied conditions of weather.

1 Roads shaded in black are main roads suitable for horse or motor ambulances under all conditions of weather, but on some of these particularly the NEUVE EGLISE - WULVERGHEM ROAD it is only possible for two motors to pass in a few places owing to the pavé been many inches, in places 18" above the level of the sides

2 Roads marked Blue are suitable for horsed wagons and in many instances motor ambulances in dry weather though they will rarely allow two motors to pass. In wet weather they would be impossible for motors and difficult or even impossible for horsed wagons which ~~would~~ should in any case be 4-horsed. If that were not feasible a spare pair should be available to hook on over the worst stretches.

3 Roads marked Red are unsuited for wheeled transport of wounded whether motor or horsed. but might be utilised for hand carriage of stretchers.
On all except the main roads (shaded black) passage of wagons might be hindered by fire control telephone lines crossing at a seven or eight foot level from the ground. I have indicated these in a couple of instances.

4 I suggest as wagon rendezvous in case of attack, on the N. side the junction of the WULVERGHEM - LINDENHOEK and N.EGLISE - LINDENHOEK roads where good cover is obtainable and whence there are roads for evacuation via DRANOUTRE: on the S. side a field on S.E. side of square of N.EGLISE whence evacuation could be effected to A.D.S. or direct via ROMARIN. Hand carriage of stretchers would in my opinion be necessary

Instructions regarding War Diaries and Intelligence Summaries are contained in F. S. Regs., Part II. and the Staff Manual respectively. Title Pages will be prepared in manuscript.

WAR DIARY
or
INTELLIGENCE SUMMARY
(Erase heading not required.)

Army Form C. 2118.

Place	Date	Hour	Summary of Events and Information	Remarks and references to Appendices
LABEUVRIERE	20	6.0 AM.	Despatched bearers in 4 motor ambulances.	
		9.45 AM	Motor ambs. all returned, not being required.	
		3.0 p.m.	Reported at ADMS office then proceeded to PONT GRENAY where Capt. MILLER was installed.	
	21		Proceeded to British Red Cross Society and was supplied with many hospital necessaries. The 24 bearers who had been on duty with the 1/2 F. Amb. returned.	
	22.		Usual routine	
	23		Usual routine. Lieut. ~~WA~~ WATERHOUSE evacuated sick and struck off the strength from 21. 6.17.	
	24		By order of A.D.M.S. despatched 2 N.C.O.s and 22 bearers to report to O.C. 1/2 N. Mid. F. Amb. also despatched 2 Ambulances to same unit. Proceeded to 46th DIV. Depot Bn. and arranged for M.O. of 1/3 N.M. F. Amb. ~~[illegible]~~ vice Capt. Lane whom I exchanged by order of ADMS to 9th Reserve Park. Capt. D.C. SUTTIE reported to duty from 46th DIV. D.A.C.	

2449 Wt. W14957/M90 750,000 1/16 J.B.C. & A. Forms/C.2118/12.

B.E.F.

1/3rd N. Mid. F.A. 46th Divn. 1st Corps. WESTERN FRONT.
O.C. Lt. Col. A.E. Hodder D.S.O. May. '17.
O.C. Maj. T.A. Barron from 15/4/17.
~~1st Army.~~ 1.

Phase "B" Battle of Arras- April- May. '17.

2nd Period Captu e of Siegfried Line May.

1917.
May. 8th. Operations Enemy. Liévin shelled with mixed H.E. and gas shells from 8 p.m. 7th to about 4 a.m. 8th between 10.30p.m. and 12.30.a.m. about 50 gas Shells fell in close proximity to A.D.S. the cellars were quickly full of gas- S.B.R. were worn by all ranks and patients and no one was gassed in the A.D.S. The gas was cleared by fires and fans the process having to be repeated 3 times

Casualties Gas. 78 cases were dealt with at M.D.S. one died and the majority of cases were slight.

11th. Operations Enemy: Gas. Enemy used gas shells freely each night necessitating wearing of S.B.R. frequently.

Decorations. Sgt. Collins and Ptes. Barlow and Conolly awarded M.M.

13th. Casualties. R.A.M.C. Lt. Col. Hodder wounded at Liévin-

15th. Appointment: Major T.A. Barron appointed O.C. vice Lt. Col. Hodder.

21st. Operations Enemy. M.D.S. shelled at 8.15 p.m. with two salvoes of 4 shells each- three of which struck the building.

The shells were of a fresh type detonating on striking the roof- sending forward a shower of splintered shell case, but spreading quite horizontally-

Transport billet(at the time unoccupied) was blown in and much clothing and equipment destroyed.

Casualties: R.A.M.C. 0 and 7 wounded.

Instructions regarding War Diaries and Intelligence Summaries are contained in F. S. Regs., Part II. and the Staff Manual respectively. Title pages will be prepared in manuscript.

WAR DIARY
or
INTELLIGENCE SUMMARY.
(Erase heading not required.)

Army Form C. 2118.

Hour, Date, Place	Summary of Events and Information	Remarks and references to Appendices
30 – 4 – 15.	Summary :- Remained 62 Admitted 10. Transferred 68 Deaths 2 Remaining 2. 8 Thermos Flasks received from the A.D.M.S – Two issued to each Battalion of the STAFFS INF BRIG for use in the Trenches for wounded – Sgt James proceeded to G.H.Q with Collapsible Wheeled Stretcher Carrier =.	

H H C Dent.
LIEUT.-COLONEL.
COMM'DG 1/3RD N. MID. FIELD AMB. R.A.M. CORPS.

(9 29 6) W 4141—463 100,000 9/14 H W V Forms/C. 2118/10

Instructions regarding War Diaries and Intelligence Summaries are contained in F. S. Regs., Part II. and the Staff Manual respectively. Title Pages will be prepared in manuscript.

WAR DIARY
or
INTELLIGENCE SUMMARY
(Erase heading not required.)

Army Form C. 2118

Place	Date	Hour	Summary of Events and Information	Remarks and references to Appendices
Lahnigrade	31/5/17		Summary of changes in personnel Month of May 1917	
			Struck off strength — Sick Wounded & regimental Duties	
			Officers 1 – 2	
			O.R. 5 6 11	
			Taken on strength Officers 4 Major Barron (from 4/R.M. [illegible] Amb) Lts Gavin, Dalton, Jack	from base
			O R 20	
			J. W. Barron Major	

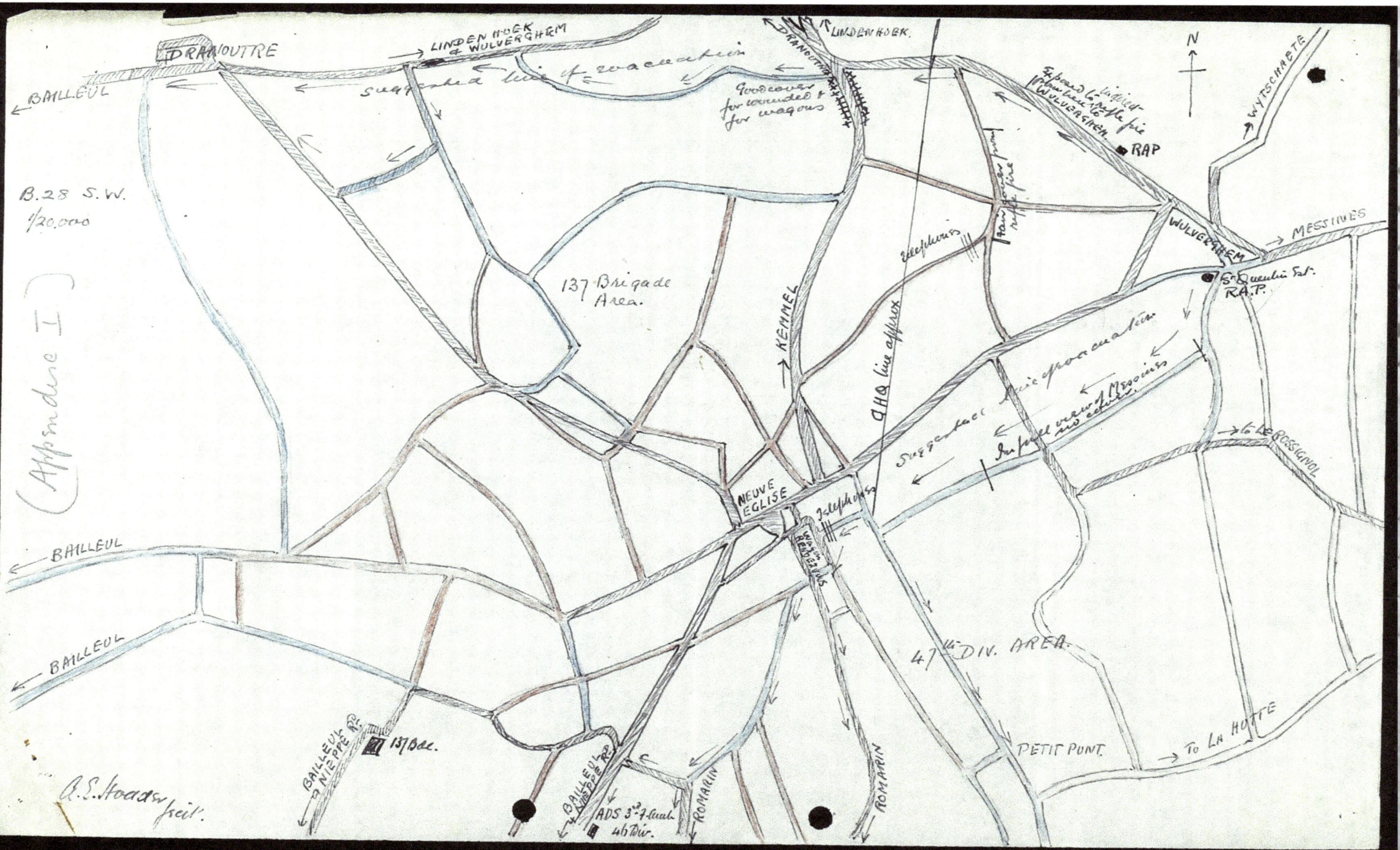

Appendix I
B.28 S.W.
1/20,000
DRANOUTRE
LINDEN HOEK & WULVERGHEM
Suggested line of evacuation
Good cover for wounded & for wagons
LINDENHOEK.
DRANOUTRE
N
WYTSCHAETE
RAP
WULVERGHEM
MESSINES
St Quentin Cat. R.A.P.
BAILLEUL
137 Brigade Area.
KEMMEL
Telephones
GHQ line approx
Suggested line of evacuation
In full view of Messines
to LE ROSSIGNOL
NEUVE EGLISE
BAILLEUL
BAILLEUL
47th DIV. AREA.
PETIT PONT.
To LA HUTTE
BAILLEUL & NIEPPE Rd
137 Bde.
BAILLEUL & NIEPPE Rd
ADS 3rd Fd Amb 46 Div.
ROMARIN
ROMARIN

Instructions regarding War Diaries and Intelligence Summaries are contained in F. S. Regs., Part II. and the Staff Manual respectively. Title Pages will be prepared in manuscript.

WAR DIARY
or
INTELLIGENCE SUMMARY
(Erase heading not required.)

Army Form C. 2118

Place	Date	Hour	Summary of Events and Information	Remarks and references to Appendices
GAUDIEMPRE	12/3/17		Visited ADMS in morning. In aft. selected site for Divisional Collecting Station on SOUASTRE - FONQUEVILLERS Road for impending operations.	
	13/3/17		Set up Divisional Collecting Station (cellar) at E25b. centre. (Sheet 57D). Capt Sturrock i/c - Sent 78 O.R. for bearer duty with 1st N. M. F. Amb.	
	14/3/17		Div Collecting Station dealt with 117 casualties on night of 13th 14th : Main dressing station 55 lying cases. - DDMS V Corps inspected both places.	
	15/3/17		78 O.R. returned from duty with 1 N M F A - Attended Conference of F Amb. commanders at ADMS Office 5.30pm	
	17/3/17		Lt Phibbs S. J. returned from temporary duty with 1/6 S. Staff	
	18/3/17		80 O.R. sent up to GOMMECOURT - BUCQUOY area to clear ground of dead.	
	19/3/17		Capt E W Strange & Lt S. J. Phibbs c 1 complete Tent Subdiv. left for temporary duty with No 4 C.C.S. VARENNES	

1/3rd N. Mid. F.A. 46th Divn. 1st Corps. WESTERN FRONT.

O.C. Lt. Col. A.E. Hodder D.S.O. April. '17.

1st Army. 2.

Phase "B" Battle of Arras_ April- May. 1917.

1st Period Attack on Vimy Ridge April.

1917.

April.19th. Transfer. To 1st Corps.

22nd. Location Field Ambulances. Br. Posts at Cité de Rollencourt M.27.b.4.2.

A.D.S. white House- Lievin- M.28.b.7.2.

Br. post- Bethune-Arras Road- R.29.b.3.0.

23rd. Operations. Enemy.attacked by 139th Bde.

Casualties. M.D.S. was kept fairly busy.

24th. OPerations Enemy. Shell of large calibre fell in courtyard of A.D.S.

Casualties R.A.M.C. O and 1 killed O and 2 wounded.

28th. Evacuation. R. Bgde. line was Approx. from M. 18.c. central to M.30.d.2.3.

R.A.Ps. at M.28.a.70.65. and M.28.b.25.0.1.

A.D.S. at White Chateau- M.28.b.7.2.

Thence by wheeled carrier to R.A.M.C. post at Cité de Rollencourt M.27.b.4.2. whence by Motor Ambulance via Angres road through M.26.c. and d.M.25.d.(Map 36c) R.30.b. and point Colonels House-R.29.d.6.6.(Map 36b) on Arras_Bethune Road to Aix-Noulette-

29th. Decorations:-

Pte. W.P. Phelan awarded Croix de Guerre for act of gallantry in rescueing 2 French Civilians whose house had been blown in by large gas shell.

Instructions regarding War Diaries and Intelligence Summaries are contained in F. S. Regs., Part II. and the Staff Manual respectively. Title pages will be prepared in manuscript.

WAR DIARY
or
INTELLIGENCE SUMMARY.
(Erase heading not required.)

Army Form C. 2118.

Place	Date	Hour	Summary of Events and Information	Remarks and references to Appendices
BRUAY	16/8/18		Day generally spent in cleaning up billets & collecting from HESDIGNEUL old salvaged R.E. material to improve at BRUAY. SEH	
	17/8/18		Major A.C.F. Turner from 1/2nd. N. Mid. F. Amb assumed command of unit. ACT	
	18/8/18		Visited A.D.S. GORRE & bearer posts. ACT	
	20/8/18		Visited ADS. ESSARS & bearer post at LE HAMEL; also walking wounded post of 1/1st. N.M. F. Amb. in BETHUNE. ACT	
	21/8/18		Enemy retiring. At 11 P.M. sent 12 extra bearers & 2 wheeled stretchers to ADS. ESSARS & 12 extra bearers & one extra motor ambulance to ADS GORRE. ACT	
	22/8/18		Visited ADS's & bearer posts & RAP's together with DDMS & ADMS. On ESSARS subsector left RAP advanced to LES FACONS (X.15.c central); right RAP to X.15.d.2.0. On GORRE subsector left RAP advanced to X.22.d.8.8; right RAP not moved. Four bearers with wheeled stretchers attached to each of the first three RAP's. Very hot day. Enemy artillery active against ESSARS & LE HAMEL ACT	

D. D. & L., London, E.C. (A8004) Wt W1771/M2031 750,000 5/17 Sch. 52 Forms/C2118/14

Instructions regarding War Diaries and Intelligence Summaries are contained in F. S. Regs., Part II. and the Staff Manual respectively. Title pages will be prepared in manuscript.

Army Form C. 2118.

WAR DIARY
or
INTELLIGENCE SUMMARY.
(Erase heading not required.)

Place	Date	Hour	Summary of Events and Information	Remarks and references to Appendices
LABOURSE	31/10		Summary of changes of personnel for month.	
			Officers – off 2 – on 2 strength unchanged	
			O.R. – off 2 – on 3 increase 1.	
			A E Hodder. LIEUT.-COL. COMM'DG 3RD N. MID. FIELD AMB. R.A.M. CORPS	

A7092 Wt. W12839/M1293 750,000. 1/17. D. D & L., Ltd. Forms/C2118/14.

May 1915.

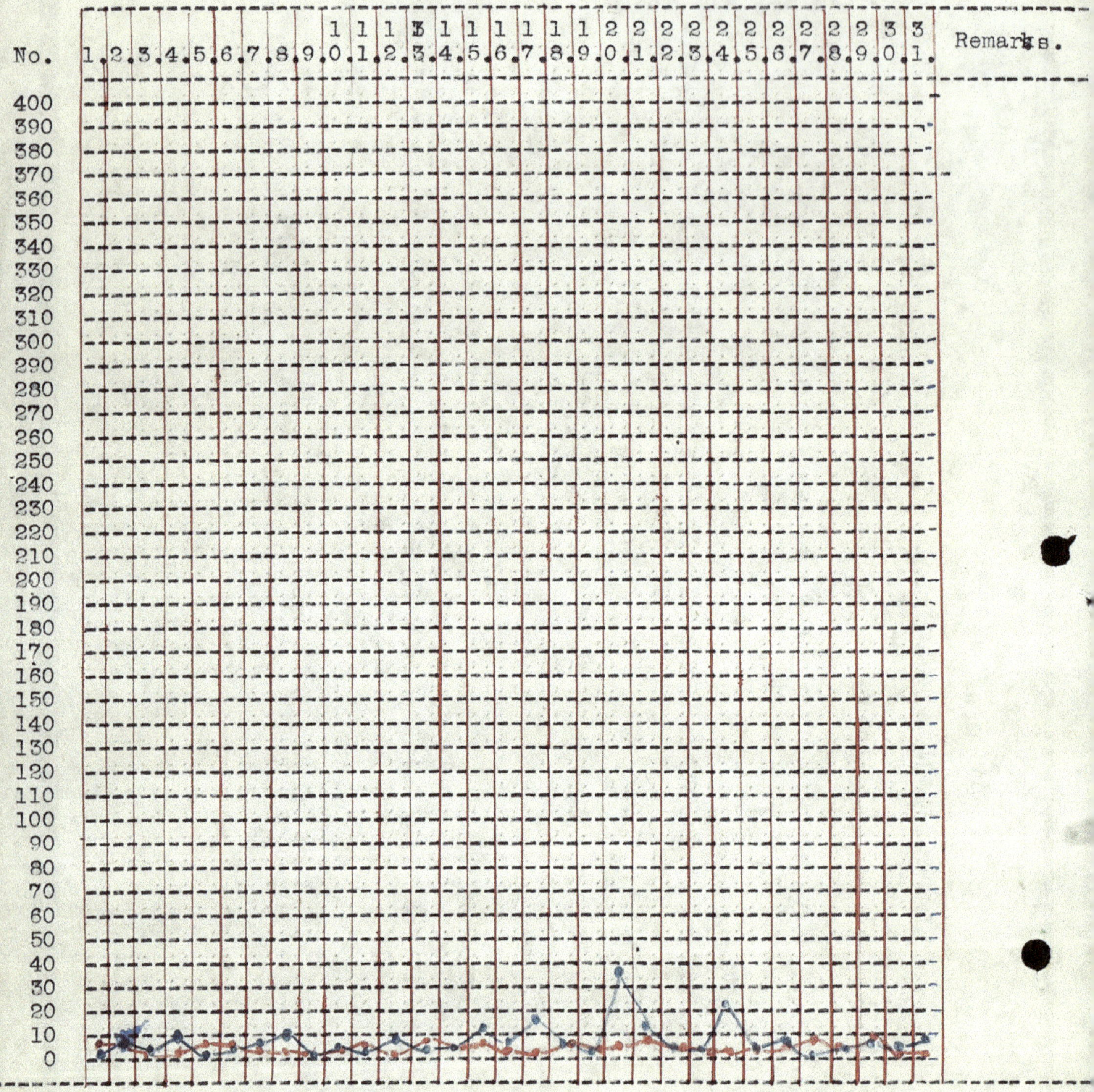

Appendix VI

~~Wounded~~
Sick ——
Wounded ——

Sick & wounded passed through the Advanced Dressing Station of the 1/3 N M F Ambce. which serves the Staffs Inf Brigade —

1/3rd North Midland F.A. May 1915

Instructions regarding War Diaries and Intelligence Summaries are contained in F. S. Regs., Part II. and the Staff Manual respectively. Title Pages will be prepared in manuscript.

WAR DIARY
or
INTELLIGENCE SUMMARY
(Erase heading not required.)

Army Form C. 2118

Place	Date	Hour	Summary of Events and Information	Remarks and references to Appendices
Aix Noulette	12/5/17		Inspected 6 reinforcements arrived from base. S Sgt Boswell T. A.S.C. left for 452 Coy A.S.C. with a view to promotion to rank of Coy Sgt Major. Capt E.E. Herga RAMC (T.C.) detached for temporary duty with 1/4 Lincolns	
	13/5/17		Visited A.D.S. & Bearer posts at Lievin – At the last post Lt Col Hodder was wounded through the explosion of a shell at the mouth of the dug out & was evacuated the same day to No. C.C.S with severe scalp wound & general contusions of body. Casualty reported to A.D.M.S.	
	14.5.17		Command was assumed by Capt G. Miller who attended conference at A.D.M.S. D.D.M.S. I Corps visited main dressing station & requested Capt Miller to continue in command. Despatched to Div Hqrs: Lieut Waterhouse & a party of 15 N.C.O.s & men when G.O.C. 46th Div presented the Military medals to Sergt Collins Privates Barlow & Connolly	

War Diary.

Unit..3rd Field Amb,46th Division.

Brigade...137th Inf Brigade.

Division..46th Division.(N.Mid).

Mobilization centre.........................Wolverhampton.

Temporary War station......................Burton.

Stations since occupied subsequent to concentration:-

Lichfield, Burton, Luton, Bishops Stortford, Saffron Walden, Newport Essex, Southampton, Havre, Arneke, Borre, Estaires, Outtersteene, Neuve Eglise, Bailleul, 1¼ South of Popereigne on the Popereigne Westoutre Road, Wipenhoek.

(a) Mobilizatión. Satisfactory.

(b) Concentration at War Station(including Railway moves), Satisfactory.

(c) Organization for Defence. ~~Satisfactory.~~(including vulnerable points) Does not apply.

(d) Training. Progressive and satisfactory.

(e) Discipline. Excellent.

(f) Administration.

1. Medical services. Satisfactory.
2. Veterinary service. Satisfactory.
3. Supply services. Satisfactory.
4. Transport. An extra limbered wagon per section necessary. The Field Ambulance has acted as a Divisional Rest Station, Clearing hospital, and Brigade Bathing establishment, extra necessaries have been purchased and there is no transport for their conveyance.

(5) Ordnance services. Satisfactory. (Extras have had to be purchased locally for duties mentioned under 4.

(6) Billets. Satisfactory.

(7) Supply of Remounts. Satisfactory. 1 Heavy draught horse deficient.

H H C Dent
Lieut Colonel,

6th Sept 1915. O.C.1/3rd Field Ambce, 46th Division.

April 1915.

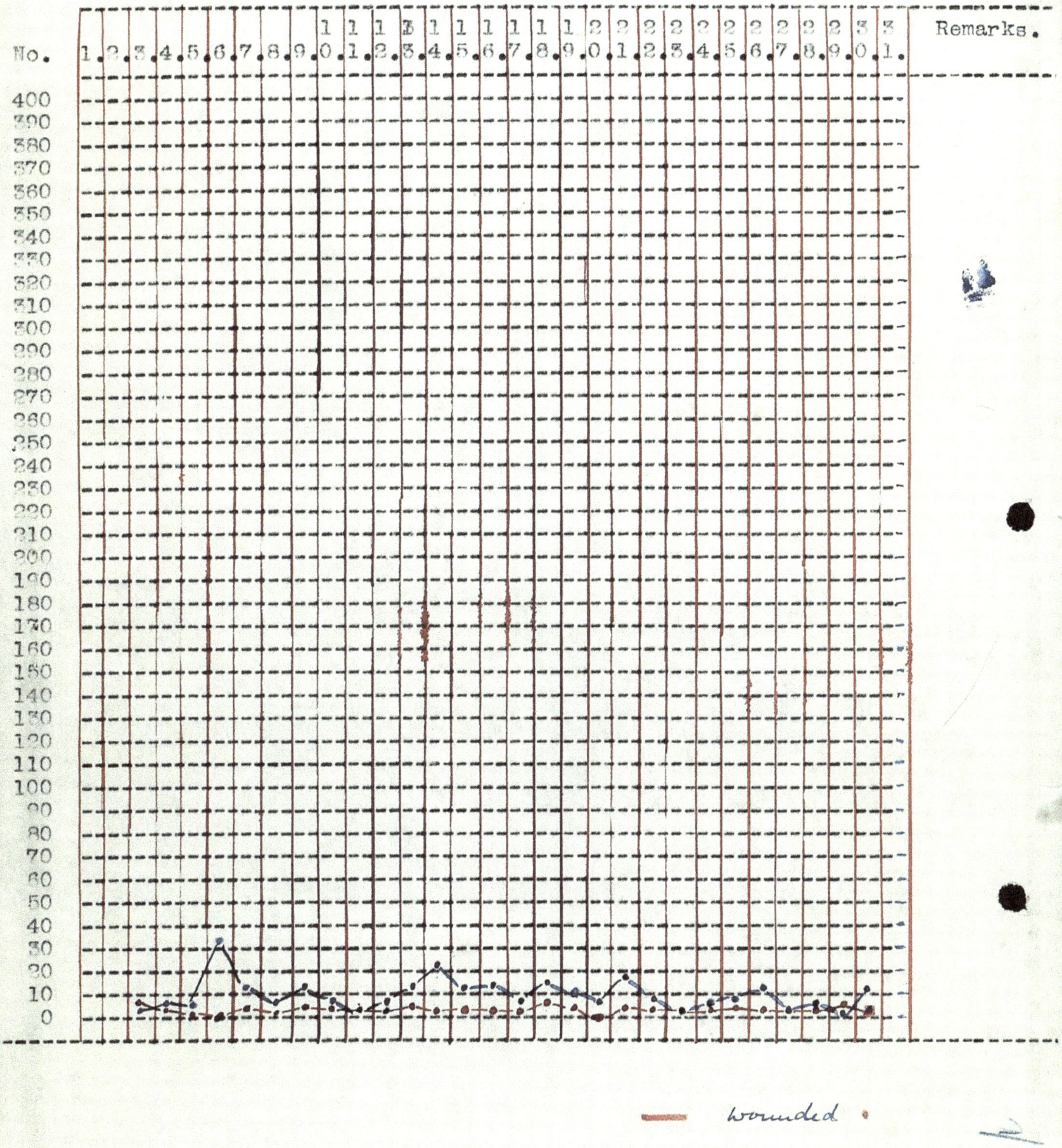

Cases Admitted to the 1/3 N. M. F. Ambce

Appendix IV

1/3rd North Midl. F.A.
May 1915

MEDICAL

Instructions regarding War Diaries and Intelligence Summaries are contained in F. S. Regs., Part II. and the Staff Manual respectively. Title Pages will be prepared in manuscript.

WAR DIARY
or
INTELLIGENCE SUMMARY

(Erase heading not required.)

Army Form C. 2118

Place	Date	Hour	Summary of Events and Information	Remarks and references to Appendices
LAHERLIÈRE	4/7/16		Capt W.D. PERRY left the unit to report for duty to 1/2 N.M. F Amb	
	5/7/16		Started on small improvements to accommodation for personnel & patients - increase of ablution facilities, of latrine accommodation and provision of trench board paths linking up the various wards of the Hospital. Total accommodation for patients 120.	
	6/7/16		Lieut D.C. SUTTIE sent to 1/5 Notts & Derby Rgt. as medical officer (permanent) vice Capt Green killed in action.	
			6 reinforcements arrived from Base - 3 of them former members of the unit	
	7/7/16		Lt J.N.J. Hartley evacuated sick to C.C.S. for Base	
	8/7/16		Held inspection of Horsed Transport in afternoon. Condition of leather parts of harness generally good but steel [illegible] require attention.	

Army Form C. 2118.

WAR DIARY
or
INTELLIGENCE SUMMARY
(Erase heading not required.)

Instructions regarding War Diaries and Intelligence Summaries are contained in F. S. Regs., Part II. and the Staff Manual respectively. Title Pages will be prepared in manuscript.

Place	Date	Hour	Summary of Events and Information	Remarks and references to Appendices
LABEUVRIERE	27	8.35 p.m.	Recd. urgent wire from ADMS ordering to detail Capt. HERGA and 1 motor amb. to report O.C. 1/2 N.M. F. Amb. at 9 p.m	
	28		Detailed 1 motor amb. to report O.C. 1/2 N.M. F. Amb. to-night at 7 p.m	
	29		Capt. HERGA returned from LIEVIN 10.30. 32 slightly wounded cases admitted. Capt. HERGA awarded the Military Cross. ADMS 46th DIV. visited Hospital.	
	30	1.0 p.m	Recd. orders from ADMS to send 2 Motor Ambulances to report for duty with 1/2 N.M. F. Amb. and to convey 12 reinforcements from 46th Div Depot also to detail 2 M.Os to report to his office. Detailed Capts. D.C. SUTTIE and HERGA.	
		8.30 p.m	Received warning order from ADMS that we should be relieved by a F. Amb. of 2nd Canadian Division on July 2.	

J. A. Barron
Major

2449 Wt. W14957/M90 750,000 1/16 J.B.C. & A. Forms/C.2118/12.

B.E.F.

1/3rd N. Mid. F.A. 46th Divn. 1st Corps. WESTERN FRONT.
O.C. Lt. Col. A.E. Hodder D.S.O. May. '17.
O.C. Maj. T.A. Barron from 15/4/17. 1.
~~1st Army.~~

Phase "B" Battle of Arras- April- May. '17.

2nd Period Capture of Siegfried Line May.

1917.
May. 8th. Operations Enemy. Liévin shelled with mixed H.E. and gas shells from 8 p.m. 7th to about 4 a.m. 8th between 10.30p.m and 12.30.a.m. about 50 gas Shells fell in close proximity to A.D.S. the cellars were quickly full of gas- S.B.R. were worn by all ranks and patients and no one was gassed in the A.D.S. The gas was cleared by fires and fans the process having to be repeated 3 times.

Casualties Gas. 78 cases were dealt with at M.D.S. one died and the majority of cases were slight.

11th. Operations Enemy: Gas. Enemy used gas shells freely each night necessitating wearing of S.B.R. frequently.

Decorations. Sgt. Collins and Ptes. Barlow and Conolly awarded M.M.

13th. Casualties. R.A.M.C. Lt. Col. Hodder wounded at Liévin-

15th. Appointment: Major T.A. Barron appointed O.C. vice Lt. Col. Hodder.

21st. Operations Enemy. M.D.S. shelled at 8.15 p.m. with two salvoes of 4 shells each- three of which struck the building.

The shells were of a fresh type detonating on striking the roof- sending forward a shower of splintered shell case, but spreading quite horizontally-

Transport billet(at the time unoccupied) was blown in and much clothing and equipment destroyed.

Casualties: R.A.M.C. 0 and 7 wounded.

April 12th 1915.

Appendix II

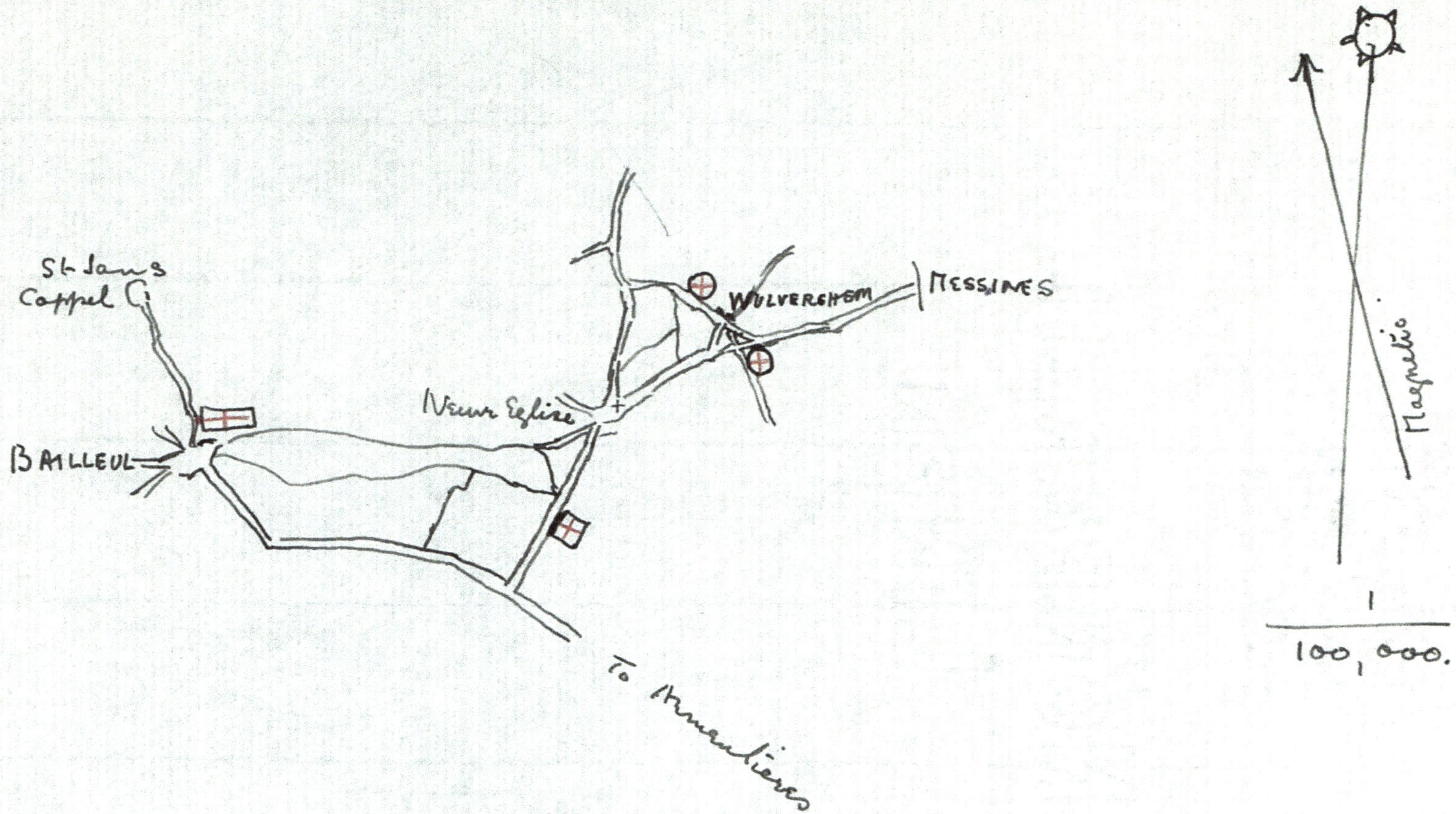

⊞ = Advanced Dressing Station

⊕ = Regimental Aid Post

⊟ = 1 Section of Field Ambulance - acting as Divisional Rest Station + Casualty Clearing Hospital - 150 beds

War Diary.
****

Unit..........................1/3rd:North.Midland.Field.Amb:

Brigade.......................Staffordshire Inf:Bdge:

Division......................1/1st:North.Midland.Division.

Mobilization.Centre...........Wolverhampton.

Temporary War Station..........Burton.

Stations since occupied subsequent to Concentration.

Lichfield,Burton,Luton,Bishops Stortford,Saffron Walden,

Newport/Essex,Southampton,Havre,Arneke,Borre,and Estaires–
Outtersteene near Merris

(a)Mobilization.
------------ Satisfactory.

(b)Concentration at War Stations(including Railway moves)
---------------------------- No difficulty experienced.

(d)Training.
-------- Progressive,and satisfactory.

(e)Discipline.
---------- Very excellent.

(f)Administration.
----

1. Medical Services-Satisfactory.
2. Veterinary Services-Satisfactory.
3. Supply Services-On the whole excelllent,but there has been great difficulty in procuring fuel since the unit left Havre.
4. Transport-The wagons supplied to the Territorial Field Ambulances are not enough to carry the extra equipment for the Expeditionary Force.In my opinion an extra G.S.Wagon per section,with horses is absolutely necessary Extra Medical necessaties are now required such as Aether,large quantities of Antiseptics,Dressings,and Medical appliances.These are bulky,and the wagons are already very much overloaded,especially the Medical Store Wagon.
5. Ordnance-Satisfactory.
6. Billets-Satisfactory.

H H C Dent
Lt Col.

LIEUT.-COLONEL
COMM'DG 3RD N. MID. FIELD AMB. R.A.M. CORPS.

Estaires
14/3/15.

Instructions regarding War Diaries and Intelligence Summaries are contained in F. S. Regs., Part II. and the Staff Manual respectively. Title Pages will be prepared in manuscript.

WAR DIARY
or
INTELLIGENCE SUMMARY
(Erase heading not required.)

Army Form C. 2118

Place	Date	Hour	Summary of Events and Information	Remarks and references to Appendices
St AMAND	9/1/17		In company of DADMS, investigated evacuation routes etc on 138 Bde sector. Conditions here fairly good: a satisfactory C.T. exists on both flanks and in the centre there is a large extent of dead ground over which bearers could move with ease: went on to inspect A.D.S. at BIENVILLERS.	
	10/1/17		Capt E.W. Strange left for temporary duty with 1/5th Lincolns. Lt. T Waterhouse left for short course at 3rd Army Sanitary School	
	11/1/17		Inspected Transport lines and Disinfecting Station LA CAUCHIE erected by this unit in August 1916: found that all constructional work was in a good order & when put up; the valve sealing of shower bath roses being still good and the steam pipes made from biscuit tin showing no leakage. Went on to inspect ADS BIENVILLERS. About 7.30 – 9 pm BIENVILLERS was shelled with 105 m. One shell hit dressing station wrecked the room used as men's mess room: ~~the~~ Brigade drying house adjacent completely wrecked. No casualties in this unit	

1875 Wt. W593/826 1,000,000 4/15 J.B.C. & A. A.D.S.S./Forms/C. 2118.

Instructions regarding War Diaries and Intelligence Summaries are contained in F. S. Regs., Part II. and the Staff Manual respectively. Title Pages will be prepared in manuscript.

WAR DIARY
or
INTELLIGENCE SUMMARY
(Erase heading not required.)

Army Form C. 2118

Place	Date	Hour	Summary of Events and Information	Remarks and references to Appendices
ECOIVRES			by GOC 46 Division and promulgated.	
	22/3/16		Supplied personnel 1 Cpl 7 men to run baths and laundry for 137 Bde in ECOIVRES and the same number to work baths at ACQ for troops in that area.	
	25/3/16		Investigated various Boyaux in order to find alternative routes for evacuation of wounded. Boyau des TERRITORIAUX available but not available to 46 Division.	
	27/3/16		Found a possible alternative route in Boyaux d'ECOIVRES and des PONTS. – Trolley railway from AUXRIETZ to ECOIVRES some help, wounded coming down by returning empty wagons.	
	13/4/16		Explored further series of Boyaux but could find none suitable for passage of wounded	
	27/4/16		Capt G W Craig RAMC T evacuated to 30 CCS for G.B.	

A. E. Stewart [signature] LIEUT.-COLONEL,
COMM'DG 3RD N. MID. FIELD AMB. R.A.M. CORPS

from the fighting line to the rendezvous suggested.
Use of the lines of evacuation here suggested would leave the main roads free for passage of ammunition and troops.

5 In case of retirement to GHQ lines R.M.O's on N side would be able to make convenient aid posts under the Railway embankment at the road junction already mentioned:
On the South side in a similar event there is no cover except in buildings such as present ADS or various estaminets till BULFORD CAMP site is reached: here cover would be obtainable in dead ground S of the Camp & behind the main road embankment on the land of Ferme La Poulouche.

I have the honour to be
Sir
Your obedient servant
A. E. Hodder.
Major RAMC T.

1/3 N. M. Field Amb.
46th Division

Ferme La Poulouche
16. 6. 15.

Instructions regarding War Diaries and Intelligence Summaries are contained in F. S. Regs., Part II. and the Staff Manual respectively. Title Pages will be prepared in manuscript.

WAR DIARY

or

~~INTELLIGENCE SUMMARY~~

(Erase heading not required.)

Army Form C. 2118

Place	Date	Hour	Summary of Events and Information	Remarks and references to Appendices
GAUDIEMPRE	31		through Field Amb in past month coming from a number of units. The number of cases of "Trench fever" is also considerable but at the stage at which they reach Field Amb it is not possible to say if any of the cases of "Fever of unknown origin" are Enteric group. They show no evidence while there of being enteric or paratyphoid. Inoculation state of unit to date with TAB - 96%.	
			A E Hodder Lt Col Cdg	

1875 Wt. W593/826 1,000,000 4/15 J.B.C. & A. A.D.S.S./Forms/C. 2118.

Instructions regarding War Diaries and Intelligence Summaries are contained in F. S. Regs., Part II. and the Staff Manual respectively. Title pages will be prepared in manuscript.

WAR DIARY
or
INTELLIGENCE SUMMARY.
(Erase heading not required.)

Army Form C. 2118.

3RD NORTH MIDLAND FIELD AMBULANCE ROYAL ARMY MEDICAL CORPS

Place	Date	Hour	Summary of Events and Information	Remarks and references to Appendices
DIVION	11/4/18		Collected sick from Battalion as usual.	
			Pack pony & saddlery returned to ADMS. have taken charge in [illegible] of 7 charger Class C2.	
			Holy Communion 7.30 am & Evening service 5.30 for all ranks.	
			Dumped 1 G.S.W. load of equipment at Billet 35 ALLOUAGNE	
	14/4/18		the Divisional troop dump. Motor Amb no 2 returning from Allouagne at night got ditched & badly damaged.	
	15/4/18		Visited 137 Bde in reference to moving orders.	
			Arranged baths for personnel at HOUDAIN	
			Collected Sick as usual.	
			Lt G.P. Sharp posted to 231 Bde RFA & struck off strength.	
			Inspected Chau VILLEFORT J26a8.6 with a view to occupying it if [illegible] by Army to vacate Chau LEGAY. Unit can get in all very close packing but the road approaches bad for cars.	
	16/4/18		All personnel bathed at HOUDAIN.	
			Wagon loads adjusted to needs of forward work in open.	
BRUAY	17/4/18		Moved unit to old site of 22 CCS BRUAY J16d central sheet 36B. at short notice 11am under orders 46 Div. Took charge for detaining whilst under observation of 108 O.R. 1 Monmouth Rgt. suffering from symptoms of gas poisoning.	

A5092. Wt. W12839/M1293. 750,000. 1/17. D. D & L., Ltd. Forms/C2118/14.

FIRE ORDERS&

****

In the event of an outbreak of fire in quarters occupied by the Field Ambulance the following procedure is to be adopted :-

1. The man in the billet will take such steps as are possible to extinguish or limet the outbreak.

2. The N.C.O. or senior soldier in charge will order out of the billet all occupants except those actually engaged in putting out the fire.

3. He will sound the alarm with whistle if available an d call up the Sergeant Major and the Officers.

4. Occupants of other billets near by will turn out and stand by outside their billets awaiting instructions from the Officer in charge, who will take steps such as organising a chain of men with buckets of water to combat the flames and prevent spread of fire to other buildings

5. Kit and equipment will be got out of the buildings by men detailed by the N.C.O. in charge who will stack it in safety and post a guard.

6. In the event of fire occurring in quarters where horses are stabled the night picquet will take steps to get all animals out and rouse all transport drivers who will remove all animals from adjacent stables to a place of safety and stand by to prevent any stampeding.

5/3/1916.

A E Hodder

LIEUT.-COLONEL
COMM'DG. 3rd N. MID FIELD AMB
R. A. M. CORPS

Instructions regarding War Diaries and Intelligence Summaries are contained in F. S. Regs., Part II. and the Staff Manual respectively. Title Pages will be prepared in manuscript.

Army Form C. 2118

WAR DIARY
or
INTELLIGENCE SUMMARY
(Erase heading not required.)

Place	Date	Hour	Summary of Events and Information	Remarks and references to Appendices
FROYELLES	14/11/16		Took over Presbytery at DOMVAST for reception of Scabies patients only:- started to erect steam bath as this was the only means of treatment at the moment available. No means of washing or disinfecting clothing available. The arrangement was useful as segregating such cases but as a means of preventing spread of the contagion or of ~~cure~~ cure almost if not quite valueless.	
	16/11/16		57 "tradesmen" members of the unit were interviewed at MONDICOURT in respect of their qualification and fitness for transfer to special corps.	
			Capt E.T. WILLANS left on temporary duty with 30th Div.	
	17/11/16		One driver left for special duty in charge of electric lighting at No 12 Stationary Hosp. St POL.	
	18/11/16		All officers attended lecture by ADMS at Div HQrs.	
	19/11/16		2 officers (C.O. + Capt Harris) attended lecture on "Night Operations on the SOMME front" by G.S.O I - 30th Div	

Instructions regarding War Diaries and Intelligence Summaries are contained in F. S. Regs., Part II. and the Staff Manual respectively. Title Pages will be prepared in manuscript.

WAR DIARY
or
INTELLIGENCE SUMMARY
(Erase heading not required.)

Army Form C. 2118

Place	Date	Hour	Summary of Events and Information	Remarks and references to Appendices
FROYELLES	20/11/16		Capt E.W. STRANGE left for course of instruction at 3rd Army Anti-gas school St POL.	
	22/11/16		Field Ambulance moved quarters to YVRENCH, carrying with them 38 sick patients: evacuated Presbytery DOMVAST. No men fell out on march.	
YVRENCH	23/11/16		Left over-nights quarters 7.15 am resuming line of march to quarters at BACHIMONT. – conditions very good for marching – No men fell out.	
BACHIMONT	24/11/16		Carried out bathing of scabies patients & members of the unit and disinfected all blankets.	
	25/11/16		Field Amb. moved to quarters at BRÉVILLERS. marching past G.O.C. 46 Div en route as part of 137 Brigade. G.O.C. expressed his satisfaction with turnout & appearance of unit – a very wet march, rain nearly all the way. No men fell out.	

Jan 1919 27
/

46 DIV

Box 2504

Check

VR 47

140/3490

WAR DIARY OF

1/3rd NORTH MIDLAND FIELD AMBULANCE.

Jan 1st to Jan 31st 1919.

B.E.F.

SUMMARY OF MEDICAL WAR DIARIES FOR 1/3rd N.Mid. F.A. 46th Divn. 2nd Corps.
1st Corps from 19/4/17.

1st Army.

WESTERN FRONT.

April-May.'17.

O.C. Lt. Col. A.E. Hodder D.S.O.
O.C. Maj. T.A. Barron from 18/4/17.

SUMMARISED UNDER THE FOLLOWING HEADINGS.

Phase "B" Battle of Arras- April- May. '17.

1st Period Attack on Vimy Ridge April.

2nd Period Capture of Siegfried Line May.

War Diary.

Unit.....................................3rd:Field.Ambulance.

Brigade..................................137th:Inf:Brigade.

Division.................................46th:Division.

Mobilization Centre......................Wolverhampton.

Temporary War Station....................BurtoN,

Stations since occupied subsequent to concentration-Lichfield, Burton, Luton, Bishops Stortford, Saffron Walden, Newport/Essex, Southampton, Havre, Arneke, Borre, Estaires, Outtersteene, Neuve Eglise, Bailleul, and 1 miles South of Poperinghe, on the Poperinghe-Westoutre Road.

(a)Mobilization.
Satisfactory.

(b)Concentration at War Stations(including Railway moves)
Satisfactory.

(c)Organization for defence(including vulnerable points)
Does no apply.

(d)Training.
Progressive, and satisfactory.

(e)Discipline.
Excellent.

(f)Administration.

1. Medical Services-Satisfactory.
2. Veterinary Services-Satisfactory.
3. Supply Services-Satisfactory.
4. Transport-An extra limbered wagon per section necessary. The Field Ambulance has acted as a Divisional Rest Station, Clearing Hospital, and Brigade Bathing Establishment; extra necessaries have been purchased, and there is no transport for their conveyance.
5. Ordnance Services-Satisfactory.
6. Billets-Satisfactory.
7. Supply of Remounts-Satisfactory, only one casualty not yet replaced.

HHCD Smt-
Lt-Col-

LIEUT.-COLONEL,
CO... 3RD N. MID. FIELD AMB. R.A.M. CORPS.

17

SECRET.
****

Sept. 1918

WAR DIARY

Of

1[illegible]North Midland Field Ambulance

For Month ending 30/9/18.

bandages are removed to incinerator at frequent intervalsby the Sanitary Squad.
He will see that the relief of nurses etc:is carried out punctually and that they get their meals and sleep at proper times.

NOTES.

****

1. Rapidity in clearing is the desideratum.
Only those cases will be dressed that ovviously need it, and only essential operations will be performed.
All necessary splinting will however be carried out and no case will be passed on that has not had A.T.S.
Medical Officers will accustom themselves to working with the same pair of dressers so that in a rush an approximation to team work is reached.

2. N.Y.D.N. cases (shell shock) will be accommodated upstairs and if possible detained 24 hours.
As only lying down cases will be dealt with at LABOURSE it is unlikely that these cases will get here in any but the smallest numbers.

3. The accommodation in Ward 4 will be increased, if necessary, by taking the larger dining room into use as a ward.

4. In addition to grading cases into more and less serious the Receiving Officer will mark the following cases by a piece of bandage round the right arm.-

Cases requiring immediate operation	-	blue.
" from whom food is to be withheld		yellow.
" not requiring dressing or A.T.S.		white.

These last will be sent straight through to the E.wards for evacuation at once and should form a considerable proportion of cases.

5. The routes wounded will take are shewn on attached plan. No patient will go over the same route twice and crossing is practically eliminated.

(sgd) A.E.Hodder. Lieut:Col:R.A.M.C.T.
C'dh:1/3rd:North.Midland.Field.Ambulance.

27/8/17.

Copies to:-
All officers (8)
S.Major.
File.

War Diary.

Unit......................................3rd Field Ambulance.

Brigade...................................137th Infantry Bde.

Division..................................46th Division.

Mobilization Centre.......................Wolverhampton.

Temporary War Station.....................Burton.

Stations since occupied subsequent to concentration, Lichfield, Burton, Luton ,Bishops Stortford, Saffron Walden, Newport Essex, Southampton, Harve, Arneke, Borre, Estaires, Outtersteene, Nerve Eglise, Bailleul, and 1½ miles south of Poperinghe on the Poperinghe Westoutre road, and ¾ mile south of Poperinghe on the same road.

(a) Mobilization. Satisfactory.

(b) Concentration at War Stations,(including Railway moves), Satisfactory.

(c) Organization for Defence. (including vulnerable points) Does not apply.

(d) Training. Progressive and Satisfactory.

(e) Discipline. Excellent.

(f) Administration.

1. Medical services. Satisfactory.

2. Veterinary services. Satisfactory.

3. Supply services. Satisfactory.

4. Transport. An extra Limbered wagon per section necessary. The Field Ambulance has acted as a Divisional Rest Station, Clearing Hospital, and Brigade Bathing Establishment; extra necessaries have been purchased and there is no Transport for their conveyance.

5. Ordnance services. Satisfactory.

6. Billets. Satisfactory.

7. Supply of remounts. Satisfactory.

July 31. 1915

H H C Dent

LIEUT.-COLONEL.
COMM'DG 3RD N. MID. FIELD AMB. R.A.M. CORPS.

War Diary.

Unit.................................3rd Field Ambulance.

Brigade..............................137th Infantry Bde.

Division.............................46th Divisi on.

Mobilization Centre..................Wolverhampto n.

Temporary War Station................Burton.

Stations since occupied subsequent to concentration, Lichfield, Burton, Luton ,Bishops Stortford, Saffron Walden, Newport Essex, Southampton, Harve, Arneke, Borre, Estaires, Outtersteene, Nerve Eglise, Bailleul, and $1\frac{1}{4}$ miles south of Poperinghe on the Poperinghe Westoutre road, and $\frac{3}{4}$ mile south of Poperinghe on the same road.

(a) Mobilization. Satisfactory.

(b) Concentration at War Stations,(including Railway moves), Satisfactory.

(c) Organization for Defence. $including vulnerable points) Does not apply.

(d) Training. Progressive and Satisfactory.

(e) Discipline. Excellent.

(f) Administration.

1. Medical services. Satisfactory.
2. Veterinary services. Satisfactory.
3. Supply services. Satisfactory.
4. Transport. An extra Limbered wagon per section necessary.

   The Field Ambulance has acted as a Divisional Rest Station, Clearing Hospital, and Brigade Bathing Establishment; extra necessaries have been purchased and there is no Transport for their conveyance.

5. Ordnance services. Satisfactory.
6. Billets. Satisfactory.
7. Supply of remounts. Satisfactory.

July 31. 1915 H H C Dent

LIEUT.-COLONEL.
COMM'DG 3RD N. MID. FIELD AMB. R.A.M. CORPS.

Appendix II

JUNE 1915

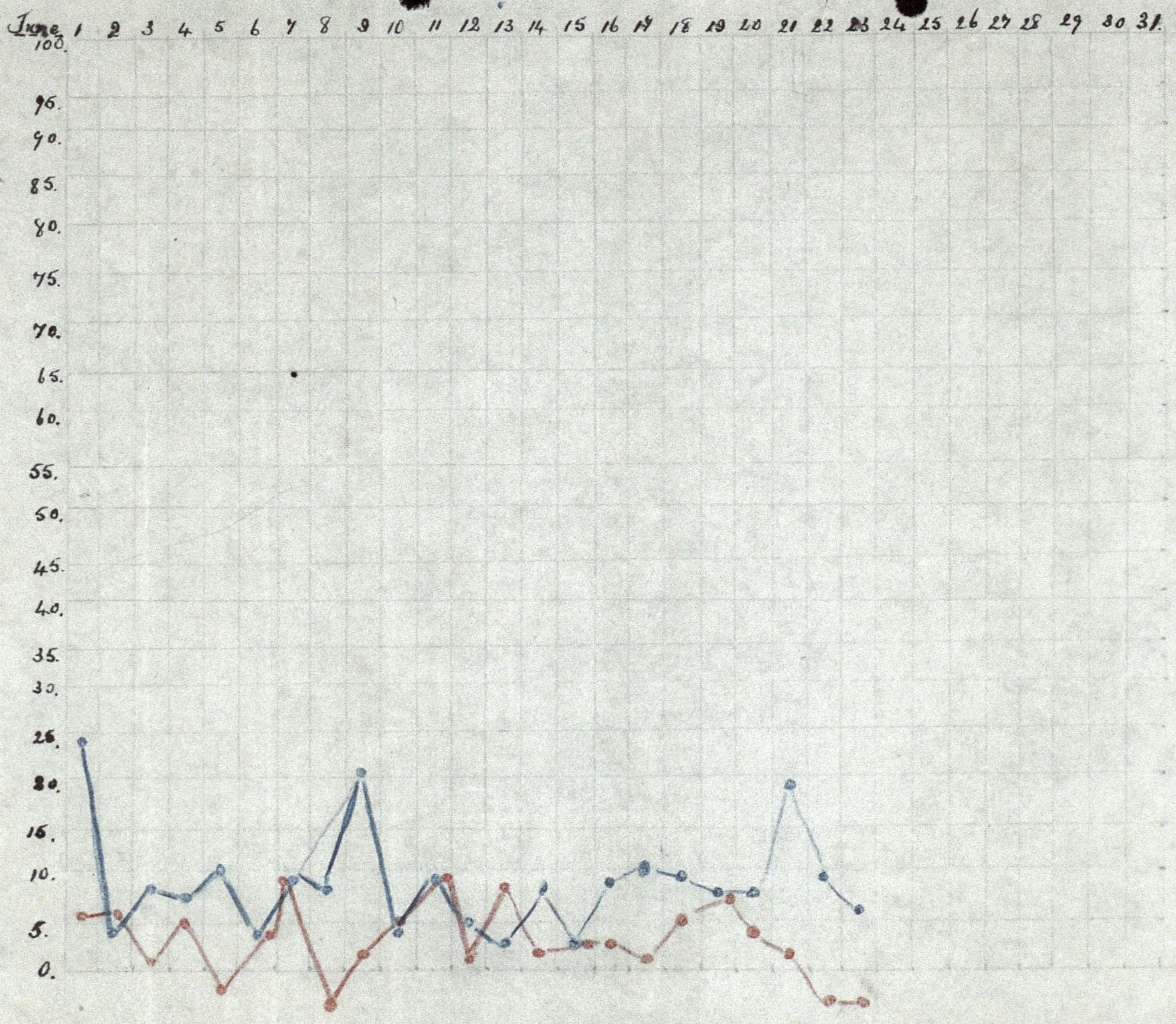

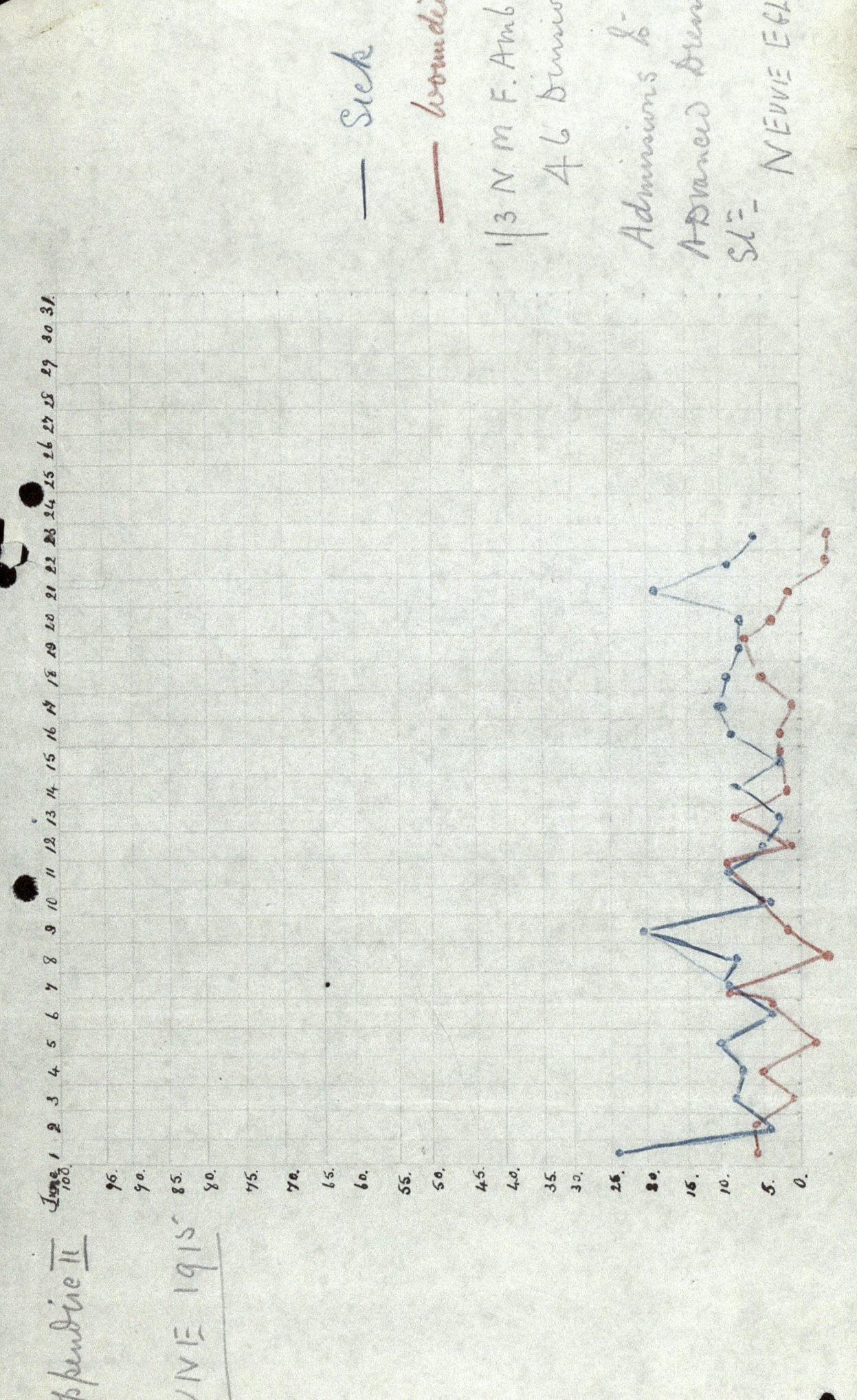

Mar 1919

140/3551

North Midland

1/3 ~~[illegible]~~ F. A.

Instructions regarding War Diaries and Intelligence Summaries are contained in F. S. Regs., Part II. and the Staff Manual respectively. Title Pages will be prepared in manuscript.

WAR DIARY
or
INTELLIGENCE SUMMARY
(Erase heading not required.)

Army Form C. 2118

Place	Date	Hour	Summary of Events and Information	Remarks and references to Appendices
Lattrayeux?	27.5.17		Made a detailed inspection of all the new quarters. The remainder of the ambulance Lieut Phillips & 40 men arrived from Lessin. Capt. E. E. Henza attached 1/4 Lincolns & Capt H. E. Gavin attached 1/8 Sherwood Foresters was struck off the strength	
	28.5.17		Attended conference at A.D.M.S. Capt E. E. Henza rejoined from 1/4 Lincolns & was taken on the strength	
	29.5.17		General routine & organisation. Commenced to build a new latrine for Sitting patients	
	30.5.17		Hospital inspected by D.D.M.S. I Corps who wished to know every detail of the routine. He thought the place looked very dingy & suggested many improvements	
	31.5.17		Hospital visited by Sanitary Officer I Corps. Inspection of Transport by O.C. 46th Div train, who was on the whole satisfied, but still thought more work could be put in on the harness.	

1875 Wt. W593/826 1,000,000 4/15 J.B.C. & A. A.D.S.S./Forms/C. 2118.

Instructions regarding War Diaries and Intelligence Summaries are contained in F. S. Regs., Part II. and the Staff Manual respectively. Title Pages will be prepared in manuscript.

WAR DIARY
or
INTELLIGENCE SUMMARY
(Erase heading not required.)

Army Form C. 2118

Place	Date	Hour	Summary of Events and Information	Remarks and references to Appendices
St AMAND	28/4/17		Inspected transport lines, vehicles & horses.	
	29/4/17		ADMS conference at which notice was received of pending transfer of collection to 1/2 N.M. F. Amb. & taking over of main dressing station GAUDIEMPRE	
			In company with ADMS visited 137 Bde in afternoon to discuss details of collection from new front about to be taken over.	
	30/4/17		Visited ADS at FONCQUEVILLERS & BIENVILLERS and took preliminary steps to handing over front line to successor.	
	31/4/17		With ADMS visited new front line & ADS with a view to its occupation by this unit.	

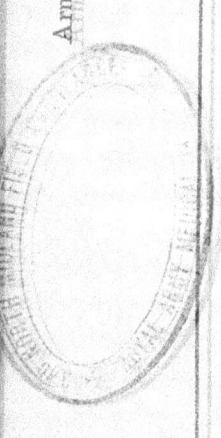

LIEUT.-COLONEL,
COMM'DG. 3rd N. MID FIELD AMB
R. A. M. CORPS

1875 Wt. W593/826 1,000,000 4/15 J.B.C. & A. A.D.S.S./Forms/C. 2118.

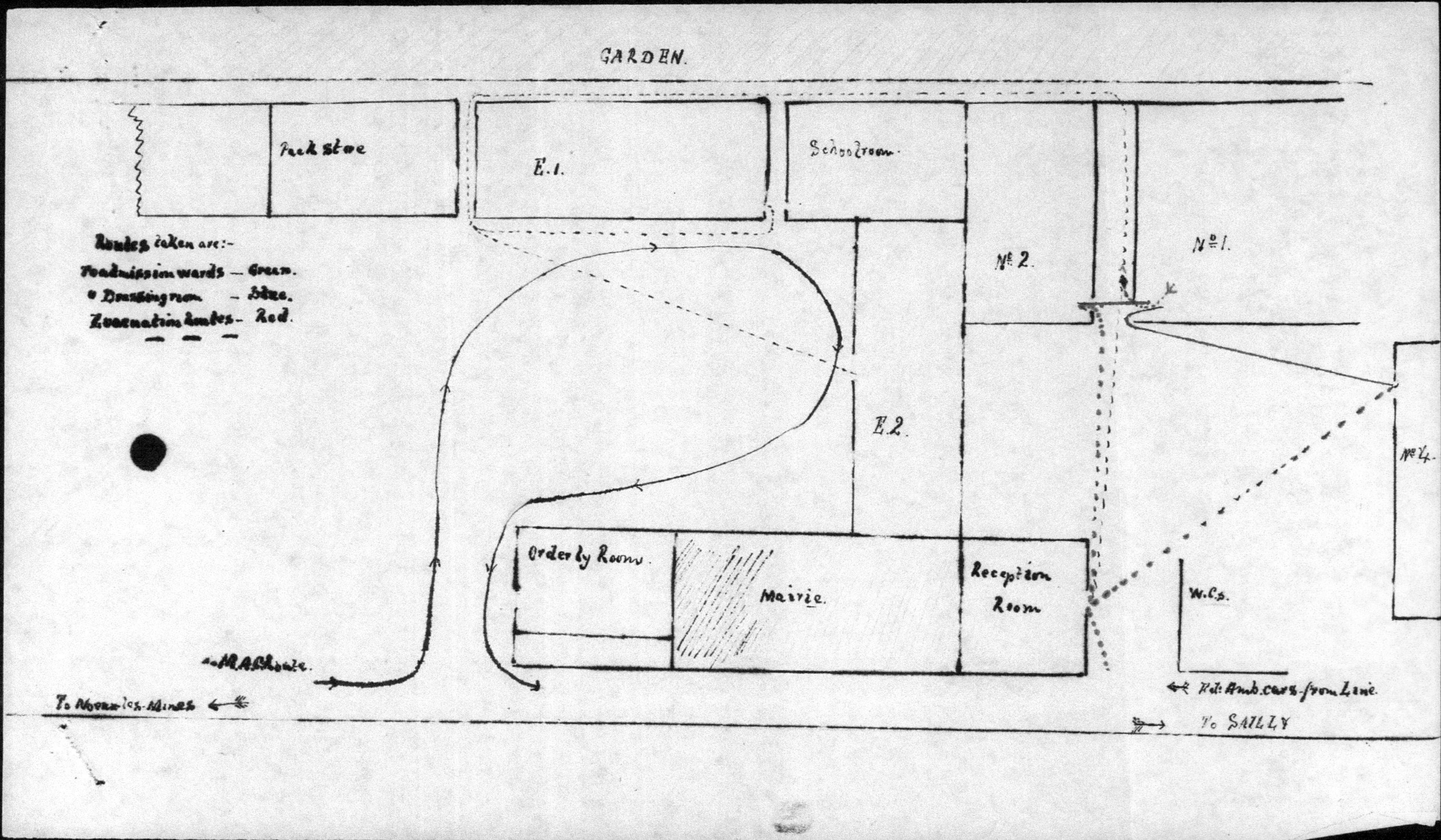
GARDEN.
Pack Store
E.1.
Schoolroom.
No. 2.
No. 1.
E.2.
No. 4.
Orderly Room.
Mairie.
Reception Room
W.Cs.
Routes taken are:-
To admission wards — Green.
" Dressing room — Blue.
Evacuation Routes — Red.
To Noeux-les-Mines
To SAILLY

Appendix I

3rd:Field.Ambulance.46th:Division.Advanced Dressing Stn:No:1.

THE WHITE MILL VLAMERTINGHE

Return shewing numbers of Sick and Wounded dealt with.

	Sick.	Wounded.	Total.
Friday.8.a.m.July 23rd:) to Saturday.July 24th:)	111.	59.	170.
Sunday..July 25th:	25.	35.	60.
Monday.. " 26th:	37.	43.	80.
Tuesday. " 27th:	23.	22.	45.
Wednesday." 28th:	37.	27.	64.
Thursday." 29th:	44.	38.	82.
Friday. " 30th:	41.	27.	68.
Total.	318.	251.	569.
Saturday.July 31st:	28.	213.	241.
Sunday. Aug: 1st:	35.	166.	201.
Monday. " 2nd:	56.	36.	92.
Tuesday. " 3rd:	50.	22.	72.
Wednsday. " 4th:	42.	21.	63.
Thursday. " 5th:	58.	15.	73.
Friday. " 6th:	34.	30.	64.
	303.	503.	806.
Saturday.Aug: 7th:	23.	25.	48.
Sunday. " 8th:	32.	13.	45.
Monday. " 9th:	17.	9.	26.
Tuesday. " 10th:	26.	50.	76.
Wednsday. " 11th:	24.	5.	29.
Thursday. " 12th:	40.	13.	53.
Friday. " 13th:	50.	16.	66.
	212.	131.	343.
Saturday.Aug: 14th:	31.	7.	38.
Sunday. " 15th:	26.	8.	34.
Monday. " 16th:	31.	18	49.
Tuesday. " 17th:	21.	15.	36.
Wednsday. " 18th:	50.	54.*	104. *26 Gassed.
Thursday. " 19th:	20.	23.	43.
Friday. " 20th:	46.	32.	73.
	225.	157.	382.

A.E. Woods(?) Major

H.H.C. Dent
Lt Col.

3rd FIELD AMBce 46th DIVISION.
Lieut. Col. Commanding.

DETAIL OF DUTIES.

****

	DAY.		NIGHT.	
Receiving Room.	Officer 1.		Officer....1	
	N.C.O. 1		N.C.O. 1	
	Bearers 6	4(10)	Bearers 6	4(10)
No:2 Ward.	N.C.O. 1		N.C.O. 1	
	Nurses. 2		Nurses. 2	
No:4 Ward.	N.C.O. 1		N.C.O. 1	
	Nurses. 2		Nurses. 2	
No:1(Theatre)	Officers.3		Officers. 3	
	N.C.O. 1		N.C.O. 1	
	Dressers.6		Dressers. 6	
E.1(Evacuation)	Nurses. 1.)		Nurses. 1)	
E.2(")	Nurses. 1)	N.C.O..1	Nurses. 1)	N.C.O..1
E.Side bearers.	N.C.O. 1.		N.C.O. 1	
	Bearers 2	4(6)	Bearers 2	4(6)

DUTIES NOT DUPLICATED.

Mortuary..	Pte:G.D.	1.
Packstore.	Cpl:	1,
	Ptes:	2.
Clerical.	Sergt:	1.
	Ptes:	6.
Cooks.	O.Rs.	6.
Q.M.Stores.	Q.M.Sgt:	1.
	Ptes.	2.
Sanitary.	Sergt:	1.
	Ptes:	4.
Dispensary.	Dispenser.	1.
	Asst:	1.

SUMMARY OF PERSONNEL EMPLOYED.

Officers..........8.
N.C.O's..........16.
Nursing..........24.
Bearers..........32.
Ptes:G.D.,etc:...22.

Grand Total.

Officers......8   C.O.   Q.Mr.
O.R's........95   Sgt:Major.

List of persons detailed for above duties will be published as under

(1) Sgt:Major.
(2) Copy posted in Admission yard.
" " " Evacuation "

War Diary.

Unit..............................1/3rd:North.Midland.Field.Amb:

Brigade...........................Staffordshire Inf:Brigade.

Division..........................1/1st:North.Midland.Division.

Mobilization Centre...............Wolverhampton.

Temporary War Station.............Burton.

Stations since occupied subsequent to Concentration..Lichfield, Burton,Luton.Bishops Stortford,Saffron Walden,Newport/Essex, Southampton,Havre,Arneke,Bo~~d~~re,Estaires,Outtersteene,Neuve Eglise. BAILLEUL

(a)Mobilization.
------------ Satisfactory.

(b)Concentration at War Stations(including Railway moves)
------------------------------ Satisfactory.

(c)Organization for Defence(including vulnerable points)
------------------------ Does not apply.

(d)Training.
-------- Progressive,and satisfactory.

(e)Excellent Discipline.

(f)Administration.

1. Medical Services-Satisfactory.
2. Veterinary Services-Satisfactory.
3. Supply Services-Satisfactory.
4. Transport-An extra limbered wagon per section necessary.The Field Ambulance has acted as a Divisional Rest Station, Clearing Hospital,and Brigade Bathing Establishment;extra necessaries have been purchased,and there is no transport for their conveyance.
5. Ordnance Services-Satisfactory.Extras have had to be purchased locally for duties mentioned under 4.
6. Billets-Satisfactory.
9. Supply of Remounts-Satisfactory,all casualties replaced.

H H Dent

April 30. 1915

LIEUT.-COLONEL,
COMM'DG 1/3RD N. MID. FIELD AMB. R.A.M. CORPS.

Continued.

Pulses tended to be slow on night of 18th.

Pulse rates did not rise in proportion to rise of temperatures - below are examples :-

PULSE.	TEMPERATURE.
75.	100°
78.	100.4°
80.	100.4°
64.	100.2°
66.	99.2°
62.	99°
96.	100.6°
66.	101.2°
78.	100.4°
80.	100.6°

Battalion was in the line on right Sector HILL 70 up to 13th. April when they were relieved, and went to COUPIGNY.

sd. A.U. MILLAR. Captain.
R.A.M.C.

Phase "B" cont.

2nd Period cont.

1917.
May.25th. Casualties. About 40 wounded dealt with during the night.

26th. Moves: To La Beuvriere.

27th.31st. General routine and organisation.

Appendix I

To:-

Colonel W.Beevor,
A.D.M.S.46th:Division.

Sir,

I have the honour to make the following suggestions for forwarding to G.H.Q.,if you think fit:-

1.That a Mobile Dentist's Surgery be instituted for each Division.

2.That this Mobile Dentist's Surgery be in charge of a Dental Surgeon with a staff of competent Dental Mechanics.

3.That this Mobile Dentist's Surgery be attached to 1 of the 3 Field Ambulances of the Division;whichever is the most convenient for the time being.

4.That the Mobile Dentist's Surgery be a large Motor Van,and be self-contained.

My reasons for these suggestions are as follows:-

a.Dental treatment could be given to men of the Division without evacuating them to Casualty Clearing Hospitals,or to the Base.

b.Daily treatment would be possible.The man returning each day to his Regiment,after treatment.
N.B.Under the present arrangement this is often impossible as the Cas:Clearing Hospitals are too far away.

c.With the above staff,plates could be quickly repaired,adjustments in their fitting made,and in some cases new plates could be provided.

d.As many men are now enlisted,and will continue to be enlisted with artificial dentures,the necessity for some arrangement of this sort is more urgent than during the early months of the War.

I have the honour to be

Sir,

16/7/15.

Your obedient Servant,

H H C D Smt-
Lt Col
OC 3 F. Ambce
46 Div

B.E.F.

1/3rd N. Mid. F.A. 46th Divn. 1st Corps. WESTERN FRONT.

O.C. Lt. Col. A.E. Hodder D.S.O. April. '17.

1st Army. 2.

Phase "B" Battle of Arras. April- May. 1917.

1st Period Attack on Vimy Ridge April.

1917.

April.19th. Transfer. To 1st Corps.

22nd. Location Field Ambulances. Br. Posts at Cite de Rollencourt M.27.b.4.2.

A.D.S. white House- Liévin- M.28.b.7.2.

Br. post- Bethune-Arras Road- R.29.b.3.0.

23rd. Operations. Enemy.attacked by 139th Bde.

Casualties. M.D.S. was kept fairly busy.

24th. OPerations Enemy. Shell of large calibre fell in courtyard of A.D.S.

Casualties R.A.M.C. 0 and 1 killed 0 and 2 wounded.

28th. Evacuation. R. Bgde. line was Approx. from M. 18.c. central to M.30.d.2.3.

R.A.Ps. at M.28.a.70.65. and M.28.b.25.0.1.

A.D.S. at White Chateau- M.28.b.7.2.

Thence by wheeled carrier to R.A.M.C. post at Cite de Rollencourt M.27.b.4.2. whence by Motor Ambulance via Angres road through M.26.c. and d.M.25.d.(Map 36c) R.30.b. and point Colonels House-R.29.d.6.6.(Map 36b) on Arras-Bethune Road to Aix-Moulette-

29th. Decoration:-

Pte. W.P. Phelan awarded Croix de Guerre for act of gallantry in rescueing 2 French Civilians whose house had been blown in by large gas shell.

19

C O N F I D E N T I A L.

V 8 44

Oct 1918

140/335

W A R D I A R Y O F

1/3 North Midland Field Ambulance

for the Month of

O C T O B E R. 1918.

Appendix II

3rd:Field Ambulance.46th:Division.Advanced Dressing Station.No:2.

CONVENT SCHOOL Brandhoek.

Return shewing numbers of sick and wounded dealt with.

			Sick.	Wounded.	Total
Sunday...	July	25th:	62.	--	62.
Wednsday.	"	28th:	1.	--	1.
Thursday.	"	29th:	1.	--	1.
Friday.	"	30th:	3.	13.	16.
		Totals.	67.	13.	80.
Saturday.	July	31st:	--	18.	18.
Sunday.	Aug:	1st:	2.	6.	8.
Monday.	"	2nd:	7.	4.	11.
Tuesday.	"	3rd:	7.	4.	11.
Wednsday.	"	4th:	14.	8.	22.
Thursday.	"	5th:	9.	--	9.
Friday.	"	6th:	8.	--	8.
		Totals.	47.	40.	87.
Saturday.	Aug:	7th:	11.	--	11.
Sunday.	"	8th:	9.	--	9.
Monday.	"	9th:	9.	22.	31.
Tuesday.	"	10th:	4.	--	4.
Wednsday.	"	11th:	1.	--	1.
Thursday.	"	12th:	9.	1.	10.
Friday.	"	13th:	13.	--	13.
		Totals.	56.	23.	79.
Saturday.	Aug:	14th:	5.	--	5.
Sunday.	"	15th:	6.	--	6.
Monday.	"	16th:	10.	--	10.
Tuesday.	"	17th:	8.	--	8.
Wednsday.	"	18th:	6.	--	6.
			35.	--	35.

H H C Dent
Lt Col

......Lieut. Col. Commanding.
3rd FIELD AMBce 46th DIVISION.

Jan. 1917

46th Div.

140/1947.

3rd N. M. Field Ambulance

WO95/2681/1

46th Division

F/208/2.

1/3rd NM Fd Amb.

Jan

Vol XI

Jan 1916

App. II

R.A.M.C.T.
****

The following men being MEASLES contacts will obey the following rules.-

1. When off duty they will keep themselves to their billet.

2. Will not enter any estaminets, or other houses in the village and will not mix with any men from other units.

3. Will be examined daily by orderly Officer: and will report at once any suspicious rash or symptoms of running at the nose and eyes that begins after the O.O's inspection.

4. They will attend to their horses and harness as usual but will turn over to "B", and "C" Sections all haulage and conveyance of sick.

5. All the contacts will wear on the left arm a white band made of a piece of bandage.

6. No: 540. L'Cpl: Butler. A., will be the N.C.O., in charge and will be responsible for the carrying out of these orders.

Roll of men referred to in above.

Cpl: Farrow.
L'Cpl: Butler.
Drv: Redditch.
" Walsh.
" Nuttall. T.
" Wakeley.
" Bradburn.
" Traves.
" Nicholls.
" Leedham.
" Preston.
" Dunn. H. P.
" Bourne.
Pte: Dawe. C.
" Hurst. H.
" Burkitt.
" Brown. H. C.
" Toy. B.
" Perry. H.

A. E. Hodder [signature]
LIEUT.-COLONEL,
COMM'DG 3RD N. MID. FIELD AMB. R.A.M. CORPS

27/2/1916.

Sept '15

46th Division

121/7052

3rd N.M. Field Ambulance

Vol VII

Sept. 15.

121/5935

46th Division

121/5935

June 1915.

No 3. N.M. Field Ambulance

Vol IV

46th Division

121
6754

Aug '15

1/3rd N. M. Field Ambulance

Vol VI

August 15

B.E.F.

SUMMARY OF MEDICAL WAR DIARIES FOR 1/3rd N.Mid. F.A. 46th Divn. 2nd Corps.

1st Corps from 19/4/17.

1st Army.

WESTERN FRONT.

April-May. '17.

O.C. Lt. Col. A.E. Hodder D.S.O.

O.C. Maj. T.A. Barron from 15/4/17.

SUMMARISED UNDER THE FOLLOWING HEADINGS.

Phase "B" Battle of Arras- April- May. '17.

1st Period Attack on Vimy Ridge April.

2nd Period Capture of Siegfried Line May.

121/4779

46th Division

121/4779
Feb 19th
to
March 26th 1915

1/3 N. Midland Field Ambulance

Vol I.

140/2696

1/3rd North Midland F.A.

Feb. 1919

19

Vol 48

144/3524

CONFIDENTIAL.

WAR DIARY

OF

1/3rd N.M.Field Ambulance.

1/2/19. to 28/2/19.

****

July 1917

140/2298

1/3rd North Midland F.A.

140/2230

May 1917.

5

1/3rd N. M. F. A.

46th Div.

140/1788

1st/3. N. M. Field Amb.

Oct 1916

46th Division

1/3 N. Midland Field Ambulance

June 1916

46th Div.

F/208/1

Dec 1915

1/3rd N.M. Fd. Amb.

Dec

Vol. X

46th Division

121
7381

Oct 7 15.

3rd North Mid: Fld: Amb:

Vol VIII

Oct 15

46th Divn

Feb } 1916
Mar }

1/3 N. Midland Field Amb

46th Division

121 / 7637

Nov 1915

1/3rd N. M. Fd Amb.

—

Nov 1915

—

Vol IX

B.E.F.

1/3rd N. Mid. F.A. 46th Divn. 2nd Corps. WESTERN FRONT.

O.C. Lt. Col. A.E. Hodder D.S.O. April. '17.

1st Army.. 1.

1st Corps from 19/4/17.

Phase "B" Battle of Arras. April- May- 1917.

1st Period Attack on Vimy Ridge April.

1917.		Headquarters. at Ecque-Decques.
April	1st.	Medical Arrangements: Temp. Hospital was opened at Malanoy Farm Map 36a O.31.a.5.5.
	13th.	Moves. To Bethune.
	18th.	Moves Detachment: A.D.S. in Liévin and Aix-Moulette taken over from Field Ambulance 24th Divn.
	19th.	Moves: To Aix-Noulette R.22.a.7.2.
		Transfer. To 1st Corps.

Oct. 1917

140/2578.

1/3rd North Midland F. A.

121/6231.

July 1915.

46th Division

121/6231

1/3rd N. M. Field Ambulance

Vol V

June 1917.

140/2250

1/3rd North Midland F.A.

46th Div

Sept. 1916

1/3rd N. M. Field Ambulance

Nov. 1917

140/2578

1/3rd North Midland F.A.

Dec 1916

46th Div.

140/1900

1/3rd N. M. Field Ambulance

Mar. 1917

46th Div.

140/2042

1/3rd N. M. Field Ambulance.

April 1917

46th Div.

140/2036

S

1/3rd North Midland F A.

Dec. 1917

140/2618.

1/3rd North Midland F.A.

Sept. 1916

46th Div

1/3rd N. M. Field Ambulance.

Nov. 1916

46th Div

140/1849

1/3rd N.M. Field Ambulance

Feb. 1917 46th Div. 140/1994.

1/3rd N. M. Field Ambulance.

March 1918

160/2849

1/3. Nth. Mid. Field Ambulance

August 1916.

1/3 N. M. F. A.

1/3rd North Midland F. A.

Sept. 1917

140/2499

1/3rd North Midland F. A.

May 1915

1/3. N. Midland F.A.

May 1915

Apr. 1918.

140/2900.

1/3 N. M. F. A.

121/5099
April 1915

46th Division

121/5099

1/3rd North Midland Field Ambulance

Vol II

46th Div
(1 M)

April 1916.

1/3rd N. Midland F. Amb.

May. 1919.

46 Div.

140/50-60

1/3rd N. Mid. Field Amb.

46th Div

May 1916

3rd. N.M. F. Amb.

Aug. 1917

140/2364

1/3rd North Midland F.A.

May 1918.

160/2983.

1/3rd. N. Mid. F. A.

Apr. 1919.

140/3550.

1/3 L. Mid F.A.

46th Division

No 3. N. M. Field Ambulance

July 1916

LIST OF APPENDICES OF WAR DIARY OF O.C. 1/3 N.MID. F.A. - MAY 1915.

1.	Photographs of Miller-James Wheeled Stretcher.	With diary.
2.	Sketch map of location of F.A. with Adv. Posts.	" "
3.	" " shewing med. posts of F.A. in Bailleul.	" "
4.	Chart of S. & W. of Staffs. Inf. Bge. passed through A.D.S. during April.	Filed under History 18 B-F.A. 1915. 21.
5.	Photograph of spray used against gas.	Filed under Medicine 19. 29.
6.	Chart of S. & W. of Staffs. Inf. Bge. passed through A.D.S. during May.	Filed under History 18 B. F.A. 1915. 21

A.D.M.S. office

To O.C. 3rd N.M. Fd Amb

As you will be under your own A.D.M.S. tomorrow please submit this report to him.

28/2/17

[illegible] Capt
D.A.D.M.S. 58th Div

2

To:- A.D.M.S. 46th Division

Forwarded

[illegible signature]

2/3/17

LIEUT.-COLONEL
COMMDG. 3rd N. MIDLAND FIELD AMB
R. A. M. CORPS

O.C. 3rd N.M. Fd Regt

46

1/3 NM Fd Amb

Vol XIV

46

3 NM Ja Arub

Fel

Vol XII

46

1/3 NM 7a amb

Vol XIII

www.ingramcontent.com/pod-product-compliance
Lightning Source LLC
Chambersburg PA
CBHW080825010526
44111CB00015B/2607